WELLINGTON'S LIEUTENANT, NAPOLEON'S GAOLER

WELLINGTON'S LIEUTENANT, NAPOLEON'S GAOLER

The Peninsula and St Helena diaries and letters of Sir George Ridout Bingham 1809–21

by

Gareth Glover

Pen & Sword
MILITARY

First published in Great Britain in 2004 by
Pen & Sword Military
an imprint of
Pen & Sword Books Ltd
47 Church Street
Barnsley
South Yorkshire
S70 2AS

ISBN 1 84415 141 7

Typeset in 11/13 Sabon by
Phoenix Typesetting, Auldgirth, Dumfriesshire

Printed and bound in England by
CPI UK

Pen & Sword Books Ltd incorporates the Imprints of Pen & Sword
Aviation, Pen & Sword Maritime, Pen & Sword Military, Wharncliffe
Local History, Pen & Sword Select, Pen & Sword Military Classics
and Leo Cooper.

For a complete list of Pen & Sword titles please contact
PEN & SWORD BOOKS LIMITED
47 Church Street, Barnsley, South Yorkshire, S70 2AS, England
E-mail: enquiries@pen-and-sword.co.uk
Website: www.pen-and-sword.co.uk

Contents

Acknowledgements

It almost goes without saying that a book of this nature requires the help and advice of numerous people and establishments. Those who were of particular help are listed here; others who helped on particular aspects of the book are mentioned in the notes that they helped compile.

I must particularly thank Miss Heather Ann Bingham, the last known direct descendant of the Bingham family, who resides in British Columbia, for graciously agreeing to my request to study and publish George Bingham's papers.

The generous help of John Montgomery, Librarian at the Royal United Services Institute for Defence Studies for identifying the whereabouts of Bingham's Peninsular letters which, it turned out, had been transferred to the Army Museum, is much appreciated.

I am eternally grateful to Dr Peter B. Boyden, Assistant Director (Collections) at the Army Museum, Chelsea, for agreeing to supply copies of Bingham's Peninsular diaries; Mrs Lesley Hamilton, Assistant Secretary to the De Lancey & De La Hanty Foundation Ltd. (the present proud owners of the original HMS *Northumberland* diary), for granting permission to obtain a copy of the diary from the photocopy of the original held by the British Library and Matthew Jones, Archivist at the Dorset Record Office for copies of the St Helena letters.

With regard to the various illustrations, I must thank the British Library for their kind permission to reproduce the only known painting of George Bingham (Reference Eg3715 f19). For the views of St Helena by Bellasis, I must thank Barry Weaver of the St Helena Virtual Library and Archive. 'The 53rd at Talavera' is reproduced by kind permission of Lieutenant Colonel P. J. Wykham and Major W. J. Spiers, RHQ, The Light Infantry. The views of Spain reproduced from Major Andrew Leith Hay's *A Narrative of the Peninsular War,* 1830 edition is from my own collection.

I must also thank Brigadier Henry Wilson, Publishing Manager for Pen & Sword Books for his support, encouragement and enthusiasm for the project, from the moment I first brought the idea to his attention.

Lastly, but certainly not least, I acknowledge the unwavering support of my incredibly understanding and patient wife Mary and dear children Sarah and Michael.

Gareth Glover
Cardiff   March 2004

Foreword

A year ago I discovered a brief reference to a copy of the Peninsula letters of Sir George Ridout Bingham having been placed in the library of the United Services Institute by Lieutenant Colonel Le M. Gretton in 1923[1] and was tempted to discover a little more.[2]

I must be brutally honest in stating that although I have studied the Napoleonic Wars for over twenty years, I was not initially aware of Sir George Bingham or his services at all. This is not too surprising, as he commanded an undeservedly less famous peninsular regiment, which was eventually so reduced in size through casualties and sickness to be amalgamated into one of those anonymous 'Provisional regiments'.[3] I was however, intrigued to discover that he had then sailed to St Helena on HMS Northumberland with Napoleon and that he commanded the army garrison on the island during most of Napoleon's final years.

On reference to that excellent internet reference tool, the National Register of Archives, run by the Historical Manuscripts Commission; I was very excited to discover two further diaries. The first was a diary written during the voyage to St Helena on HMS

---

1. Journal of the Society for Army Historical Research Volume 26, pp. 106–111 *The Bingham Manuscripts* 'by T.H. McGuffie.
2. Held at the Army Museum as files NAM6807–163.
3. Wellington was not keen on letting such valuable experienced veteran troops return home. He arranged that battalions would draft all the remaining men into a few companies, sending the superfluous officers and NCOs home to recruit for the battalion. Two such reduced battalions were then amalgamated as a Provisional regiment. Four such regiments were formed in Spain.

Northumberland and now held by the British Library;[1] the second a copy of his diary and letters from St Helena held by the Dorset Record Office.[2]

My appetite now well and truly whetted, I unknowingly embarked on a great treasure trail for copies of the diaries.

Having eventually obtained a full set of copies of the known surviving letters and diaries of Sir George Bingham, after tortuous negotiations, I proceeded to evaluate them, being a little afraid that they might prove to be of little real historical value. This fear was heightened, following the realization that George Bingham had edited the diaries in the 1820s, removing all personal family details. Had he amended the diaries in any way to protect reputations or to avoid offence?

I need not have worried, the letters sent to his family 'for their eyes only' from the peninsula are vibrant, immediate and honest. His letters are packed with information regarding the situation of the army; they include his thoughts and fears for the campaigns, untainted by the dreaded 'hindsight' of memoirs written much later; a full description of the country he travelled through and of the people and customs he met without prejudice; his honest and unfettered views of the officers and men he served with and full explanations of the trivia of daily life on campaign too often missing from such memoirs.

He describes the horrors of war; the unforgiving, inhuman war fought by the French and Spanish and the gentlemanly but no less deadly conflict between his own army and the enemy. Embarrassing incidents and the absurdities of war are retold for amusement, such as a regiment blazing away for twenty minutes at a strong line of French infantry, until the fog lifted to reveal a long stone wall! He is just as honest about his own troops, even describing when the soldiers recoil from the enemy and fail. These letters were not written with posterity in mind, simply to aid the understanding of his kin folk to the situation he found in a strange land.

His later diaries and letters, covering the voyage to St Helena and service on the island, are packed with information regarding

1. Held at the Dorset Record Office as D/MPL: 43 amongst the Mansel-Pleydell Archive.
2. Held in the Manuscript Collection at the British Library, reference RP1718.

Napoleon and his entourage, with whom he seems to have built a very good rapport, unlike the governor, Sir Hudson Lowe. His reports of conversations with the ex-Emperor are fascinating, being written down immediately afterwards, again simply for the amusement of his family. This is no political piece as so much written by players at St Helena is; Bingham refreshingly reports the situation honestly, finding fault with both sides. His views are very important in the continuing debate to this day regarding the treatment of Napoleon on that South Atlantic rock.

I am frankly amazed that this gem has not been published before and I feel very privileged to be able to bring it into the limelight that it so thoroughly deserves. I am certain that these letters and diaries will be viewed as some of the most important to have surfaced in the last century and can stand proudly alongside any other peninsula diary that has been published to date.

It is therefore not before time that George Bingham's able views and comments on all these matters were brought to the attention of the public at large.

Introduction

A history of George Bingham

George Ridout Bingham was born on 21 July 1777. He joined the army as an ensign in the 69 Foot in June 1793, serving with it in Corsica and as one of the detachments embarked as marines under Admiral Hotham in the Gulf of Genoa. He was promoted to captain of a company in the 81 Foot in 1796, serving with that regiment at the Cape[1] and took part in the Kaffir war on the Sundays River in 1800.

In 1801 he became a major in the 82 Foot, serving with it on the island of Minorca, until it was returned to Spain under the terms of the Peace of Amiens in 1802.

In 1805 he transferred to the newly raised 2nd Battalion 53 Shropshire Regiment in Ireland. The 53rd had been serving in the West Indies as a single battalion regiment but on its return home was ordered to form a second battalion. This was raised quite quickly from men who had only volunteered for limited service and was sent to Ireland in 1804. In 1805 the first battalion was ordered to the East Indies where they were to remain until 1823 and a large number of men were drafted from the second battalion to ensure it sailed at full strength. It was at this time that Lieutenant Colonel George Ridout Bingham took command of the 2nd battalion, a post he held until 1817. The remnants of the battalion were moved to Shrewsbury where they recruited hard throughout North Wales

1. The Cape Colony was wrested from the Dutch in 1796.

1

and Shropshire, and when moved to Sussex in 1808, numbered 705 rank and file.

The *Star* records their march through Chichester at this time.

A Grenadier of that regiment attracted much attention; he measures seven feet and three inches in height, and is only nineteen years of age. He is allowed to be the tallest man in the army.

In March 1809 the second battalion was ordered to Spain, anchoring in the Tagus on 4 April. The 2/53rd served in the pursuit of Soult after Oporto, Talavera, Fuentes d'Onoro, covered the siege of Badajoz, Salamanca and siege of Burgos. George was severely wounded at the Battle of Salamanca having rallied the battalion by grasping the King's Colour and waving it over the heads of the men. He was mentioned in Wellington's Salamanca dispatch of 24 July 1812 and was awarded a gold medal.

Following the terrible retreat to Portugal in 1812, the regiment was reduced to a mere shadow, but Wellington, wishing to retain such veteran troops with his army, the few remaining men were placed into four companies and the skeleton staff of the other six companies sent home to recruit. A similar exercise having taken place in the 2 (Queen's Royal) Regiment, the two were combined as the '2 Provisional Regiment' which George commanded. This combined regiment fought at Vitoria, the Pyrenees, Nivelle and the Nive. The six companies in England returned to Spain fully recruited again in 1814 and the 2/53rd took the field as a full battalion for the Battle of Toulouse.

George Bingham was with the regiment throughout this period, until the ill health of his mother forced him to return home at the beginning of 1814, thus missing the Battle of Toulouse, where it was commanded by Lieutenant Colonel Mansel. More importantly to George, he arrived in England a few days too late to see his mother again before she passed away, aged sixty, at Melcombe on 31 December 1813.

Returning to his family home, George discovered a number of carefully preserved bundles of papers, which contained the letters he had sent to his family; he was to edit these in the 1820s.

He married Emma Septima Pleydell of Whatcombe House, Dorset, in September 1814, but unfortunately the couple were to be childless. George was promoted to colonel in 1814 and received the KCB for his distinguished services, thus becoming Sir George Bingham. Called back to war by the escape of Napoleon from Elba, the 53rd were not involved in the Waterloo campaign. However orders were sent for the 2/53rd to proceed with Napoleon to St Helena and to form part of the garrison there. George was promoted brigadier general and commanded all of the troops on the island under Sir Hudson Lowe. Sir George and Lady Bingham are known by the pseudonyms Swell and Lady Swell in Gorrequer's pithy diaries.

George returned to England in 1819 and was soon after promoted major general of the 2nd battalion 95 Rifles and was succeeded at St Helena by Brigadier General Sir Pine Coffin.

He lived at Dean's Leage[1] which family estate he appears to have inherited from his mother and which he retained as his family home until his death. He afterwards was placed on the Irish staff and commanded the Cork district from 1827–1832. This was a period of great tension in Ireland, discord being fomented by the debates in Parliament regarding Catholic emancipation, famine and later pestilence. In Ireland as at St Helena, Sir George Bingham's tact and kindliness of disposition appear to have won general esteem and he seems to have been regarded by all as a 'thorough gentleman'.

Whilst on a visit to his London home at Charles Street, Manchester Square, he suddenly died on 3 January 1833 when he was only fifty-five years of age.

The Bingham family

The Binghams have always had strong links with Dorset, and particularly Melcombe, since Norman times. The manor house is first mentioned in 1056 when Goda, wife of Eustace, Count of Bologne and sister to Edward the Confessor, bequeathed the manor of Nethermelcombe, as it was then known, to the Abbey at

1. The mansion of Dean's Leage lay one mile west of Witchampton village. At one time the land was owned by Tomas Pearce, Commissioner of the Navy and Member of Parliament for Weymouth. He sold it to Thomas Ridout who built himself a house that became known as Dean's Lease, and sometimes Dean's Leaze. On the death of Sir George Bingham the property was sold. The mansion was pulled down, but the stable block was converted into a farmhouse, which stands today.

Shaftesbury. Harold, Earl of Wessex seized it from the abbey but on his death at the Battle of Hastings, the manor became crown property.

By 1115 the manor is recorded as belonging to the Turbevilles and the neighbouring church is first mentioned in 1150.

In 1228 Robert de Bingham was elected Bishop of Salisbury, and in 1246 his nephew, also Robert, married Lucy, the daughter and heir of Sir Robert Turbeville. The family is also in the Hundred Rolls of 1273, when a Robert de Bingham is for the first time recorded as residing at what was then called Melcombe Bingham.[1]

Like many a noble family, service in the army seems to have become a long-standing tradition. One John de Bingham was knighted by Edward IV in the field, after the battle of Tewkesbury in 1471.

In the Civil War, the family sided with the Parliamentarians. John Bingham was a member of the Long Parliament until its dissolution in 1653. He became colonel of a regiment, Governor of Poole and commanded the parliamentary forces at the last siege of Corfe Castle and oversaw its demolition.

Richard Bingham, born in 1741, took the family seat on the death of his barrister father in 1755. He became colonel of the Dorset militia and married Sophia Halsey of Great Gaddesden, Hertfordshire in 1766. They had four children which they named Richard (born 1768), William (1771), Charles Cox (1772) and Sophia (1773) before his wife Sophia died in 1773. Richard soon married again, as he wed Elizabeth Ridout of Dean's Leage near Witchampton in Dorset on 26 October 1775. A further four children resulted from this second marriage before the death of Elizabeth in 1813, George Ridout (1777), John (1785), Mary and Leonora (dates unknown).

George's father eventually died in 1823 and the estate passed to his first born. George's half brother Richard resided at the ancestral home at Melcombe Bingham; he had joined the army and eventually rose to the rank of lieutenant colonel. He married Priscilla Carden but died without issue in 1829; the estate consisting of the manor and 66 hectares of parkland, being inherited by his nephew, the Reverend George Bingham. The family seat

---

1. It is unclear why and when the name changed to its modern version, Bingham's Melcombe.

of Bingham's Melcombe was sold in 1895 and following a number of barren marriages, the title eventually passed to the family branch in Canada, where their descendants remain to this day.

The diaries and letters

It must be stated that all of the records that I have used from the various sources are copies of the originals, of which I have been unable to discover the whereabouts. The letters from Spain held by the Army Museum were obviously copied on a typewriter from the originals in the early twentieth century. They, however, have the air of authenticity and despite spelling mistakes and some obvious copying errors, there is nothing within them to cause one to question their validity.

The copy of the *Northumberland* diary at the British Library is known to be a direct copy from the original. The St Helena diaries from the Dorset Record Office, also containing a further copy of the *Northumberland* diaries, have been compiled in a format obviously designed for publishing in her own hand, by a Margaret Pleydell, a descendant of Lady Emma Bingham's family. It is not known why it was not published as interest in Napoleon has always been strong, although extracts were published in *Blackwood's Magazine* in October 1896 and *Cornhill Magazine* in January 1901.

The copy of the *Northumberland* diary obtained here has been compared with the copy in the British Library and is the same, giving confidence in the remainder.

My contribution to these letters and diaries has been simply to draw them together into one coherent mass and to add explanatory notes wherever I felt it was necessary or helpful.

The only changes I have made to the scripts have been to alter spelling of names of people and places where the correct version has been accurately identified. George Bingham also had a very irritating habit of apostrophizing all sorts of words; these have been written in full.

I trust that the reader finds these letters and diaries as interesting, illuminating and enthralling as I have found them. It has been both a privilege and a delight to get to know Sir George Ridout Bingham so intimately.

Covering letter by Sir George Ridout Bingham as a foreword to his Peninsula letter books

On my return to England in 1814 after my mother's death, I found in her dressing room, carefully put together, a great many letters, I had written to her, and my father, during the time I was serving on the peninsula, viz., from April 1809, till January 1814, as well as a few letters, I had written to other friends, which had been sent to her, for her perusal. Having much leisure time on my hands, when I settled at Dean's Leage in 1820, I began to enter these letters into this book, leaving out everything relating to my privates affairs, or that had no connexion with the service on which I was engaged, or to the countries which these letters attempt to describe. But I have made no alterations in the letters themselves although they contain predictions that were never verified, although my sentiments on several subjects underwent frequent variations, as I became better acquainted with the countries, in which I served. I left the impressions as they were first made, and as I first expressed them, and as they were chiefly collected for my own amusement, I look with pleasure to these alterations in my sentiments; and more particularly to the gradual increase of confidence in our commander, which it will be seen, was not so unlimited at first, as it afterwards became when we had better opportunities of being acquainted with the brilliant talents he possessed. For the same reasons I have not attempted to alter the style of the letters, which were frequently written in haste, and with a carelessness which has always marked my correspondence; they are intended only for the perusal of a few of my most intimate friends, who would perhaps like to look over an interesting period of my life, and the scenes I was an eye witness to, and would rather do it through the medium of letters written on the spot, than a more laboured production.

The period contained in this first book, is one twelvemonth, from the beginning of April 1809, when we landed on the banks of the Tagus, to the end of March, in the year 1810; it embraces three very interesting points, viz., the campaign in the north part of Portugal, with the expulsion of Marechal

Soult from that country, and the rapid return of the Army to Abrantes; the advance to Talavera, the sanguinary contest at that place, and the retreat of the Army to the neighbourhood of Badajoz after it; and lastly the long winter march from the banks of the Guadiana, to the northern frontiers of Portugal. In these marches we traversed (in a hasty manner to be sure) the greater part of Portugal, and some miles in Spain; and saw much of the country we passed through, and although we wanted the leisure and opportunity afforded ordinary travellers to examine every point worth seeing, as much of my time was necessarily occupied in the duties of my profession; yet the grand manoeuvres in which we were engaged will make up for this deficiency, and render the whole more interesting and worth the trouble of perusing

G. R. Bingham

Dean's Leage

Began May 1820

Chapter One

The Peninsular letters

Although Britain and France had been almost continually at war since 1793, except during the short lived Peace of Amiens of 1802, it had in many ways been a limited war. Britain, through its navy, had gained complete supremacy of the seas; whilst Napoleon and his ever growing French Empire dominated the European land mass. For most of this period, therefore, neither was in a position to seriously challenge the others' control of their given element. France had cowed all of the major powers in Europe, frustrating Britain's attempts to bring her Empire to its knees through grand alliances with the other traditional power houses of Austria, Prussia or Russia. Britain had used her navy to capture virtually all of the French, Dutch and Danish outposts throughout the world. This had a hugely beneficial effect on the economy of Britain but was extremely detrimental to the British forces, which had to be thinly spread across these pestilential islands and suffered frighteningly high mortality rates. The few attempts to land a substantial British army on the continent of Europe generally led to abject failure or, where victory was gained over the local French forces such as at the Battle of Maida in Southern Italy, the inability to maintain sufficient numbers to stand against the French forces summoned to counter the threat, caused a rapid re-embarkation. Such pyrrhic victories gave some cheer to the besieged British populace, but proved a merely temporary irritant to Napoleon's driving ambition and Britain could only look upon the minor peripheral states of Sweden and Portugal as her allies.

This all suddenly changed in 1807–8, when Napoleon made the

fatal decision not merely to eradicate Portugal but also to enforce his own brand of 'democracy' on his erstwhile ally, Spain, the final bastion of the venal and arrogant Bourbon dynasty. His usurping of the Spanish throne for his brother Joseph was the catalyst for a general insurrection throughout the country. Spanish representatives were soon in London demanding support in the form of money and arms, which they did receive in copious amounts; but were reluctant about troops, as the enthusiastic insurgents were convinced that they were capable of defeating the French hordes alone; a belief that was unfortunately strengthened by the fortuitous defeat of a French corps at Bailen.

Ten thousand troops under the command of Sir Arthur Wellesley, later to become famous as the Duke of Wellington, was formed into an expedition to aid Portugal oust the French invaders. This army landed at Mondego Bay in August 1808 and, following victories at Rolica and Vimiero, General Jean Andoche Junot agreed to sign the Convention of Cintra by which the French forces would leave Portugal on British ships! The convention was heavily criticized in Britain and Generals Sir Hew Dalrymple and Sir Harry Burrard with Wellesley, who had been supplanted by these senior officers as the British Army in Portugal significantly increased in numbers, were called home to face an enquiry. Only Wellesley was exonerated although the agreement had achieved the complete removal of French troops from Portugal including two significant fortresses, without further loss.

Sir John Moore took command of the forces in Portugal and, believing in the promises of support from the Spanish juntas, he boldly led the army deep into Spain. Napoleon and his overwhelming forces reacted swiftly to this threat to their communications and turned en masse to trap the British Army and destroy it. Warned at the last moment of his impending doom, Moore was forced to retreat rapidly to Corunna and fought a rearguard action in which he was killed before the army re-embarked.

Despite reports of the horrors of the retreat and visions of the cadaverous wreck of an army that arrived at Plymouth and Portsmouth, the British Government did not falter in its determination to continue the struggle. Wellesley was sent back to Portugal with the promise of significant reinforcements to the meagre force Moore had left to protect Lisbon. The 2/53rd formed part of this force sent to Portugal in 1809, where they arrived in April, and so began the great adventure so ably described here in the letters of their commanding officer, George Bingham.

Chapter Two

The Campaign of 1809

Wellesley soon formed his new army and set Marshal Beresford to work training the Portuguese army to British standards. As soon as he was happy that the army was in a condition to fight, he launched a surprise attack on the forces of Marshal Nicolas Soult, who was established around Oporto, Portugal's second city. Having succeeded in driving this force away, the army returned to the Tagus and prepared for a bold move into Spain. Wellesley had been promised abundant supplies from the Spanish juntas and advanced along the Tagus where he joined forces with the Spanish army commanded by General Gregorio de la Cuesta.

The French attacked at Talavera sure of success, but were beaten off by the British. However, acute supply problems and the imminent threat of having his lines of communication severed by Soult, forced Wellesley to leave his wounded to the mercy of the French and cross the Tagus, rapidly retreating by mountain tracks to Portugal. The following letters describe the part played by George Bingham and the 53 Regiment during these operations.

Letter 1   **Tagus, 5 April 1809**

Dear Madam,[1]

You will be much surprised (if this ever does reach you) at the receipt of a letter so soon from this place. I wrote my last letter to you from the Cove of Cork on Tuesday se'nnight, we were at that time uncertain when we were to sail. On Wednesday morning the

1. As with the majority of the letters this is written to his mother.

wind came round and we all got under weigh with a fresh breeze which fortunately continued, first blowing strong, afterwards more moderately till we came to this river yesterday at about half past four o'clock. I do not know that I ever was better pleased with anything than the passage up the Tagus, the genial warmth of the climate, the advanced state of vegetation, forming so great a contrast to the country we had left, to which the shortness of the passage added greatly, and the beauty of the building, the clearness of the atmosphere was quite delightful, we had scarcely time to eat the fresh bread we took on board at Cork before we got a supply here.

One transport having on board a part of the 30th Regiment is missing but great hopes are entertained that she will reach the harbour in safety. We had no idea that this was our destination, it would have been well for us if we had, as we laid in stock of fresh provision to last us to Cadiz, Gibraltar, or even further, which we shall now dispose of to a great loss. I should not have written so soon, that is not until I was able to give you some idea how we are to be disposed of but that a convoy is expected to sail tomorrow, and if we disembark immediately I cannot answer for time. Reports here are various; from what I can learn the French are at Oporto, we have a position about five miles from this, and we expect to join the Camp there. What our force is likely to be I have no idea, most probably not more than sufficient to hold the country as long as the French choose to allow us, that is, till the Emperor has settled his affairs in the North of Europe, and has nothing left to do but to think of us. We shall then re-embark, perhaps as quickly as at Corunna; I should think therefore our campaign would not be of a long continuance and I may have the pleasure of shaking you by the hand yet before the end of the year.

Letter 2   Fonte del Pipo, 9 April 1809

Dear Sir, [1]

We had an uncommonly fine passage from the Cove of Cork to this place, only six days; the two first it blew pretty fresh; the rest more moderate. One day passed after our arrival in the Tagus

1. Written to his father.

without orders; on the following (the 6th) we landed here. Being on the opposite side of the river to Lisbon, we are a little in the dark as to news, as our Brigadier[1] lives on the other side of the water; but there seems to be generally speaking, a want of intelligence. I hope it does not extend to our chief Sir John Cradock,[2] who does not, from the conversations I have heard going on, enjoy the confidence of the army, which a general about to take the field ought to do. At present there exists certainly no small degree of confusion, orders given and countermanded &c. &c. We have been in expectation of moving every day since we came here; the French are at Oporto near which place they surprised the Portuguese a short time since, who consoled themselves with putting their General Freire to death.[3]

Against this division of their army we were to have marched till it was ascertained that another column was advancing on Extremadura. We are now therefore from what I can learn, to take up a position to cover Lisbon, about thirty miles from it. Part of the Army are already on their march and the rest is to follow. Much is expected from the Portuguese, but I am afraid little reliance can be placed on them; certainly some of the new levies commanded by British officers appear tolerably well, but I am afraid want the necessary spirit. There certainly exists a hatred towards the French, and if the enemy were to be kept off by the warlike spirit of the natives they would never get to Lisbon, for every body is in arms. Such as have not muskets, fowling pieces; and such as have no fire arms, pikes. They are a motley group, and so armed and dressed as

1. The 2/53rd was in the 5 Brigade with the 2/7th (Fusiliers) and 1 Company of the 5/60th commanded by Brigadier Alexander Campbell.
2. Sir John Cradock assumed command of the troops at Lisbon following Sir John Moore's march into Spain with the bulk of the army. He was a timid commander with a small force of about 10,000 effective men. He achieved little and happily handed over command to Arthur Wellesley on 22 April 1809.
3. As Marshal Soult marched on Oporto, the Portuguese forces led by General Freire stood near Braga in an attempt to block the French advance. The wreck of the Portuguese ordenanza units defeated at Salamonde arrived at this camp, loudly declaiming Freire for failing to support them and accusing him of cowardice. On the arrival of the French forces, Freire fled, but was recognized and captured. Baron Eben, who had assumed command of the Portuguese forces, took up a defensive position at Monte Adaufe. Freire was placed in the gaol at Braga, where a group of ordenanza returned to drag him out and murder him with their pikes.

to be quite ludicrous; they have some engineers who are making a show of fortifying every point but such fortifications were never yet seen in this or any country.[1]

We are to proceed for some way up the river in boats, the Fusiliers[2] and 53rd form our brigade and we are in the same division with the Brigade of Guards and the brigade composed of the 2nd Battalion 48th, 60th, and 66th,[3] under the orders of General Hill.[4] We are to move without baggage or impediments of any description, our women[5] &c, are left on board. Some of the regiments have behaved exceedingly ill, first getting drunk, then committing every sort of outrage. We have escaped this, having fortunately been placed in an isolated situation; we are near the town of Almada close to the banks of the Tagus, with a beautiful garden at the back of the house, which (with warehouses &c.) contains the whole regiment. We parade in a long walk covered with vines; the climate is delightful.

Letter 3   Rio Maior, 17 April 1809

My dear Madam,

I wrote last from on board, the day before we landed which letter I hope you will soon get. I shall continue to give you from time to time a relation of our proceedings in a sort of journal. We have travelled by easy stages, and have had therefore a good opportunity of observing the country but not of the inhabitants, who keep aloof

---

1. This refers to works planned around Almada to prevent shipping in the Tagus being fired upon.
2. The 7 Regiment was titled the 'Royal Fusiliers'.
3. The 1 Brigade actually consisted of the 2/48th, 2/66th, 1 company of 5/60th but also the 1/3rd which Bingham appears to have omitted. His statement that the three brigades (Guards, 1 and 5) were all in a division commanded by Hill is at variance with Oman, who states that the army was not placed into divisions until 18 June 1809.
4. General Sir Rowland Hill, affectionately known by the troops as 'Daddy' Hill, for his paternal care of his men. He was a very able officer and was really the only one that Wellington would trust with a major independent command.
5. An official allowance of six women (plus any accompanying children) per 100 men was allowed to proceed with the regiment when going overseas. The selection was made by the drawing of lots on the quayside and often led to scenes of near riot and hysteria. Women left behind were left virtually destitute and would usually be forced to return to the bosom of their families.

and though they wish (I believe) success to our cause, dare not venture near us. Not that in reality we are so formidable, but the country we pass through tasted the French last year. For though the French can behave well if they like, yet on what account I can say not, they treated poor Portugal but badly, and not only plundered whatever they could lay their hands on, but did a great deal of wanton unnecessary mischief.

On the 6th, we had orders to disembark, the same day; which we did about four o'clock in the afternoon, on the left bank of the Tagus, opposite Lisbon. The 7th Regiment occupied the town of Almada, situated on the height, whilst we were put into a house and store houses on the sea shore. The bank rises very steep behind it, so that what is the fourth storey towards the river is the ground floor above. It has been a beautiful place and the gardens though much out of order, show what it has been. A long alley with a treillage of vines, near a flower garden in which was a fountain, containing silver and gold fish, with a view of the City of Lisbon also the fleet and river between, was our breakfasting place. The house was almost destitute of furniture, but the British Consul provided me with a small furnished house in the town. You will accuse me of great want of curiosity in having stayed four days, at this place without having crossed the water to Lisbon, but the momentary expectation of moving, and the anxiety I was under that my regiment should take the field complete in its equipment, made me forget or rather put it off till it was too late to think of it.

Almada is a large town and take this picture of it as a specimen of all Portuguese towns that I have seen; irregularly built so that it is more a collection of houses thrown together than a town, the streets narrow, filthy, and almost impassable for any sort of carriage. The houses had however the luxury of glass windows, which we have now lost; the churches neither large nor striking, a good deal of gilding, but less painting than in Italy, nor much taste displayed in either.

On Tuesday the 11th, at five in the morning we bid adieu to Almada and embarked on the Tagus in fourteen boats of different sizes and although the wind was not fair, yet with the resistance of the tide about one o'clock we reached our destination. The river is very broad just above Lisbon and the right bank beautifully wooded, cultivated, and interspersed with villages, at one of which

I touched and landed, called Sacavem[1] situated on a small creek that runs into the river. The left bank is quite flat but covered with firs. We marched on landing through Vila Franca de Xira, a large town not less filthy but with better houses and apparently better inhabited than Almada, and after a short march of three miles through a most delightful country; being an orange grove nearly the whole way, arrived at Castanheira [do Ribatejo] a small town with only one street, at the foot of some high hills on the borders of the fertile country watered by the Tagus. I was quartered at a religious house belonging to some large convent, the two friars that inhabited it were both good looking young men and did not appear to practise the austerities of their order; they were very civil and gave us every accommodation their house was able to afford. How great a loss a person experiences in not knowing the language of the country he is in! Obliged to judge by appearances, you can gain no information and you merely look over it as you would a fine picture, without anyone at hand to explain it; you try to guess what it is intended for.

In the two days we remained at Castanheira I bought a mule for my baggage, and my horse having got safe on shore I am quite set up.

On Friday the 14th, we moved off again; our route was for Alconchel [2] (the first day), after marching five miles through the same rich country, we entered on a large sandy plain, with a few pines scattered here and there; the road broad, but frequently sandy, and deep. We were ordered to halt at a solitary convent, Nostra Senora de Mexocira with scarcely any cultivation or dwelling of any kind near it. The Brigade of Guards had filled the town and we were put up in the church of this convent which was much handsomer than we expected to find in so lonely a place, lined entirely with what in England we call Dutch tile but very large; a very handsome altar with a profusion of gilding round it. I am happy to say we left it in as good a condition as we found it, for I put the colours of the regiment on the high altar and two

1. The transcript reads 'Santarem' but that town is much further north, it must have been Sacavem.
2. I cannot positively identify this town but believe it should read Alcoentre as neither of the two towns with names similar to Alconchel are anywhere near the route between Castanheira and Rio Maior.

sentries to prevent any of the soldiers coming within the rails. The rest of the people we stowed away as well as we could, under the portico belonging to the convent; fortunately the night was fine so that some who slept out were not the worse for it. We marched an hour before day light on the 15th, over the same sort of sterile country we had left, till day light showed us the pleasant valley that Alconchel stands in, and the fine strong Brigade of Guards quitting the town. We did not halt in it; it appeared very small and near it, was the only chateau I have yet seen in the country; it was prettily situated, much out of repair, the gardens well planted and looked like the lower gardens at Melcombe.

We left the cultivated land with the village, and crossing another sandy heath, entered three miles before we came to this place a large forest, the wood chiefly pine. I was surprised to find so much fir in a southern country as I thought it confined to northern regions. The trees were tall but not in general large. The opening on this town was beautiful; it stands in a valley surrounded almost on every side with this forest, and formed a delightful contrast to the country we had just passed over. This town was occupied last year by the French, who committed horrible excesses, which has so much alarmed the inhabitants that the first day we entered the town it was almost depopulated; the people that remained received us very hospitably. Conceive a town about the size of Cerne[1] with nearly five thousand soldiers in it and you may form a judgement of what Rio Maior now is. I am fortunate, and have a tolerable house; here we have been now two days, it has rained a good deal and we have suffered from cold, there being no glass in the windows, so to have light you must leave the casement open. We are obliged to keep a sharp look out to get anything to eat, for so many mouths devour the land; I think however we fare as well as our neighbours. We caught some excellent fish in the stream yesterday. What the French are about, or where they are, no one knows, nor no one seems to care; as for me I am only a passenger.

This is the right division of our army; the centre is at Caldas [da Rainha], the left at Obidos, the reserve and cavalry at Alcobaca.

I shall send this by the post, and let it take its chance; the latter part is written on the 18th, the bad weather continues, and we know nothing of when we are to move or to what place.

1. The town of Cerne Abbas in Dorset.

Letter 4

Dear Madam,

I wrote you a long letter from our last halting quarter, and although I have not much to say yet I take advantage of a civil land-lord (who promises to convey this to Lisbon) to write, as it may be some time before I shall have leisure again.

Poor Harrison [1] met with a sad misfortune at Rio Maior; he broke his leg in jumping over a stick, and it was with great concern I was obliged to leave him behind. His situation is a melancholy one, heightened by his not being able to speak a word of the language, and having no medical attendance.

After eleven hours marching on the 21st, the greater part good but the latter part execrable road, we came to a small town most romantically situated in the mountains, called Porto de Mos. We were quartered at an Augustine convent, where they gave us an excellent dinner, comfortable beds, and a hearty welcome. The situation is delightful, very like the Vale of Llangollen in North Wales, the ruins of a Moorish castle with its light and fretted battlements is at the head of the valley. The convent is a spacious building with a handsome church.

The 22nd, we marched in here; a tolerable town or rather city, it being a Bishop's see; the cathedral is certainly handsome but has been plundered of all its valuables by the French; gilt candlesticks, and glass chandeliers are substituted for silver, the effect however is not much lessened by it; the organ is a very good one, and they have a tolerable choir.

We are very much crowded having four other brigades in the town, besides our own, the market however has been well supplied, and the people who have suffered much from the French have shown an uncommon good disposition towards us. The week has been past [sic] in rumours and expectations; Sir John Cradock has (much to the satisfaction of both army and people) resigned the command to Sir Arthur Wellesley who is not yet come up. We may now expect something decisive, three brigades of the army are just getting under arms to march in the direction of Oporto; we follow at day break tomorrow. You can expect to hear great news soon, should it be my good fortune to gladden your

1. Lieutenant Charles Harrison of the 53rd.

18

heart with a sight of my name in the Gazette, how happy it will make me.

All this country is beautifully picturesque, here are the ruins of a castle that people in England would go three hundred miles to see; the Bishop's garden rich, and well stocked with oranges, is under the walls.

I have been quartered at the house of a medical man who speaks French. I have written to Tryon[1] and have desired him to communicate what I know of the movements of the army; if we halt before we reach Oporto, I will write again.

Letter 5   Coimbra, 5 May 1809

My dear Madam,

It is very possible, I may not have an opportunity of writing after I leave this for some time as it is expected we shall march tomorrow, and take the field. We left Leiria, and my good friend the doctor, in a hurry, and marched on Sunday last to Pombal, a town that has the appearance of having been heretofore of greater consequence than at present; a very pretty river runs at the bottom of the town, to which you enter by a good bridge of three arches. On Monday we came to Condeixa [a Nova] a beautiful village in which there are a great many good houses, a natural cascade situated amidst orange groves, which have both blossoms and fruit in perfection at this season. I was quartered just without the village at a farm house, and was most handsomely and hospitably treated. From Condeixa to this place is two leagues; a paved road through a beautiful country. This town (the Oxford of Portugal) is as well situated as any city in Europe; it stands on several small hills on the banks of the Mondego, which is as broad though not so deep as the Thames at Blackfriars, winding through hills covered with wood and crowned with convents or other large buildings. We entered the city over a long low bridge (built by the Romans) crowded with inhabitants, and as we passed under temporary triumphal arches, they welcomed us with 'Viva's', and covered us with roses, orange flowers, and sugar plums; a number of well dressed pretty women amongst them. Of the size of the buildings of the university you

---

1. Captain Nathaniel Tryon Still, 3 Foot, was brother-in-law to George, having married his sister Mary. He retired on half pay 25 September 1814.

19

may form an idea when I tell you one college contains our whole division consisting of five regiments. The two days we have been here, have been spent in seeing the public buildings. These fall very short in point of architecture, as well as every thing else to those of our own universities, but there are many things really worth looking at. I am quartered at St. Peter's College, the students of which (such as remain, for most of them have either entered the army or have gone home on account of the war) are exceedingly civil, and entertain us very hospitably. They have acted as cicerones, and have pointed out to us all worth seeing; they have an excellent library belonging to the college, and have a number of new publications both in French and Italian. Amongst others I noticed a superb work published at Naples, with coloured prints of pictures discovered in the ruins of Herculaneum.

From my apartment I command a view of the Mondego and the Convent of Santa Anna,[1] on the other side of the river. The quadrangle in which it stands has on one side the observatory, on another the library of the university and chapel; opposite the observatory are the schools and hall of examination, and the Rector's Palace, and opposite the library this college. The other three sides are very well ornamented; having porticoes with noble pillars and handsome doors to each of the buildings; but this college is like an old white-washed barn and forms a disagreeable contrast to the whole.

In the library a number of good books yet remain, although the best have been sent to Lisbon to be out of the way of the French. It is a large hall with the books very well arranged, the ceilings handsomely painted, and a gallery running round the whole; it is rather dark and perhaps has too much gilding for a building of the sort. At the head of the room is a very good picture of John the V the founder. The books are in every language.[2]

The museum is a very fine building, and was formerly the convent of the Jesuits; it has also suffered by the most valuable articles having been sent out of the way. There is a very fine collection of fossils and shells. The birds appear in bad preservation; the beasts are few in number, and are badly stuffed; the reptiles are excellent; some

1. Actually the Convent de Santa Clara.
2. The Biblioteca Joanina; a baroque fantasy with its mass of rare books remains to this day.

snakes from Brazil nineteen and twenty feet long and there is an enormous alligator from the same country. The apparatus for electricity appeared to me to be very good, and there are two excellent rooms fitted up as theatres, with seats &c, for lectures.

From the museum, we went to the Convent of Santa Cruz, one of the richest in Portugal.[1] There are fifty friars besides lay brethren and servants. These fifty must all be noblesse; they never go beyond the walls of the convent unless they choose to attend the studies of the university. To make them amends for not quitting the convent they have every luxury within the walls; a garden for a warm climate delightfully laid out in what we should call bad taste, with straight alleys, cascades, and some good jets d'eau, a pleasure house that contains a concert room and billiard table. In this convent they entertain three General Officers and their staff; and it is supposed not less than sixty officers live in their house at present. Their refectory is a superb room, before the French came they were served off silver. At present they must be content with porcelain. The cathedral[2] is not so fine a building as that at Leiria or so well fitted up. The Bishop, who is also the rector of the university is at Paris, where he was sent last year by Junot to ask a King,[3] and where he has been kept ever since.

It is supposed we shall advance tomorrow towards Oporto; if Soult chooses to run the risk of remaining, we shall go there. If he moves off before we arrive, it is supposed we shall turn to our right, and go to the frontiers of Spain to see after Victor. Hitherto our campaign has been no more than a party of pleasure. Hereafter we must expect to meet with some difficulties and greater inconvenience.

Letter 6   **Convent of Santa Tirja, near Oporto,**
20 May 1809

My dear Mother,

I have not had an opportunity of writing to you since I left Coimbra, nor have I time at present to do more than to tell you that

---

1. The Igreja de Santa Cruz is a riot of excessive sculpture.
2. The Sé Nova is an unprepossessing Cathedral which replaced the Sé Velha as Cathedral in 1772.
3. Junot sought the throne of Portugal from Napoleon.

I am safe and well, and have not felt the fatigues and privations of the campaign. I have not yet been in action, our brigade having been in the rear on the 10th, 11th, and 12th, although we used our utmost endeavours to get up, but were not fortunate enough to share in the brilliant exploit, of the passage of the Douro;[1] we crossed the river the evening of the 12th, but after the French had retired. We have made very long marches in excessively wet weather, and on roads scarcely broad enough to admit of more than one man abreast, and literally knee deep in mud; frequently without bread, and seldom less than twelve hours under arms. We have had but one days halt since we left Coimbra, nor are we likely to be better off hereafter, as we are now on our march to oppose Victor, whom report says is marching with 40,000 men on Lisbon. The weather however is about to be better we hope, and the roads and resources improve every day. I dine today with Sir Arthur Wellesley who is at present here. The packet goes off tomorrow. I just write now to send by it; if we halt a day at Oporto I will write a longer letter. We attended the shattered remains of Soult's Army nearly to the frontiers of Spain, and by the time we get back to Lisbon, shall have marched five hundred miles.

Letter 7   Coimbra, 28 May 1809

My dear Madam,

I take the opportunity a short halt affords, to give you an account of all that has happened since we left this place, from whence I wrote last, for I can scarcely call the short billet I sent from Santa Tirja anything, although it may have afforded you the satisfaction of knowing that I was safe and sound, though somewhat fatigued by incessant marching and bad weather. We left this on the 9th and returned yesterday and have had but three halting days. Our marches have been long and the roads we have passed over much worse than the worst cross roads you ever had an idea of in England. We left this at four o'clock on Tuesday 9th, a part of the

---

1. Soult had pulled all his forces north of the River Douro during 10/11 May and broke the bridge. Having discovered some hidden wine barges, Wellesley sent over troops on the 12th to the seminary on an isolated hill on the eastern edge of the city. This movement was not discovered until too late; an attempted counter-attack was defeated and the French army was forced to flee Oporto precipitately.

Army having marched the day before; and after a short march of three leagues, reached Mealhada, nothing remarkable occurred this day, except that the roads began to be worse than those we had been accustomed to, long, narrow watery lanes; the country rich and well cultivated, and from an old castle in ruins near the town the view was very fine. We resumed our march on the morning of the 10th at two o'clock, and passed about one, a good town, situated on a river navigable for boats to the bridge, over which we crossed. Here we first heard that the cavalry and troops that were in advance, were engaged with the enemy. About three we crossed the Vouga where the advanced post of the French had been in the morning, and at five o'clock arrived at Albergaria-a-Velha, where we halted for the night. We marched again however soon after midnight, and at one o'clock on the 11th reached Oliveira [de Azemeis], where first the desolation made by the French became apparent, the wine casks all stove in, the furniture and houses all torn to pieces, the town looked like a desert. Several wounded French and some prisoners were left there. They had been taken the day before; they said they were completely surprised, having had no idea the English had been so near them; being without a friend in the country they had been unable to gain any intelligence what ever. We did not march on the morning of the 12th till eight o'clock, owing to the horse of the officer sent with the orders having fallen lame. It had been intended we should have moved at four. We passed over the ground where a skirmish had taken place the day before; the peasants encouraged by a priest, were employed in burying the dead. The French in their retreat shot all the natives they saw; an old priest with venerable white hairs, lay by the road side with his throat cut by these barbarians. At one o'clock we arrived at Cavalhos, where we had hardly been dismissed when the drum again beat to arms. We were informed that the leading brigade had crossed the Douro, and were engaged with the enemy, and we were ordered up to support them. We lost no time in moving off and almost ran the whole way to Villa Nova di Porto, for the last three miles amidst crowds of people anxiously waiting the result of the combat, which the roar of distant artillery and musketry assured us was not yet terminated. The fine quays on the bank of the river were thronged with people, and a sacred white standard of an immense size displayed. The boats carried us over quickly but it was not till our arrival in Oporto, that we learnt our

23

exertions to arrive had been of no avail; that we were too late to have a share in that glorious day, which will do so much credit to the handful of troops engaged in it. We were billeted in a street in the north part of the town and I was most hospitably received by a Mr Ribeira, a Desembengador or Judge, to whom I am under many obligations. It is not possible to describe the horrors committed by the French during the four days the place was given up to pillage; the unfortunate inhabitants of this opulent town were left to the mercy of the most brutal soldiery in the world, the most wanton barbarities were committed. Women with infants at their breasts were shot in the streets in the open face of day, and the unfortunate people were in hourly expectation that the whole town would have been burnt; no one durst go out into the streets, or even look out at the windows without being shot at. Five musket shots had been fired into the house I was at, one of which passed within a foot of the head of old Mr Ribeira whom they had thrown the day before over the garden wall.

The 13th we remained the whole day at Oporto. The weather was cold, wet and uncomfortable, but on the morning of the 14th the day we left Oporto, the rain descended in torrents, the lanes we had to march through were scarcely passable. At five in the afternoon we arrived at Casal di Pedro, a few houses scarcely deserving the name of a village, where we passed the night. The country in this province is much richer and in a higher state of cultivation than any we have yet seen. From Casal di Pedro we could see Vila do Conde about three miles from us, with a magnificent aqueduct two or three miles in length; the country beautifully wooded, and a quantity of fine oak timber. On the morning of the 15th we marched on the road to Barcelos, but before we had got three miles which we were nearly three hours in accomplishing, we received a counter order and returned to Casal di Pedro. It seems it was expected that the French would have retreated by Tui, but when it was found they had taken the road to Chaves, it was necessary we also should change our route; so we marched that evening to Villa Nova de Famalicao in excessive heavy rain, and over roads almost impassable. This bad weather the French experienced as well as ourselves, but as it spoilt all the bread in the haversacks, our men were nearly starved; it besides destroyed our shoes so fast that the men were almost bare foot. At four o'clock on the morning of the 14th, we marched in the same weather and over the same description of roads; at three in the afternoon we arrived at the beautiful city of Braga where we halted for two hours, got some wine and a little bread for the men, and moved on again. It was ten o'clock at night before we arrived at the village we were to rest at; the darkest night I ever remember to have been out in, so that I wonder we ever got there at all. Many men from fatigue were left behind; so that when we paraded the next morning, sixty men were absent and the rest were so jaded and knocked up, so hungry and bare foot, that they looked very unequal to continue the chase. The French had been at Povoa [de Lanhoso] two nights before; they had left manifest tokens of their having been there. Amongst other acts of wanton cruelty they had destroyed the wine casks (which are here very large and expensive) burnt the implements of husbandry so that the poor people, impoverished by the march of two armies will run the risk of starving. Tired as we were, the next day carried us on (in the hopes of overtaking Marshal Soult) to Padroes, nine miles. On our arrival we met an order to remain where we were; the misapprehension of this order carried us back to Povoa, the weather equally bad, supplies very scanty and both officers as well as men suffering from hunger, wet, and want of rest. The 18th to rectify the mistake made the day before, we went on again the nine miles to Padroes, a place more wretched than you can conceive, and lying more on the direct road, more exhausted than the village we had quitted. We halted here the 19th, the weather continuing the same, and hardly a waterproof house in the place. We now began to lament our hard fate; there was nothing to keep up our spirits; all hope of overtaking Soult was at an end, as he had now forty-eight hours start of us. The Brigade of Guards had fallen in with their rear guard the night before, and had dispersed them; the want of bread prevented our further pursuit, besides it was known to the army that Victor, taking advantages of our being so far to the northward, was advancing on Lisbon. Under these circumstances it was deemed necessary to retrograde; which we began to do on the 20th, we reached Guimaraes a very good town, after rather a long march through the mountains. It had suffered from the French in their retreat; at a large nunnery now occupied by our men; they committed their usual depredations. The convent was strewed with broken fans, the remains of artificial flowers, and trifles of this description which they had wantonly destroyed, because they could not or would not carry them away. On the 21st, we moved through

25

the most beautiful country we had seen in Portugal, to the Convent of Santo Tirso, which contained three regiments within its walls.

The Commander-in-Chief arrived in the afternoon with all his staff and we dined with him in the refectory. The 22nd, brought us to Oporto, and to the very kind host Ribeira, who sent out to meet us, and who had a dinner ready for us at four o'clock, the time of our arrival; and with whom we stayed the next day. Amongst the other miseries of this campaign, is the want of money. We have scarcely ever been able to get as much from the Pay Master General as would mend the soldier's shoes, and both officers and men will soon be naked. I experienced a sad misfortune here in losing my mule, which was stolen from a field in which she was turned out; a great loss, as the beast had been of considerable use to me in the mountains; the back of my own horse having been sore, from the length of time we were performing the marches, the wetness of the weather, and the steepness and badness of the roads.

Mr Ribeira having furnished me with letters of recommendation for this place, I left him on the morning of the 24th, with regret, as I should much have liked to have remained with him some time longer. After a march of four leagues (the league in this country are four and sometimes five miles) we halted at a miserable village, that formed a perfect contrast to the quarters we had just left; as did the deep sand roads near the sea, the large fir woods with only occasional patches of cultivation, to the country we had passed over north of the Douro.

On the 25th, we marched through Ovar, a good town, and embarked on the lake of Aveiro. This lake communicates with the sea, by a narrow and shallow passage through which boats only in fine weather can enter. The passage was far from pleasant, it rained the whole time and it was dark before we reached Aveiro. Sir William Myers [1] and myself were billeted on the Superintendent of Tobacco, where we found a party of well dressed people playing cards. We left Aveiro in the morning at day break, without having been able to see anything of the town, but we press on so rapidly we have no time to look at anything.

---

1. Sir William James Myers had become Lieutenant Colonel of the 7 Foot on 15 August 1804. For a brief period after Talavera, he commanded the Brigade. He was severely wounded at the Battle of Albuera and died of his wounds the next day, 17 May 1811.

A march of five long leagues, which took nearly all our day light to perform, brought us to Cantanhede; this town was unfortunately full of wine, in very ill-secured cellars, into which our people broke, and committed great excesses, which I was very much grieved at, as hitherto we had behaved ourselves very well; but our men are so harassed by incessant marching without appearing to derive any benefit from it, or without any prospect of its termination, that they are become careless and do not mind what becomes of them. On the 27th, we marched in here, where I hope we shall at least have one weeks rest, after which where we shall go is uncertain. I suppose not to Spain, if the news of the defeat of the Austrians is correct.[1]

Letter 8   Abrantes, 7 June 1809

My dear Madam,

I have an officer going down to Lisbon by the Tagus and cannot let him go without giving you a line, although I had not intended to have written till I had obtained a little more intelligence respecting our future plans. We came here in six days easy marches from Coimbra with little interesting on the road; too little indeed to make a continuance of my journal anything but tedious. The first three days were to the small villages of Rabacal, Ansiao and Pechins, at neither of which was there anything remarkable. The weather generally wet, but more so after the march was over than during the time we were out. The fourth day brought us to Tomar, a good town; we were quartered in the Convento de Cristo.[2] This convent is very ancient and has beautiful remains of gothic architecture, especially the gate of the chapel and the choir, which is

1. This letter being dated 28 May must refer to the battles of Abensberg (20 April), Eckmühl (22 April) and storming of Ratisbon (23 April) which formed the opening phase of Napoleon's war against Austria. The surrender of Vienna (13 May) and the French defeat at Aspern Essling (21–22 May) would not be known of for a month or more and would have given more hope.
2. Originally built in 1162 by the Knights Templar as their headquarters. Following the papal suppression of the order in 1314, many knights fled here from France and Spain. The Portuguese King Dom Dinis coolly side stepped the papal ban by renaming the knights the 'Order of Christ'. King João III later transformed the convent from a neo political headquarters of the order into a monastic community.

27

fitted up in the style of Henry the Seventh's chapel in Westminster Abbey; the carved work of the stalls in the same manner. The Kings of Spain, Philip II and his successor were great benefactors to this convent, when they had possession of Portugal. Amongst other things they brought water to the convent from the distance of a league, carrying it over deep ravines by a handsome aqueduct of two tiers of arches one above the other.[1] One of these we fell in with on our march and being unconnected with any other building had a very good effect. The people of the convents were not so civil as others we have met with. The farther from danger the less civility; the French, however had paid them a visit, the year before, and had taken all the money they had in their strong box; all their plate and jewels. They estimated their loss at sixty thousand cruzados; a cruzado is worth about three shillings, English. They left them two silver pixes for sacrament, and their rich stock of embroidered velvet dresses, which as they were in a hurry they did not think worth the trouble of carrying away. The country about Tomar is beautiful, and there is a very good river, which about four miles below the town is contracted by two mountains, and make a handsome fall. Over this is thrown a bridge of one arch. This scene with the surrounding country would do no discredit to Wales. We crossed this river near where it entered the Tagus, by a bridge of boats, to Punhente,[2] a small dirty town on the side of a steep hill. It is close to the Tagus, which is here a fine river, with a beautiful turn into another reach just above. The sombre appearance of the olive, formed a good contrast with the bright green of the corn, and the view was altogether very striking. An old lady asked Sir William Myers and myself to tea at the house where we were billeted. She was highly powdered and with a carnation stuck in her head, which by the bye, is the height of the 'ton' in Portugal; she had two daughters, one of whom spoke French, so we had a pleasant evening; at least a little variety. This morning brought us in here; all I can say of the place, is, that it stands on the summit of a mountain that overlooks the Tagus, and surrounding country, which shall be the subject of a future letter. Victor is one hundred and sixty miles from this; whether we shall follow him into Spain remains to be proved.

1. The Pegoes aqueduct built in the seventeenth century is still an impressive sight.
2. The town of Punhente is now known as Constancia.

My dear Sir,

I have been kept so constantly moving, that I have hardly had a moment to spare, but having written by every favourable opportunity to my mother, I hope my letters have afforded amusement to you as well as herself. You will have heard from her that although we came in for no share of the honor [sic] obtained in the passage of the Douro, we had our share of the fatigue, which you may suppose was great especially after we left Oporto in chase of the Duke of Dalmatia.[1] The weather was very bad, and we traversed roads supposed heretofore impassable for armies.

Our principal cause of failure in not completely annihilating that corps, arose from Marshal Beresford's [2] not having timely intimation of our having crossed the Douro; he first heard of it forty-eight hours after, by a French Commissary who had been taken prisoner. Could he have had earlier notice of our success, he might have interposed between Soult and Galicia, when nothing could have prevented his having been taken prisoner, with his whole force. The French did not behave well at Oporto; they were completely panic struck, and ran; though much superior to the force that first crossed the river, hardly attempting to defend themselves. I met with great

1. Marshal Nicolas Jean de Dieu Soult, Duke of Dalmatia.
2. Marshal William Carr Beresford had been tasked with the reform of the Portuguese army in 1809. By the time of the Oporto campaign there were some signs of improvement and Wellesley ordered Beresford with a largely Portuguese force, (which including Wilson's and Silveira's detachments picked up en route, amounted to some 11,000 men) to make a turning movement to the east of Oporto to attempt to cut off Soult's line of retreat to Spain. Soult had placed a force commanded by Loison at the bridge of Amarante to protect this crossing but on the arrival of Beresford's force he retired without contesting the crossing. Soult hearing of this too late to remedy the situation was forced to flee Oporto northwards via the mountainous region of the Entre Douro to link up with the forces of Marshal Ney in Galicia. This was only accomplished by rapid marching over the mountains having abandoned virtually all their cannon and equipment. It has been suggested that a rapid advance by Beresford's force to Amarante and beyond could have sealed Soult in Oporto. However it is clear that Wellesley and Beresford had not expected Loison to flee so meekly and the defeat of Soult was far from certain. A drive north westward by Beresford could have been disastrous to the Portuguese troops if attacked in isolation and even in the event that they could have stood in the way of Soult's retreat, were they really strong enough to stem the flow of a larger and very desperate French army?

civility and most hospitable entertainment from a Mr Ribeira, a judge, which I should be glad if hereafter, I could in any way repay.

We have now moved to this part of the country, to oppose Marshal Victor,[1] who entered Portugal while we were in pursuit of Soult; he has already returned, and is at Talavera de la Reina 160 miles from this, where it is reported we are to follow him; time will show whether this measure is likely to be successful. If Bonaparte can succeed in Austria, and of his ultimate success who can doubt, he will enter Spain and fall upon us when we are at that distance from the sea that there will be no retreat, and we shall be in a greater scrape than the Corunna army.

We hope to stay here at any rate some days to refit, as we have been marching without intercession these last six weeks, and in that time have traversed [a] great part of the Kingdom. We have had a great deal of wet weather; it is now fine, and today is quite summer, and we may shortly expect to suffer from heat. The army has been exceedingly healthy, perhaps if we rest; the seeds of disease which fatigue and wet may have engendered, may at some future time break forth. At present we have scarce as many sick as we should have had in England or Ireland. The whole Army have behaved very ill, and the men have committed outrages that have disgraced them. The excessive long marches, frequently by night, narrow roads, want of bread, and other causes, occasioned straggling and plunder, and having the example of the French before their eyes, they have signalised themselves to the great annoyance of the inhabitants we came to protect. Severe examples have restrained it for the time; it is still however very bad.

Letter 10   Camp near Abrantes, 16 June 1809

Dear Still,

What are to be our future operations? Is not this a curious

---

1. Marshal Claude Victor-Perrin, Duke of Belluno commanded the I Corps of the French Army in Extremadura. In the absence of the main British force at Oporto, Victor had probed the Portuguese border, advancing to Alcantara but had been deterred from advancing further, being unsure of the size of the British and Portuguese Corps of observation under Mackenzie stationed on the River Zezere and the Spanish Army of Cuesta hovering to the south. Victor eventually retired to Talavera de la Reina.

question for a man on the spot, to ask of you who are at such a distance? But, the fact is, we can know nothing. We expect to advance into Spain, but cannot learn whether we wait for our reinforcements, or whether we move as soon as our commissariat arrangements are complete. The bridge of Alcantara has (it is said) been blown up.[1] If this is the case I take it for granted Victor, who is on the Tagus with 24,000 men, means to attack Cuesta before we can join him. I am told the latter has a better organized force than any of the Spaniards have hitherto had. Victor's Army is represented as being composed of two thirds Germans and Italians. It is from a deserter of the latter nation I have this account. His artillery, forty pieces, said as well as his cavalry to be very good. In the latter arm we may be a match for him, but our artillery has been beat to pieces by our chase after Soult, and it will take some time to put it to rights again. I understand Sir Arthur has been very much displeased at the statistism [sic]. Two regiments are going from this to Gibraltar; 2nd Battalions 27th, and 9th. They are to be replaced by two more effective battalions 48th and 61st.[2]

The position of our army at present is as follows, Mackenzie's Brigade [3] at Sobreira Formosa and Cardigos, between this and Castelo Branco; at which place it is said, the Portuguese Army is to assemble. Fane's Brigade of Heavy cavalry [4] in the highest order, and horses in as good condition as when they left England, halted on the left bank of the Tagus, under the magnificent position of Abrantes, the communication kept up by a bridge of boats. Hill's,[5]

1. Colonel William Mayne commanding a battalion of the Loyal Lusitanian Legion and the Idanha Militia, bravely attempted to hinder the advance of Victor but was forced to give way, blowing up the centre of the bridge as he retired. The impressive bridge still exists.
2. Bingham gets a little confused here. Oman states that 1/61st and 1/48th did indeed arrive from Gibraltar. The 2/9th went to Gibraltar to relieve the 1/61st, but the 3/27th (not 2/27th) were sent to Lisbon not Gibraltar.
3. Major General Alexander Mackenzie was General Officer Commanding 3rd Division in which he commanded a brigade consisting of 3/27th, 2/31st and 1/45th. (The 2/24th replacing the 3/27th before Talavera).
4. Major General Sir Henry Fane 1st Dragoon Guards, commanded a cavalry brigade consisting of 3 Dragoon Guards and 4 Dragoons.
5. Major General Sir Rowland Hill commanded 2nd Division and a brigade within consisting of 1/3rd, 2/48th, 3/66th and 1 company 5/60th.

Stewart's,[1] A. Campbell's,[2] and Sontag's[3] (now commanded by Colonel Peacock of the Guards[4]) Brigades of infantry in two lines in rear of the cavalry. The Brigade of Guards[5] at Punhente two leagues further down the river. Where Cameron's[6] and Tilson's[7] Brigades are, I do not exactly know; one is in advance, somewhere near Mackenzie's, the other in rear of the Guards. General Tilson it is reported has had permission sent to him to return home in consequence of some strong remonstrance on his part relative to serving with the Portuguese troops. They are indeed wretched, and miserably non-effective, but has a young officer a right to remonstrate too strongly on what every one is aware of? And in case of failure make allowance for Colonel Donkin,[8] our late Quarter Master General is to have his Brigade.

1. General Richard Stewart commanded a brigade in the 2nd Division, consisting of 29th and 1st Regiment of detachments (the 1/48th was added before Talavera on its arrival from Gibraltar). The regiments of detachments were made up of convalescents and men left behind from the units in Moore's Corunna campaign. They were broken up after Talavera and the men returned to their parent units.
2. Brigadier General Alexander Campbell commanded 4th Division and a brigade within consisting of 2/7th, 1 company 5/60th and 2/53rd.
3. Brigadier General John Sontag, a Hanoverian officer, commanded a brigade in the 4th Division, consisting of 97th, 1 company 5/60th and 2nd Regiment of detachments.
4. A Brigadier General Sir Warren Peacocke of the Guards was the Commandant at Lisbon. There is no reference to his having taken a field command vice Sontag in Oman or any other reference that I can find. Indeed Schaumann states that he was 'incapable of taking command in the field'.
5. The Brigade of Guards of Brigadier General Henry Campbell in the 1st Division consisted of 1 Coldstream, 1 Scots Guards and 1 company 5/60th.
6. The Brigade of Colonel Alexander Cameron in the 1st Division consisted of 2/9th, 2/83rd and 1 company 5/60th. (The 2/9th was replaced by the 1/40th before Talavera.)
7. Major General Christopher Tilson commanded a brigade in the 3rd Division consisting of 5 companies 5/60th, 2/87th and 1/88th.
8. On 21 June, Tilson moved to the command of Hill's brigade in 2nd Division, Donkin replaced him in command of the brigade in the 3rd Division. Bingham's comments regarding the move are not readily understood but can be explained. Oman does not show any Portuguese regiments incorporated into the British Divisions until February 1810, but I believe he is in error here. Wellington clearly mentions 16 Portuguese regiment as forming a part of Stewart's brigade at Oporto (see Gurwood Vol. IV page 323) and it is likely that Tilson had a regiment attached to his brigade as well. Whatever the reason Tilson certainly disappears from the list of officers commanding brigades in Spain before 1810.

I will just give you two anecdotes, for the first I can vouch its being authentic. A battalion of the 40th Regiment was put into our Brigade,[1] on our advance from Coimbra their strength was 750 on paper, nearly complete; the effectives were 350, of whom about fifty were left in hospital at Coimbra, when we left it. The 2nd Battalion was attached to Cameron's Brigade, and when nearly up with the French at Ruivaes, could only muster forty-six rank and file. The 16th Regiment you know is mentioned in the despatch as having behaved well on the 11th May, but no notice is taken of the command having devolved on Doyle,[2] in consequence of the Colonel having been taken ill five minutes before the action began!

We have been two days in our huts, and our camp is hardly complete. Yesterday morning about five o'clock, to prove if our huts were waterproof, we had a thunder shower, which has cooled the air to that degree that there was no sleeping before sunrise; the climate of Portugal is far from being what I expected, we have had nearly as much rain and it has been quite as cold as it would have been in England. We have been remarkably healthy as yet, and have only lost one man by sickness since we landed, but we have had a man shot by the Portuguese, as he was employed pressing bullocks; his name was Richard Drew.[3] I lament him, as he belonged to the Parish of Rushton, and lived in the Chase near Deans Leage. I have no means of sending this letter, therefore shall not conclude in hopes of having something more to say before I close it.

June 17th, Mellish[4] arrived the night before last from Cuesta's[5] army. Victor has retired; they say on the Ebro, he is most likely only

---

1. The copy states the 10th, but this is an obvious mistake as they did not serve in Spain at this time. I have corrected it to the 40th which was added to the brigade at the time described by Bingham.
2. The 16th Portuguese Line Regiment is mentioned by Wellington in his Oporto Despatch of 12 May 1809. Wellington states that the regiment was commanded by Colonel Machado and ably seconded by Lieutenant Colonel Doyle. Bingham indicates that Machado did not command that day, but that all the glory should have been Doyle's.
3. Private Richard Drew is simply marked in the Return as 'Dead 7 June'.
4. Captain Mellish was Assistant Adjutant General.
5. General Gregorio Garcia de la Cuesta was the Spanish commander of the Army of Extremadura. He was heavily defeated by the French at the Battles of Rio Seco and Medellin. He suffered a stroke on 12 August 1809 and retired to Majorca where he died in 1812.

falling back on reinforcements, for how they can foresee he is to retire so far as the Ebro I can not tell.

I dined with General Hill, yesterday, he seems to think we shall not move for some days; there is however a report today that we are to enter Spain immediately. Don't set me down as a grumbler, when I say I do not look forward to a march into Spain with any confidence. What are 20,000 British troops to do in the heart of that country? For can any reasonable man suppose that with this force, if aided to the utmost by the Spaniards, we can drive the French beyond the Pyrenees before they have reinforcements?

The business of the Bridge of Alcantara happened as follows:- The French before they retired sent a strong column in that direction, probably with the intention of destroying the bridge. The Portuguese Colonel Mayne, who commanded a force on the right bank of the river, thought he should sleep much better with the river between him and the enemy, and saved them the trouble by springing the mines previously prepared and destroyed eighty feet of that most beautiful fabric; one of the most perfect and finest of the roman bridges. I have now completed my allowance of baggage animals, five; three would answer if their backs were made of iron, but unfortunately they will get sore occasionally.

Letter 11   Camp near Abrantes, 21 June 1809

My dear Sir,

I received yesterday your letter of the 12th of May, which is the only one I have had since I landed, except one directed to the Cove of Cork. I have written every week to my mother, with a regular journal of our marches and proceedings, and from her you may have heard how well I have stood the fatigue attending on long marches and wet weather.

The army is at present collected in this neighbourhood where we have remained a fortnight, to refresh after our short campaign in the north, and we are now preparing (I think) to undertake a very hazardous expedition, to advance into Spain.

I much fear that even supposing Bonaparte had his hands full of employment, the French force now in Spain, when concentrated would oppose to us three or four times our number. That they will draw this force together, I have no doubt, and we have already seen how little dependence can be placed on our allies. The Portuguese army are (it is said) moving towards the north of Portugal, to prevent Soult and some corps with whom he has formed a junction, moving on Oporto. His dragoons have already been seen on the Minho, and should the Portuguese be forced, we should have this Army in our rear.

Marshal Victor, who was in our front, has retired, perhaps with a view of drawing us on further into the country. We have quitted the houses for the fields. Last week we were marched into a large fir grove, and were ordered to cover ourselves as well as possible. We have now very comfortable huts, which keep out some rain, and are certainly cooler than tents. The first night we got exceedingly wet, but although we have had thunder showers every day since, we have felt no great inconvenience since that time.

The force in camp at this place consists of nine regiments of infantry, and two of cavalry; the rest of the army are also in huts in the neighbourhood of the Tagus, for the convenience of supplies. It is now reported we are to march on Sunday, but whether we enter Spain by Alcantara or Badajoz, we have no idea. We shall have seen a good deal of the world before we return, we have already marched upwards of five hundred miles, and shall I dare say add some thousands to it before we return. How I shall enjoy a walk on the Downs with you, and a long palaver on all that has happened. Richard Drew who came from Dorset, has been shot, by our good allies the Portuguese, as he was recovering some bullocks that had strayed from the cars.

We have been very healthy, and have lost only one man by sickness since we landed.

Letter 12   **Camp near Abrantes, 22 June 1809**

My dear Mother,

I wrote to you when we first arrived at this place, and fearful lest we should move immediately I write again although I have no present prospect of sending it. We are to advance into Spain and my next letter may be from Madrid; if you ask me how I like this measure, I will tell you, 'not at all'.

With what happened last year, we ought to be careful, as we may make ourselves certain we shall be outnumbered, and the farther we advance, the farther we get from our own resources, and the more difficult it will become, to make any retrograde movement; and I am afraid our faithful allies would be ready to turn against us.

We remained one week in Abrantes, a dirty but beautifully situated town, standing on a very high and steep hill above the Tagus. I do not know that it is celebrated for anything but having furnished the title of Duke to Bonaparte's friend Junot; in consequence, the town was exempted from military contribution. The scaffolding of the illumination on the occasion still remains at the court house, where a brilliant star of coloured lamps was exhibited. The people of this place in consequence of this honour conferred on them are very much in the French interest; the poor Marquess, who bore the title before, was sent to France, where he is now living in great penury, and teaching music for his subsistence. On the side of the hill, next to the river, are plantations of the olive, and though the olive is not of a lively colour, the tout ensemble from the opposite bank of the river, is very grand and picturesque.

After having been in the town a week, we marched out to this place, which is on the left bank of the Tagus, and about a mile and a half from Abrantes. We have constructed a very neat little town of fir huts, thatched with heather; and I assure you some of them are very pretty; they don't keep out the heavy rains that fall at this time of the year altogether, but they are very cool, much more so than tents. We have nine regiments of infantry and two of cavalry, the 4th Dragoons is one. Colonel Dalbiac [1] called on me yesterday and made very kind enquiries after you. If we were not very busy in preparations for our march, this life would be very dull; we live a good deal by ourselves, no opportunity of having a mess; generally eat our pittance of salt or fresh beef alone. I was introduced the other day to Brigadier General Fane, who was very civil; he is much looked up to in this Army and considered a promising officer.

Letter 13   Under a tree near Castelo Branco, 1 July 1809

My dear Madam,

I hear a mail for England is to be made up this evening, and although I have not time to write a long letter, I never let an oppor-

1. Lieutenant Colonel John Charles Dalbiac 4 Dragoons.

tunity pass without at least letting you know how I am. I like this sort of marching much better than being in quarters; I have now a soldier's round tent, which I carry on my mule, and which makes me very comfortable. We have passed over a most uninteresting mountain country, since we left Abrantes, but the roads have been better than those we have been accustomed to. The first day we go to Gaviao, the second to Nisa, where we were put into quarters, and where the people were so uncivil they would hardly give me a glass of water. The third day we crossed the Tagus again on a flying bridge, and encamped near Vila Velha [de Rodao], (the wind blows my paper about so I can scarcely write) where we encountered one of the heaviest thunder storms, I ever remember to have experienced. Yesterday we were near the village of Sarnadas [de Rodao], and this morning we came here. This part of Portugal is very miserable; the country nearly one barren heath, or covered with gum cistus; scarcely any signs of cultivation, except near the few scattered hamlets, and I think we have hardly seen ten in the sixty miles we have traversed; neither wine nor bread to be purchased. We carry every thing with us, each man carries four day's bread, and the oxen we eat march with us. We have not hitherto suffered much from heat, but must expect soon to do so. We are to enter Spain on Tuesday, and halt near Zarza la Mayor, (the first town in Spain) one day, after which it is said, five days will carry us to Plasencia. The report today is, the French have retired from Madrid, eight days since. I hope we shall get to Madrid, as I shall have great pleasure in giving you an account of that celebrated city. You must not expect my letters from bivouac's to be long, as I have none of the conveniences for writing; such as table, chair, &c.

Letter 14   Camp near Plasencia, 11 July 1809

My dear Sir,

We have arrived here after a long but not tiresome march from Abrantes, halting every night on our route, which has been to the neighbourhood of the following towns and villages, which will enable you to trace us on a map.

Gaviao, Nisa, Vila Velha, Sarnadas, Castelo Branco, Ladoeira, Zebreira.

Enter Spain to Zarza la Mayor, and halt one day. Moraleja,

Coria, Galisteo, Plasencia, in a wood about three miles from which I am now writing. Having had my health very well, I have enjoyed this march very much; we have passed over a great variety of country, and encamped in several most beautiful and picturesque situations. We arrived here on the 9th and it will be the 19th before the whole army will have assembled; we shall then have 20,000 men. Nine leagues from this is Cuesta with an army of 40,000 men, very well appointed. Sir Arthur Wellesley went yesterday to concert measures with him, for the attack of Victor who is at Talavera de la Reina, with some say 50, some 40, some 30,000 men.[1] When we first entered Spain it was said Joseph Bonaparte commanded the army in person and that it amounted to 52,000 men; it is now reported he has left Madrid for the purpose of pushing on to Seville; indeed both parties appear ignorant of the other's plans or movements. Nor can we wonder at the scantiness of intelligence in a country where each town is ten miles and often at a greater distance from the other; and you never meet with a single house, and seldom a single person between one and the other. We hear that Blake's army, formed at Valencia, have dispersed, having hardly fired a single shot and this is not very encouraging at our first starting. The people of Spain are I dare say well affected to the cause, that is to say if <u>wishing</u> would drive the French out of their country, but no exertion do they seem disposed to make. Tomorrow, on Sir Arthur's return we shall know something but should Victor retreat, I doubt if we shall be able to follow him. If we attack at Talavera, we shall be eight days march from the frontiers of Portugal, nor can it be concealed that this army is chiefly composed of young soldiers, hardly fit to undertake a campaign of marches, and manoeuvres, as this is likely to be; and Cuesta has it is said, already complained of the slowness of our movements. We are badly off for Generals. After the Commander of the Forces you must descend very low before you meet much talent.

Our movements on this last march have been on rather a grand scale; a column of nine battalions. Fortunately, the roads have been in general good, so that we have had few stops. Here we take things very easily; we have no outlying picquets, or guards of any description. All the General Officers live in the town of Plasencia, nearly three miles off, with only one Captain's Guard in the town. Our

1. Before the arrival of King Joseph's Army, Victor had only 23,000 men.

only advance is <u>under</u> Sir Robert Wilson, who has the Lusitanian Legion[1] and one squadron of hussars <u>under</u> him.

Our camp which is irregular, is most beautifully situated in two and sometimes three lines, in a forest of cork trees, the spot where my own tent is pitched is exactly like that described in Don Quixote, where the divine Atltisidora makes her appearance at the funeral of the shepherd, I forget his name. The valley is closed with mountains, even now tipped with snow; a pellucid river, deep enough to swim in, passes within fifty paces of the front line. You shall hear again as soon as anything is decided.

Letter 15   Camp near Plasencia, 11 July 1809

My dear Madam,

My last was written to you from under a tree near Castelo Branco, three days after which we entered Spain, by Zarza la Mayor. The river or rather rivulet which divides the two kingdoms is not very broad, and at present scarcely above the ankles. There are no tokens either by custom houses, or otherwise to denote the division. The frontier town on the side of Portugal is Salvaterra [do Extremo], the second days march after we passed the border was to the banks of the Alagon, near the town of Moraleja, which has once been fortified that is to say, somewhat in the modern manner, for all the towns we have yet seen are walled. The situation of our bivouac was beautiful, on a plain with many large trees scattered here and there, in the most picturesque manner. The third day brought us to the neighbourhood of Coria a large town with a handsome cathedral. It stands on the banks of the Alagon, a considerable (but not navigable) river; the appearance of this part of Spain is striking. Vast plains, some of them well cultivated, destitute of enclosures, and without a single house or even cottage without the walls of the towns, which are themselves thinly

1. Sir Robert Wilson with the Loyal Lusitanian Legion and a number of Spanish troops totalling 4,000 men had advanced as far as Escalona, only twenty miles from Madrid. This movement disconcerted Victor until King Joseph arrived with reinforcements and ordered a move forward against the allied army at Talavera. Hearing that Soult had passed the Puerto de Banos and the allied army was in retreat, Wilson fled back through the mountains eventually reaching Portugal after a number of near misses.

scattered; so that the population of this fine country with its advantages of soil and climate is smaller than you can conceive. The towns are much better built and greatly cleaner than the towns in Portugal; but the environs are not so pleasant, or so much improved. There are neither gardens nor fruit trees, but a high wall with sometimes a steeple rising above it, stands alone in the midst of a large plain, covered with grain, which has on the whole a dreary appearance.

Friday the 8th, the fourth days march in Spain, we encamped on the banks of the same river. On the 9th we forded this same river just under our encampment; it was about three feet deep, and very rapid, and after a tedious march, arrived here.

Plasencia is the best town we have seen, prettily situated, walled around, and with a handsome cathedral. Our camp is in a wood, about two miles or more from the town. The scenery about is delightful; high mountains tipped with snow, terminate a valley well wooded, with our old friend the Alagon, winding down it. We know not how long we are to remain here, or what we are to do; the certain intelligence that Blake's Army have dispersed without having hardly fired a shot is but a bad greeting to us on our arrival.[1] Marshal Victor is about four days march from us, at Talavera. Various are the reports as to his strength. Sir Arthur Wellesley went yesterday to consult with Cuesta who is with his army nine leagues from us. What the result of their deliberations may be, we are anxiously looking for. The weather has been very hot, and both men and officers are beginning to suffer from it. I (I thank God) have kept my health and have suffered no inconvenience from the climate, but having my face completely peeled.

Letter 16   **Camp near Talavera, 26 July 1809**

My dear Madam,

Our means of sending letters to England become every day more difficult. The distance from this to Lisbon is so great and the numbers of the army have so much increased, that no notice is now ever given in orders, of a mail, or bag, being made up; as letters

1. Having fought bravely although defeated at the Battle of Maria, Blake made his army stand against a reinforced Marshal Suchet at Belchite and was completely routed.

40

would pour in so fast, that it would require more mules than can be spared to carry them.

It will, I know, give you great pleasure to hear that (thank God) I continue to enjoy uninterrupted good health, and that although generally speaking the army may be said to be sickly, I have never been absent a day from my duty. I wrote both to yourself and my father from Plasencia, which place we left on the 17th, the whole army having assembled, and we moved together. Our first day's march was a short one, not more than nine miles to Malpartida [de Plasencia] near which we were placed in the open plain, without tree or bush to shelter us, exposed to the hottest sun we had as yet felt; not a breath of air, and the tents much hotter than the open plain. Near us crawled a half stagnant stream which conveyed no sensation of coolness or refreshment. In the midst of the mis-fortunes it was impossible to forbear laughing at an officer of the Guards, just from the shady side of Pall Mall, reposing under the shade of a green silk umbrella, and coiling up his legs that they might partake of the benefit of the shade. After some search, some four or five of us, thought ourselves happy in finding a miserable hovel which had been a mill which did afford a little shelter from the powerful rays of the sun. The only reason we can think of for the bad choice of this bivouac, was that the general officer might be accommodated in the village; as a short distance in advance would have brought us to a forest through which runs the clear and rapid River Teitar and where we should have avoided the extreme heat to which we were thus uselessly exposed.

On the 18th another provoking mistake was made; the army, for the same reason as influenced the choice of ground on the day before, was ordered to Majadas, but on our arrival there, the wise heads of the Quarter Master General's department found out that a fine river laid down in the map was perfectly dry; and that there were only two wells to supply twenty thousand men, besides the horses and cattle. This discovery was not made till the head of the column had nearly arrived on the ground, and we had to return nearly four miles to a most beautiful situation on the banks of the Teitar; where large forest trees were covered nearly to their summit with wild vines, falling in beautiful festoons. The river was nearly as broad as the Stour at Blandford, and the view was bounded by mountains covered with snow. This day was also very hot, and we were twelve hours under arms. The next day's march (19th) was a

41

very tedious one. We were in the rear of a column of twenty-four battalions; all the cool part of the morning we marched very slow, on account of narrow bridges; all the heat of the day, very fast. Twelve hours brought us to a stream in the same forest which had contained the whole distance, to the neighbourhood of a solitary inn, called Venta di Sentinella. Here we lived in great luxury; we bought a pig on the march, and we caught a hare. As we came on our ground, our situation was again most picturesque, on a small island, surrounded by the brook, covered with large trees, and so wild that it appeared as if human footsteps had never penetrated these shades before. We marched as usual the next day (20th) and about three o'clock the whole Army debouched on one of the plains of Castille in four columns, forming as they drew out of the wood, the most beautiful spectacle I ever beheld. After passing some miles over these plains, which in spring would maintain large herds of cattle, or might be turned to any purpose of cultivation, we arrived at Oropesa, and were quartered in a convent which stood at the foot of the hill on which the town (a venerable structure surrounded with walls and battlements) was seated.

The French had retired from it that morning, carrying away all the bread, and doing as usual, as much wanton mischief as lay in their power. Not a vestige of the wood work of the church of the convent we were quartered at remained, the doors, the windows, and even some of the rafters of the roof, had been taken to make fires of. The library had not escaped, and the books and manuscripts, the collection of ages, were scattered all over the field. At three the morning of the 21st we were under arms, expecting to meet the French at this place. Just however as we were on the point of moving off, an order came for us to pile arms, and the advance of the Spanish Army made its appearance. It continued to pass till 12 o'clock; 40,000 men it was said. Their infantry was good, and their artillery appeared better, and the cavalry looked tolerably well, but of them you will hear more hereafter. About 8 o'clock we received intimation we were not to march, and that General Cuesta was to see the army at five o'clock in the afternoon, at which time the line turned out for him. He rode along the line from left to right, a stupid, mean looking old man, paralytic, with no appearance of the hero about him.[1] We understood he expressed himself very well

1. Descriptions of Cuesta all agree in describing a corpulent and indolent man.

satisfied with the looks of our troops, and certainly considering all the fatigues and constant marching since they landed, they looked remarkably well. On the 22nd we marched at 8 am, having previously heard a good deal of firing, we shortly passed the Spanish Army drawn out in two lines in the plain on the left of the road. These cavalry had been reinforced that morning by the Duke D'Albuquerque's Corps.[1] Shortly after the spires of the town of Talavera, appeared in sight and a good [deal] of firing in front of it, led us to suppose we should soon fall in with the French. At four however, we came to our ground for the night in the olive groves near the town, and to the left of it, the Spanish Army passed through the town and encamped in front of it. It appears the main body of the French Army had retired early in the day, taking up a position behind the Alberche, which runs into the Tagus near this place. They had left a small rearguard of cavalry, and some horse artillery, for the sake of discovering the strength of the allied army. This rearguard checked the whole Spanish Army. In vain the Adjutant General of our army, Stewart[2], tried to get 7,000 Spanish cavalry to charge. They would undertake nothing decisive and would only skirmish; the French cavalry small as their numbers were, would have driven them off the plain, if the English cavalry had not come up. The French then immediately retreated, and covered by the fire of their artillery, escaped in face of so superior a force without loss. As soon as they were well off they were followed in a most gallant manner, by the Spanish cavalry, who galloped through the town, as if they were about to eat the whole French Army. The next day, (23rd) was lost, <u>why</u>, we could not tell. It was said the Spaniards were not ready. We certainly were without bread, but, we could have fought without bread, although we could not have advanced without it. On the 24th we got silently under arms at 1 o'clock in the morning, to commence the attack. We were formed before day light in the rear of a wood about half cannon shot of the enemy's position. We had the river which was not knee deep to cross, and were in breathless expectation of being ordered to advance. When the day broke the bird was flown; the last division of the French

1. Major General the Duke de Albuquerque commanded a division in the Spanish Army of the Centre.
2. Major General, the Honourable Charles Stewart (later Lord Londonderry, the writer of the first history of the Peninsula War).

had left their ground at the same hour we left ours. I had the satisfaction however to have seen the whole French Army the evening
before they retreated, with an excellent glass, from the steeple of
the principal church of Talavera. Here we are now in a sad
dilemma; the 'Junta' promised Sir Arthur forty thousand rations at
this place instead of which, they only gave him six thousand. We
have scarcely any bread, and yesterday killed the last bullocks we
brought with us from Portugal, and today have been obliged to
serve the men with bacon. What we are to get tomorrow, God
knows. We are nearly as badly off as the men ourselves, as neither
bread nor meat is to be bought. Under these circumstances what
our future operations are likely to be, it is hard to say. We understand four day's bread is expected up from Plasencia, in which case
on its arrival, we shall push on to Madrid, which is only four days
march from this; but there again we shall not be better off than we
are here, we cannot stay here, and to fall back is nearly as bad, as
we have eat [sic] up the country behind us. Had we been fortunate
enough to have attacked the enemy on the 23rd things would have
worn a better appearance, we could have retired with credit.
Perhaps we should have been better supplied after the defeat of the
French Grand Army.

The Spanish Army <u>did</u> follow the French, and today we hear a
heavy cannonade in that direction. Perhaps the Spaniards have
been defeated, in which case we shall have to manage the French
alone.

Letter 17   Field of action, near Talavera, 29 July 1809

My dear Mother,
I am thankful to be able to give you early information of my
doing well, after the most severely contested action that English
troops have for some time seen. We were engaged from four o'clock
on the afternoon of the 27th till sunset on the 28th. Our Brigade
has been fortunate enough to distinguish itself and that with little
loss, and we have captured several guns.

Had the Spaniards made any sort of movement, or shown any
disposition to have engaged, the loss on our part would not have
been so heavy as it has been. But the British stood the whole attack
of the French, without assistance. And the Spaniards eat [sic] up,
during the action, all the bread that had been prepared for us; so

that our men have been forty eight hours with scarcely any food. Our extreme want of provisions will prevent our following up our victory, which has cost too much for the results that are likely to be obtained in consequence of it.

The French retired in very good order on the night of the 28th unmolested. We have suffered much in superior officer. Hardly a general officer of infantry but what is either killed or wounded. Generals Mackenzie[1] and Langwerth[2] are killed. Hill[3] and the two Campbells wounded[4], and our total loss will amount to 5,000 killed and wounded. The French fought with great bravery and obstinacy and had eight well served pieces of artillery in the field, and their loss must be at least equal to, if not superior to our own.[5] In the 53rd we had six men killed and thirty two wounded. Martin Crew and Seth Bishop are severely, Corporal Muslewaite,[6] and Jacob Durnet, slightly wounded;[7] these men came from the Dorset [Militia] and I mention their names, that you may satisfy enquiries. At the close of the action yesterday I was so overcome with fatigue and heat that I fainted, and they all thought me killed. I shall write to my father or Still an account of the action, which however you will know more of from the Gazette. At this moment the Spaniards are murdering the wounded Frenchmen in the woods in our front. I must hasten to prevent them. Adieu.

Letter 18   Camp near Talavera, 1 August 1809

Dear Tryon,

As I know that you will expect that I should attempt to describe the sanguinary action that took place on the spot from which I am

1. Major General John Randell Mackenzie, 78 Foot commanded the 3rd Division.
2. Brigadier General Ernhest Eberhard Kuno von Langwerth of the 4th Line Regiment King's German Legion was on the General Staff.
3. Sir Rowland Hill was slightly wounded.
4. Lieutenant General Alexander Campbell commanding 4th Division and Brigadier General Henry Campbell commanding the 1st Division were wounded.
5. Oman states the respective loss as British 5,365 and French 7,268.
6. Privates Crew, Bishop and Corporal Muslewaite all belonged to Captain Poppleton's company; none are recorded on the Talavera return as wounded.
7. Private Durnet belonged to Captain McCaskin's company and is recorded on the Talavera return as 'Absent on duty'.

now writing; and having in some measure recovered the fatigue, collected my scattered ideas, and having gone over the ground once or twice, I sit down to use my best endeavours. You will see at Wycombe a great many accounts,[1] and this may serve to add a little to the stock of general information.

The whole army having assembled at Plasencia, moved from that on the 17th and on the 22nd, having joined Cuesta's Army, came to this place. The French who were not in strength, retired on our approach behind the Alberche. The 23rd, for some reason or other yet unknown on the part of the Spaniards, we remained idle. On the 24th, we intended to have made our attack, but on our arrival on the ground, we found the enemy gone. We were unable to follow for want of provisions, in the mean time the French who had retired in the direction of Toledo, having received reinforcements and being honoured with the presence of their King Joseph Napoleon returned on the Spaniards who had followed them singly, and drove them before them like sheep. On the 27th, they made their appearance on the Alberche, the dragoons and General Mackenzie's Division were sent to cover the retreat of the Spaniards, which they did, closely followed by the French, who advanced so rapidly, that we had hardly time to occupy the position, which was as follows. Our right was on the town of Talavera and the Tagus, a perfect flat for about three quarters of a mile, much intersected with ditches, vineyards and covered with olive trees. This space was occupied by the Spaniards in two lines three deep, and with reserves. Just on the left of their line was a small eminence that commanded the plain. On this a battery was established and a work hardly more than traced out, having been interrupted by the unlooked for rapid advance of the enemy. In front of this, were two small enclosures, and beyond that, all the enemy's movements were obscured by olive trees. On the left of the battery a small plain began to extend itself with olive groves on each side, and with a dry watercourse running through it. As you went on to the left, the plain widened and the olive groves ceased, where the ground began to rise which it did suddenly, and terminated in a high conical hill; beyond this was a deep narrow valley with bold

1. High Wycombe was the site of the Royal Military College Senior Department. Here officers were instructed before being appointed to Staff posts.

46

rocky mountains on the other side. The round hill was our extreme left, and the extent we had to occupy, was so great that the army was in some places two, and in others only in one line. I before observed that the French followed our troops very close. About 7 o'clock they appeared in force on our left, and after a cannonade that lasted till sunset, as soon as it was dark brought up their columns to charge. They had succeeded in getting possession of the hill, but the 2nd Division coming up, drove them from it. This hill was of the utmost consequence to us. It commanded, and was in fact the key of the position, and we retained it against several attacks the enemy made on it. About ten o'clock the firing ceased for the night, which we passed under arms, occasionally entertained by a heavy fire from the Spanish line, which they kept up on being disturbed by the enemy's patrols. At day break the army appeared in nearly the same position as the night before, except that our line a little to the left of our centre, was rather farther advanced and stood on the edge of a ravine, that there separated the two armies, and was very much exposed to the fire of the French batteries, which had not yet opened. There was nearly an hour of suspense after daylight, before the least movement was to be seen on either side. About the expiration of that time the French filed a strong body of chasseurs into a wood in front of our centre, and on the advanced part of our line falling back, opened a tremendous cannonade on them, which was soon directed to the whole left of the line, and did great execution. Some guns we had on the circular hill commanded theirs and dismounted several of their guns, and there were frequent explosions of ammunition wagons, but they had so many guns in the field that they maintained the superiority of fire, and under cover of which they made another unsuccessful attempt to possess themselves of the hill on the left.

About 12 o'clock the fire ceased and the French cooked their dinners. At 2 o'clock they had completed their arrangements for a general attack along the whole front of the British line; they moved down under a plunging cannonade from our batteries on the left, they drove in our light companies in front, and coming on the flank of the Fusiliers drove them back also; some of them penetrated nearly to the work in front. They were immediately repulsed by a charge made by the Fusiliers, who had instantly rallied, aided by the 2nd right company of the 53rd, supported by the remaining seven companies of that battalion.[1] In this charge, we passed at first the outermost of the two enclosures in front of the work, and in the retreat of the enemy they left a brigade of ten guns and some tumbrils of musket ammunition. The brigade then lined the ditches of the enclosures, and thus formed a flanking fire on the column that attacked our line more to the left, by which the Nassau Regiment suffered severely. We were aided in our charge by the Spanish Regiment of Cavalry Princessa, who charging down a road in our front, just came on the French as they were retiring before us, and took several prisoners.[2] The attack of the enemy on the centre was more favourable to them.

The Brigade of Guards moved forward to charge about the same time as we did; the French columns had not entered on the plain, they lined an enclosure on their side, and as the Guards were broken in crossing the dry watercourse, gave them a tremendous volley and then quitting the enclosure charged in their turn. This crisis might have been fatal; the enemy were near or rather beyond the centre of our position, when the 48th Regiment further to the left was thrown forward and brought on their flank, which movement was decisive. They retired with loss and the attacks were not repeated; on the left of the whole, they tried to pass a strong body along the valley on the left of the position, their force was charged in the most gallant manner by the 23rd Light Dragoons and the 1st Hussars of the German Legion. Although these regiments made no impression on the squares which the enemy promptly formed, and suffered (especially the former) a very serious loss, yet it effectually stopped the advance of the enemy.[3]

Failing in all these attacks they retired to their original position and kept up a cannonade directed more towards our part of the line, till sunset, when all was quiet, and during the night they crossed the Alberche unmolested. It was intimated to the Spaniards that not having been engaged and the French Army being much

1. This presumably means the eight centre companies of the battalion, the light company being out in front skirmishing. It is unclear where the grenadier company was.
2. This is a rare comment praising the efforts of the Spanish cavalry. Oman records this incident but states that it was the regiment Del Rey.
3. Here there is no mention of the fabled 'hidden ravine' which is sometimes blamed for the losses of the 23rd. Bingham would have been well aware of such an incident if it had been true.

crippled it afforded them a good opportunity of achieving something; Cuesta flatly refused to move, and the want of supplies prevented our profiting by our success. Thus ended an action, which though perhaps not so useful, has been as brilliant and as glorious as any we have ever (in these late wars) been engaged in, when it is considered the numbers with whom we had to contend; which from the accounts of the wounded amounted to 40,000. We had not in the field more than 18,000.[1]

The brigade of light infantry did not arrive till the day after the action (29th).[2] Of what service to the cause this victory may prove, I cannot venture to say. The Spanish Army is in so disorganised a state, the under officers such poltroons, the superior such traitors, I am afraid one day or other they will lead us into a scrape, from which it will be difficult to extricate ourselves. We are now without a day's provision in advance, without magazines and (notwithstanding what you may hear in England) with a population very lukewarm in our behalf. This ought to have been foreseen before we left Portugal. The whole day of the action our people were without provisions, and we have been detained here ever since for want of it. Our loss has been considerable, which considering the length of time we were engaged is not to be wondered at; two Generals killed and three wounded. Your regiment the 3rd has suffered much, as have the Guards, 24th, 48th, 61st and 83rd Regiments. The total number is said to be 5,100; the loss of the enemy is variously stated. About 1,000 prisoners mostly wounded have been brought in; these fell in the last attack only, for those who were wounded on the evening of the 27th, and in the first attacks on the morning of the 28th, had been removed.

Letter 19   Camp near Deleitosa, 10 August 1809

My dear Madam,

I wrote you a short note on the morning of the 29th, just after the battle at Talavera, which I have since heard went off with the

1. Oman states that the Spanish army numbered some 32,000 men; the British just over 20,000 and the French 46,000 at Talavera. In mere numbers the allies look to have had a reasonable advantage, however in terms of quality the French had a marked superiority and the Spanish barely took part in the battle.
2. The Brigade of Major General Robert Craufurd consisted of 1/43rd, 1/52nd and 1/95th.

despatches, and I hope arrived in time to have quietened any fears you might have entertained for my safety; so that I now continue my journal from that time, not entering into the details of the action, having written very largely to Still on that subject. I shall only say it was hardly contested, was a very sanguinary one, and that we appear to have gained nothing by it, but the honor [sic] of the victory dearly purchased by the loss of so many good officers, and brave soldiers.

On the 3rd of August we were to have moved forward in the direction of Madrid, and were to have formed a junction with another Spanish Army commanded by Vanegas, of 25,000 men.[1] However we fortunately heard (I say fortunately because after the specimen we have had of the Spaniards, much was not to have been expected of them) that Marshals Soult and Ney had moved from the north of Spain, and had interrupted our line of communication with Portugal by Plasencia;[2] had got possession of our magazines, and were advancing in our rear. It now became necessary to make some decided movement. We were living at Talavera from hand to mouth that is we were obliged to thrash the corn ourselves, grind the flour, and bake the bread. On the morning of the 3rd, therefore we left our ground near Talavera, and moved to Oropesa, on the Plasencia road, the Spanish Army being left at Talavera, to endeavour to maintain itself there, till we had opened the road to the rear for our reinforcements and provisions. However to our great surprise, on the morning of the 4th we found the Spanish Army thronging in upon us at Oropesa, Cuesta having two hours after we left Talavera, given his orders to retreat, notwithstanding the promises he had made to Sir Arthur Wellesley to remain, and there not being at the time the order was given, a French soldier within six leagues of him. Our situation now became an unpleasant one; if we attacked Soult, we had Victor in our rear. It was consequently determined to cross the Tagus and by passing over a range of mountains called the Sierra de Villuercas, to fall back on supplies known to be on the road from Seville. After some short time lost

1. Vanegas commanded the Army of La Mancha of about 23,000 men which stood just south of Seville.
2. The combined divisions of Soult and Ney numbered 37,000 men. Hearing of Wellesley's advance along the Tagus, they had rushed south and were now on the lines of communication of the British army.

in coming to this determination, we crossed the Tagus by the beautiful bridge of [El Puente del] Arzobispo, thirteen arches, and encamped on the left bank. On the morning of the 5th, we entered these defiles, leaving our allies to defend the bridge we had just crossed. As the guns, spare ammunition wagons and carts were to be dragged over some of the mountains by hand, you may guess our progress is not very rapid. The excessive heat of the weather, the total want of bread and salt, and the constant exposure of our people to the sun, has already begun to diminish our numbers. The 6th, we were the whole day employed in getting the guns &c, over a river, and up a mountain. In this too we were retarded by a false alarm circulated by Colonel Hawker 14th Dragoons.[1] On the 7th, we marched only one mile. On the 8th, we got on eight miles, on the 9th, six miles, and this day two. We have now succeeded in getting the whole of the carriages out of the passes, and shall hereafter proceed (though we know not whither) with greater ease. In the meantime the Spaniards, on the 7th, allowed themselves to be surprised in their camp at Arzobispo, and retired in confusion without destroying the bridge, and with the loss of nine pieces of cannon. They are now attempting to make a stand at the River Ibor, a pass so strong by nature that if they only roll stones down they may keep off the whole French Army in Spain. But, I have no doubt that Cuesta is (as he has been supposed to be) a traitor, and that in the same manner the position of Talavera (by which we lost 3,000 of our sick and wounded[2]) and the bridge at Arzobispo were given up, so the present fine position would be relinquished on the first appearance of the enemy, and we shall have another battle to fight, of the result of which there is no doubt; but the apprehension of falling (if wounded) into the enemy's hands, weighs down the spirits of both officers and men. And thus then is likely to end this ill advised expedition, entered on without foresight and conducted without firmness. The value of Spanish assistance ought to have been fully known and duly appreciated by the experience of Sir John Moore's expedition, and it was madness to think of penetrating to Madrid, with 20,000 men, when it was known what a much superior force the enemy had in the country.

1. Author of a 'Journal of the campaign of 1809', he had been wounded at the passage of the Douro.
2. Oman states only 1,500–2,000 prisoners fell into the hands of the French.

The star of the Wellesley's will carry us through everything and we shall meet again in the course of next winter in England. It has pleased God to grant me excellent health and spirits although we have suffered privations of every description, but water agrees with me as well as wine, and although bread is considered as a necessary of life, we find, for a few days it may be dispensed with.

The scenery in the mountains is beautiful, as fine as the wildest part of Wales, but the country always miserable is rendered doubly so, by the horrors of the war. Villages burnt, peasants starving; it would be worse but for the extraordinary fertility of the soil, that yields almost without labour the necessaries of life. Oh, could these people, who wish to see an enemy landed in England, behold the wretched situation of this district, and these depopulated places. Wherever an army is, without its regular supplies, it cannot starve, it must help itself. License to do so immediately becomes licentiousness, and more is wasted by an army let loose on a people, that would subsist treble the number in a regular way. We have just heard that the French did not enter Talavera, till three days after we had left it, and have treated our wounded with the greatest attention; we have left them a supply of provision, and have provided against a further want. We understand we are to fall back by Trujillo, to Badajoz and Elvas, in Portugal.

Adieu.

Letter 20   Camp near Lobon, 27 August 1809

My dear Madam,

I wrote to you from Deleitosa on the 10th, since which it has pleased God to continue to me uninterrupted good health, although sickness made great ravages in our Army during our stay on the banks of the Rio Almonte, a scarcity of every thing, and a total want of vegetables and salt, introduced dysentery amongst both officers and men to rather an alarming degree. On the 20th, we left it, and marched to Trujillo, a large old town about fourteen miles from our former position. It was a favourite residence of the Emperor Charles V, and still retains some portion of its former magnificence. The house of Pizarro[1] is still shown, and in one of

1. The house is now the 'Casa Museo Pizarro'.

the churches are the tombs of both him and Cervantes.[1] The vicinity of the town (as indeed most of the towns are) is barren beyond description, not a tree within miles of it.

The 20th, brought us to Santa Cruz [de la Sierra], a village situated at the foot of a steep isolated mountain which had some appearance of vegetation on it.

The 22nd, we encamped near the village of Escurial. The 23rd, on the banks of the Guadiana near Medellin, where the Spaniards had been defeated by the French in March last. There is a beautiful bridge over the river of eighteen arches. The 24th, we took up our ground close to Merida, by much the most interesting town I have seen in Spain. It was founded by Augustus under the name of Emerita Augusta, and was a flourishing town under the Romans,[2] and there are considerable and very perfect remains of temples and other magnificent buildings yet in existence. We halted on the 25th, and I spent the whole day, and part of a beautiful moonlight night, in examining these rarities. Several arches of an aqueduct on so grand a scale that the Spaniards call them los milagros (the miracles) are very perfect,[3] one of the gates of the Roman town, the Temple of Mars, now a chapel; another of Diana,[4] three beautiful altars of white marble, which piled one on the other, now serve as a pillar to uphold a saint; two bridges, one of nearly forty arches, a naumachia, and other precious vestiges. Indeed there is scarcely a house that has not some beautiful fragment used as stone in the building of it. In a field not far from the town, a Corinthian capital of white marble, and the shaft of the same column laying near it, compose a part of the fence. Some time since Count Florida Blanca, sent a connoisseur, to search for antiquities, but was prevented by the inhabitants. It will now remain a treat for the first French General whose taste and inclination may lead that way. We hear nothing of the French or their movements, but are leisurely retiring to the frontiers of Portugal.

Arronches is to be our station, only four short marches from this. What we are to do when we get there, we know not. We are now rather better off, as to necessaries, but I am tired of camp and shall

1. The church of Santa Maria Mayor.
2. The city ranked as tenth in the Roman Empire.
3. It is still known as the 'Acueducto de los Milagros'.
4. The Temple of Diana had been adapted into a renaissance mansion.

be glad to be once again in quarters. We want a complete refit; we have hardly a shoe to our feet or a coat to our backs.

Letter 21   Camp near Badajoz, 13 September 1809

My dear Sir,

We have been here now nearly a fortnight (a long period of rest for us), in a very pleasantly situated camp, with no other disadvantage than being eight miles from any town. We are however plentifully supplied, having an excellent market established on the ground, and the weather being somewhat cooler, the cessation from our toils and marching is very agreeable.

I have received no letter from my mother since that dated 20th July, consequently am without your congratulations on my escape at Talavera; we are all to have medals.

What we are now to do we cannot conjecture, the army is still sickly, nor is it to be wondered at considering our men have been six months without having had their clothes off at night, and have not had a blanket to cover them. The days have been excessively hot, and the nights again as cold and disease naturally follows bad living and violent fatigue. We know nothing of the movements of the French; it is indeed reported they are about to pass the Tagus at the Bridge of Alcantara. Our cavalry is completely knocked up, and the artillery have hardly a horse to put in harness. Brigadier General Catlin Craufurd marched in yesterday with a reinforcement of five regiments,[1] and this will make our infantry about the same number they were, when we were further in advance; but if the present sickness continues our numbers will rapidly decrease.

Letter 22   Camp near Badajoz, 18 September 1809

My dear Madam,

I do not recollect that I have written to you since I left Lobon, that is to say about three weeks since. On leaving that place, we

---

1. The reinforcement consisted of 1/11th, 1/57th, 2/28th, 2/34th and 2/39th. The latter three were brigaded together under Brigadier General James Catlin Craufurd in the 2nd Division. He died of natural causes at Abrantes 25 September 1810. This Craufurd should not be confused with Robert Craufurd of Light Brigade fame, who died later at Ciudad Rodrigo.

marched the first day to the neighbourhood of Talavera [la] Real, and afterwards to Badajoz, and from Badajoz to this place which is about eight miles from it. The same gloomy uninteresting scenery that I have so often described characterizes this part of the country; vast plains, now so thoroughly burnt up as not to exhibit the least appearance of vegetation, without a feature of any kind, and here and there woods of the cork and ilex of stinted growth, and without a house or living animal between one town and the other to enliven the scene. Badajoz is the best town we have yet seen in Spain, and is the only one from which we are enabled to form a correct judgement of what the towns were in this country before the invasion, as the French have never been in it. As a frontier town to Portugal, it has always had a garrison, and although strong enough to have resisted the incursions of the Portuguese, would not hold out five days if the French were seriously to attack it. The bridge over the Guadiana (a Roman work) is of twenty-two arches, and very handsome, and as the river on this side of the town has been dammed to serve as a defence on the part next Portugal, it is even in this dry season, very respectable, as to breadth and depth.

The cathedral which is hung with crimson velvet has nothing worth notice, except that, and two immense silver lamps which seem waiting for the French to convert into cash.[1] The streets of the town are narrow, but exceedingly clean. Near the Elvas gate is a public walk, which of an evening is frequented by a number of well dressed women, that is to say, well dressed for the fashion of the country, which is always in black. The promenade is however sufficiently enlivened by the variety of colour the Spaniards have adopted for their uniforms. One of the regiments of hussars are dressed in yellow, another in light blue; their infantry are in dark blue, green, red, white, black and brown. The officers on duty are much more respectable looking men than we have been accustomed to see with the Army, but their regiments, with the exception of one battalion of grenadiers, are a motley crew, and exactly of the appearance of Falstaff's ragged regiment. Our situation here is a pleasant one; the only disadvantage is our distance from the town. We are in a thick wood, with a stream about 500 paces in our front, on an island formed by this rivulet, and shaded by large ash trees,

1. The Cathedral is a fortress like building dating from the thirteenth century.

and beautified by the oleander, now in full bloom. Sir William Myers has built a hut in which we mess, and from which I write, and I am now enjoying the murmuring of the stream, close beneath my feet; we have a table, a rough one indeed, made of an old box, but to people accustomed to eat their victuals on the ground, a luxury. Round this table are two canteens, and four little casks as seats; what would you wish for more in the best dining room? An excellent market is established; we get tolerably good wine, capital fruit, butter, eggs, cheese, a few vegetables, and rice. I hope [one?] of these days to be able to introduce my present messmate to you; he was Still's junior at Winchester, and although only twenty-six, is a senior Lieutenant Colonel to myself. He is good looking, animated, and very gentlemanly in his manner and address; but uninterrupted prosperity, his early rank, his title, and the society he has been accustomed to, gives him (to people unacquainted with him) an air of pride and hauteur, which prevents his being so popular as he deserves to be. He is clever, but unsteady, an ardent friend, a bitter enemy; but take Sir William Myers as he is (and no men are without faults, time will correct his) and he bids fair, if his life is spared, to become a splendid character.

Another messmate is the Major of Brigade Auchmuty[1], who with perhaps fewer splendid qualities has more serviceable ones. His knowledge is extensive, of undaunted courage, without vanity, or ambition, and fond of retirement. We miss his society much at present, but he has been obliged by an attack of intermittent fever to go into town, and we hardly hope to see him with us again till we go into winter quarters, which we expect to do shortly, and I should not wonder if we fell back nearer to Lisbon on account of our supplies. The fatigue our men have experienced is now beginning to tell, and we have in the regiment alone, upwards of two hundred sick, seventy of whom have been sent to the hospital since we have been here. Amongst the number are eleven officers, who are less able to bear the privations and hardships. Our great want at present is books. The heat of the day, and the necessity of not exposing ourselves unnecessarily to it, makes the time hang somewhat heavy on our hands. If this campaign should terminate our

1. Samuel Benjamin Auchmuty, 7 Fusiliers, became DAQMG and AAG to the Division.

expedition, I should like to return to England, to enjoy once more the pleasure of your society.

Letter 23   Camp near Badajoz, 2 October 1809

My dear Madam,

I am at a loss how to fill so formidable a sheet of paper as this I am about to attack, not having moved from our camp in the wood, since I last wrote, which I think was about a fortnight ago. The weather has been exceedingly hot and the Army sickly, and being at so great a distance as eight miles from town, I have hardly left the camp.

I have hitherto (thank God) escaped both ague and fever, which has cost us so many officers and men, and has ruined the constitution of so many more. You can have no idea how ignorant we are with the army, and we begin to think the packet must have been taken. The next arrival from home is the more anxiously looked for, as it will determine whether we are to undertake a winter campaign. If we do not receive these orders soon we expect to break up from our camp, and to go into quarters at Vila Vicosa with the Division (4th) to which we belong. It is in Portugal, about two or three days march from this. I am not anxious to leave the camp, for although the regiment is sickly, having upwards of two hundred men in different hospitals, we are a good deal more healthy than those troops that are in towns; indeed if the men had blankets, they would be very well off, but both their clothing and greatcoats are worn very thin by hard service; for the last six months, the men have never had their clothes off.

You can scarcely form an idea of the solitude of this wood. Beyond the environs of the camp you may ride ten miles in almost any direction except Badajoz, without meeting the habitation of man. A solitary church about two miles from this, whose whitened tower just peeps above the trees, makes the dreariness more apparent; it is called Nostra Señora di Botoa.[1] In this large expanse of forest, we enjoy no autumnal tints, except just on the banks of the stream. It is one dark green of stunted cork trees; wherever the

1. Presumably near present day Botoa, approximately eight miles north-east of Badajoz.

trees are cleared and the plain appears, there is at present no signs of vegetation, which indeed is not to be wondered at, as we have scarcely had the sun obscured by clouds since we left Portugal four months ago. The French are said to be as quiet as we are, waiting for reinforcements and collecting provisions. We are pretty well supplied but the Spaniards make us pay for bringing their articles to so out of the way a place, and our living is more expensive than it was in Ireland. Fruit is very plentiful and very good, that is to say melons, grapes and pears.

October 3rd, I have just received your letter &c; we understand we are not to leave this camp till the rains set in, which will be the latter end of this month, or beginning of November. We are to go either to Olivenza, which is in Spain, or to Vila Vicosa; unless the despatches arrived today make any alteration; as we hear that a fleet of transports, supposed for the purpose of carrying us to England, has arrived.

Commanding officers are to have medals for Talavera, as the Captains of the Navy have had after distinguished actions.[1]

Letter 24   Olivenza, 16 October 1809

My dear Madam,

You will perceive by this date, that since my last letter we have changed our residence, from the fields to the town, and enjoy all the luxuries of tables, chairs, clean houses, glass windows &c, &c. Last Monday the rains began, and in a few hours set our camp literally afloat. At 10 o'clock we got the order to move, and marched through the wet to Badajoz, where we were most inhospitably received by our good allies, the Spanish patriots; who in return for all the benefits, subscriptions &c, conferred by England on them, would hardly open a door to shelter us from the pelting, pitiless storm. I believe I should have slept in the street, deluged as it was, had it not been for Frank Cockburn,[2] who performed the part of the Good Samaritan by me, and who gave me a good dinner, and

1. Gold medals were issued to the commanding officers of units that were engaged in battles. All other ranks had to wait until 1848 when the General Service Medal was launched and issued retrospectively back to the Egyptian campaign of 1801.
2. Captain Sir Francis Cockburn 60 Regiment was DAAG to the 4th Division in 1809 but left the Peninsula in 1810.

permitted me to lay my mattress in one corner of his room. The next day the 11th, we marched in here. This town had always been (although situated on the left of the Guadiana, here become the frontier) a part of Portugal, until ceded to Spain by the Peace of 1801. The inhabitants, who are Portuguese, retain all the national prejudice against their present masters, and they received us with open arms. The men are comfortably lodged in the barracks and arsenal, and the officers only billeted on the inhabitants. I am quartered on one of the chief fidalgos of the place, in the Largo di Santa Maria, and just opposite the church of that name.[1] The fortifications which are extensive, have been dismantled by the Spaniards, and are falling to decay. The town is a very neat one, the streets broad and the houses exceedingly clean. The churches, three or four in number, handsomely filled up, and as the French have never been here, are ornamented with silver lamps. The cathedral is old and has remarkable pillars, twisted and running in a spiral manner from the bottom to the top.[2] I should be well contented to remain in this quarter for the winter. The climate delightful, and the neighbouring country cultivated and picturesque; but we are not likely to meet with such good fortune, as it is reported and believed, Bonaparte is either at Madrid, or on his way to it, and his active disposition will not allow us much rest, and I fancy preparations are already making for our retreat. It is reported we are to occupy a position near Lisbon, and to defend that city, but how are we to feed the immense population, and will it be worth our while to retain it? We are burthened with an army of sick, and if the French were to advance with rapidity, and in force, not less than seven or eight thousand would fall into their hands; Elvas is full, and another hospital is now opened at Vila Vicosa. At these two hospitals the average number of deaths are eighty in each week, nor is there any chance of this mortality decreasing, before the cool weather sets in. These are but melancholy prospects but I trust providence, who has hitherto preserved me in all these dangers and difficulties, will carry me through them, and bless me at last, with a sight of home. If we remain here I will write again about the latter end of the month. If we move, from the first halting place. Adieu.

1. The Santa Maria del Castillo, a sober seventeenth century Renaissance church.
2. The Santa Maria Magdalena is an eighteenth century church built in the Portuguese style.

Letter 25   Olivenza, 31 October 1809

To N. Gundry Esq.[1]
South Lodge
Near Enfield

Dear Sir,

My mother was good enough to send me a letter you wrote to her, on reading the Gazette account of the Battle of Talavera, containing on the part of Mrs Gundry and yourself, congratulations on my fortunate escape. I have in return, to request you will accept my sincere thanks for the interest you take in my welfare, and I hope some day or other to return you my personal acknowledgements for this additional proof of your kindness.

We have been suffering very much for these last two months from sickness, the natural effect of rest after a very arduous and fatiguing campaign, and of the privations we suffered; principally in Spain. This state of sickness is at present the more unfortunate as we understand the French are retiring behind the Ebro, and that Joseph Bonaparte has established his court at Vitoria. What his reasons for this extraordinary step may be, you who know what is going on in the northern parts of Europe can best tell. But should a coalition of the northern powers against France have taken place, (which is the report here) prompt measures, and a winter campaign whilst the passes of the Pyrenees are shut, which would prevent the enemy from receiving reinforcements, might recover us the Peninsula. But there is a defect in the Spanish system, (which time only could extirpate) that would always lay them open as a prey to France, whenever she recovers her preponderance. That the faults of the old government are not at an end, the following anecdote, which perhaps may not find its way into the papers will show.

Desertion has arrived at that height in the Spanish Army that strong measures have become necessary to put a stop to it; a party

---

1. Mr Nathaniel Gundry lived at South Lodge, a large house on Enfield Chase (previously owned by William Pitt the Elder) throughout the period of these letters. His wife was reportedly robbed by a highwayman on Enfield Chase in 1800. There is however, no clear link between the Gundrys and the Bingham family. I must thank Mr Graham Dalling, the Local History Officer for Enfield Council, for this information.

of deserters were marched into Badajoz with an escort, who not being so alert as they might have been, allowed one of their prisoners in passing a church to slip from them, and to seize hold of an immense knocker, placed there for the purpose of affording criminals the right of sanctuary, and an opportunity of evading the law. Having once hold of this, he was safe; a priest soon made his appearance, and conducted him in triumph into the body of the church, to the manifest satisfaction of the bystanders to view an action tending to subvert the establishment of their government with gratification. We are now quartered in a pleasant town, the inhabitants of which are very civil, the country about it pleasant, and the climate at this period of the year delicious. The jasmines are in full flower, and we sit all the evenings with the windows open; we have had as yet but little rain, but expect more in the month that is to come.

Letter 26   Olivenza, 14 November 1809

To my Mother,

You will no doubt be surprised my dear Mother, at not having heard from me for so long a period. The day after I last wrote to you from this place, I received two letters from you, and one from Nora.[1] I was then vexed that I had sent my letter only the day before, and I determined not to write again till after the next packet arrived. Now we have never been so long without a mail as this last time. Three were due, and the day before yesterday two arrived, but no letter from Melcombe; I have therefore now sat down, confident that as soon as I have closed and sent this, that a letter now lying in some of the post offices will make its appearance. We have been living a very quiet, comfortable life, forgetting the war, and all about it, here in Olivenza. The weather continued hot during the whole month of October. The rain set in very partially, the beginning of this month, and the weather is now delightfully cool and pleasant, and I take my walks and rides exactly as if I were in England. We have established a mess also, not indeed a very splendid one, but everything is by comparison; and people who for some months have been eating their dinners on the ground, if indeed they had any to eat, were glad enough to be once more

1. His youngest sister Leonora; she married twice but without issue.

assembled at a table. We have also, but with some difficulty, provided our mess with knives and forks &c. everything is plentiful, and was when we first entered the town cheap; the market (as is always the case where the English are) now rises; still we have as yet no right to complain. Two things however are yet wanted to make us completely comfortable; books, and the society of pleasant women. I have read Sir John Moore's correspondence, but I was obliged to sit up nearly the whole night to get through it, for it was only lent me for twelve hours, and except that, and the 'Tales of the Castle'[1] I have not had a book since I have been here. Speaking the language, would bring no society with it. The people of the town have the national antipathy of the Portuguese against the Spaniards, which the having fallen under the dominion of the latter has rather increased. The people of condition who could manage it, retired into Portugal, the remainder, as they could not associate with one another without admitting the Spaniards, chose to confine themselves to their own houses, and I begin to think they are right, for no society is preferable to that which is disagreeable. Except then, on a religious festival or at a procession, they never leave their houses to mix one with another. We have card parties amongst ourselves, and suppers, to which the master of the house in which we live is generally invited; their admiration is excited by the quantities of solids consumed at these suppers, as they are excessively abstemious themselves. They are very fond of news and swallow with avidity anything, however extravagant. I think both Joseph, and Napoleon Bonaparte, have each been killed three times since we have been here. The Emperor of all the Russias has been twice dethroned, and murdered; the armistice between the Austrians and French constantly broken, and the latter always defeated. Anything as an excuse for their apathy. I have frequent opportunities of attending the church service here; the great church being exactly opposite my house. They have a good organ, and some tolerable voices. Their service on Sundays appears less frequented than those on other days. The service is performed with great decorum, and although one cannot but despise the mummery of their ceremonies, we cannot but be struck with the appearances

1. *Tales of the Castle* or *Stories of Instruction and Delight*, originally *Les Veuilles du Chateau* by Madame le Comtesse de Genlis 1785 and translated by Thomas Holcroft.

at least of attention and devotion. I have never seen any one go into the church, but for the purpose of saying their prayers; all seem devoutly to join in the service, and after it is over, go away. On All Saint's day, a sermon was preached, the only one I have heard. A Franciscan friar attended by a brother of the same order, having been first anointed with oil, at the great altar by the priest who said Mass, mounted the pulpit. He might be about forty-five years of age; of an expressive countenance, his face meagre and emaciated. On ascending the pulpit he threw aside a large cloak that enveloped him, and having said a short prayer, began his sermon extempore, with very good action, though perhaps more than we have been accustomed to, or should like. He was fluent in his expressions, and never stopped or hesitated, for a word. I did not understand enough of the language to follow him through his discourse, but I found he was much commended, and considered a popular preacher.

Lord Wellington returned from Seville[1] last night, (that is to say, to the headquarters at Badajoz) where it is said he was very coolly received. The Spanish Army have again crossed the Tagus. If they risk an action, which it is reported they mean to do, they will be playing the game Bonaparte wishes them to do. He would be glad to have an opportunity given him of disposing of the Spanish armies in detail, to enable him to turn his arms on us. Our future operations are kept very secret, but I cannot help thinking that an early move towards Lisbon is intended, although there appears to be no intention of evacuating the country altogether, which perhaps it would be better to do in good time before we were much perplexed, and obliged to embark in face of a superior force, always a hazardous operation. Frank Cockburn, whom you may recollect at Exeter, is here; he is the life of the place. He holds the situation of Assistant Adjutant General to the division. General Cole has assumed the command of the division,[2] and appears a good sort of a man and is not very troublesome. Adieu.

1. The seat of the Central Junta of Spain; its effective government.
2. Brigadier General the Honourable Galbraith Lowry Cole, Colonel of the 27 Foot. Later he was wounded at Albuera and severely in the arm at Salamanca.

My dear Madam,

As I predicted in my letter to Nora, your long letter from Deans Leage of the 24th, came to hand the day after I had written to her. I should indeed have been well pleased to have been with you there, but it seldom has happened that I have been able to avail myself of the interval that occurs, by the frequent change of tenants, which however cannot be either pleasant to you or beneficial to the concern. I hope Colonel Godfrey [1] may prove a better tenant than Mr. Linthorn and reside there some time.

The affairs of this country are quite inexplicable. The Spanish armies are advancing on all sides, and if credit can be given to the reports in circulation, the Duke D'Albuquerque is near Talavera de la Reina, Vanegas near Aranjuez, and the Duke del Parque at Porta de Banos; the French retiring before them. Whether this is done with a view of enticing us once more to advance, or whether they are willing to draw near their strongholds, and reinforcements, no one can tell. As far as regards ourselves, it has failed in its effect, for I see no symptoms of advancing. We are still sickly, the cold weather may have prevented the fever and ague from spreading further, but the convalescents recover slowly, and they amount to half the Army. I have now 214 sick, present and absent. Sixty-four have died since we came to the country, out of seven hundred, the number that embarked; chiefly in the months of August, September and October.

It is reported the Spanish general officer who commanded in Badajoz, has been discovered in a correspondence with the French, and has been sent to Seville, where he will most likely meet the punishment he deserves. Badajoz, having been so long the head-quarters of our Army; if he is clever he may do some mischief.

Since I last wrote I have been living quietly, so much so that I have not wherewithal to make out a letter. The turkeys have suffered considerably and we have had nothing but mess dinner society. I hope at any rate, we may remain in this country till the spring, as a winter passage is not desirable. I propose going over to Elvas in a day or two, for one night, as well to see the town which

1. I have not been able to identify this officer as he does not appear in the 1809/10 Army List.

is a considerable one, as a beautiful fort near it, called La Lippe, and which is considered a masterpiece of fortification.[1]

Letter 28   Olivenza, 29 November 1809

My dear Madam,

I received your letter of the 12th two days ago; you cannot tell how pleased I was to receive a letter in so short a time. It lessens the distance between us so much, especially when I recollect that I was frequently longer last year in Ireland without a letter. As we have few books, and not much evening society, you can form no idea of the joy a letter from home gives. On the contrary if a mail does arrive without a letter it is quite a disappointment.

Before this letter reaches you, you will have heard of the misfortunes that have attended our cause in Spain; yet as Tryon and perhaps my father may be with you, I cannot help trying to give you a feint outline of what has been passing. After the retreat of our Army everything was quiet. The French were as unable to move as ourselves, from sickness and want of provisions, as well as want of transport, if they had them. They contented themselves with forcing the bridge of Arzobispo early in August, and having possession of this passage of the Tagus they did not choose to avail themselves of it by following our army into Extremadura. The Spaniards, who never begin to exert themselves till it is too late, began to augment their armies about the time they heard of the success of the French in Austria, and of the battle of Wagram.[2] They got together three armies, respectable only in numbers, and anxious to strike a blow before the arrival of the French reinforcements, they advanced again. They put at the head of these armies, new, and (as they gave out) more dashing commanders, and the first movements seeming to justify their expectations, they began to think they were able to do great things. The Northern Army commanded by the Duke Del Parque obtained some trifling success near Salamanca.[3] The Duke D'Albequerque passed the Tagus at

1. Fort La Lippe guarded the southern gateway to Portugal and was considered to be impregnable.
2. The Battle of Wagram (5–6 July 1809) was Napoleon's revenge over the Archduke Charles of Austria for his defeat at Aspern-Essling in May. This costly victory soon led to the end of the war with Austria.
3. The Battle of Tamames fought on 18 October 1809.

Arzobispo, without opposition, and got to Oropesa, where he began to complain of the want of provisions. The Army of La Mancha, taken from Vanegas, (who seemed to be aware of what sort of troops he had to deal with, and who risked little) was given to a man who had served with Blake, and who in a proclamation he issued on taking the command, was, (as he said) to wipe off the stain of eleven defeats. This army, so commanded, advanced to Aranjuez, five leagues from Madrid, where the French (who know these gentlemen pretty well) retired, concentrating their force. On the 19th Marshal Victor, with 35,000 men fell on this army of La Mancha, which consisted of 75,000 men and seventy pieces of cannon. His attack was so rapid the Spaniards had not time to deploy their heavy columns, and as might be expected in raw troops, soon got into confusion; they lost 8,000 killed, 15,000 prisoners, and fifty pieces of cannon. The remainder dispersed and here ends their great effort.[1] The Duke D'Albequerque recrossed the Tagus, and what has become of the Duke del Parque no one can tell. I am afraid our councils have tended to make the Spaniards depart from their true line of policy, viz, retaining the strong country and not venturing on the plains where they are certain of being beat. As soon as the reinforcements arrive from France, we may expect to take the field. We can have but little chance of obtaining any decisive success, and I am afraid if some good fortune does not befriend us the months of December and January will not be either more pleasant or profitable than they were last year to Sir John Moore; except the distance we shall have to go is not so great, and we may have, if we keep a good look out, a better start. Adieu.

Letter 29   Olivenza, 9 December 1809

My dear Madam,

In my last I told you of the defeat of the right of the Spanish line near Aranjuez on the 19th of last month. I have now to tell you that a similar fate has befallen the Duke del Parque, who commanded their left army near Salamanca. Of the date and details we are as yet ignorant, it however would appear as if the French were inclined to push forward in that direction into Portugal, and that our army was put in motion to meet them. The first division moved from Badajoz

1. The Battle of Ocaña fought on 19 November 1809.

today, and I think about next Tuesday (12th) we shall be in motion also. It is conjectured Abrantes will be the point at which we shall cross the Tagus, and should the French be in any force, fall back on Lisbon and perhaps try the fortune of another action before we embark, to leave the country altogether. Or it may be that their movement on the northern frontier of Portugal is only a feint to draw our attention to that point, and to prevent our falling back on Cadiz, for they do not appear to have followed up the blow given to the Army of La Mancha, at the battle of Ocana, except from reassembling.

We have had for the last six weeks the most beautiful weather, not a cloud in the sky, with a slight white frost at night. I hope it will please God to continue the weather for the march, as rain such as falls in this country would destroy our sick, which I am sorry to say are yet very numerous, the fine weather not having done us the good we expected it would. On the contrary, our sick are greater in number than they have been since our arrival here. We have eighty in the 53rd, many of whom are certainly not in a state to be moved; however, moved they must be, as we have no one to leave with them. This is very distressing, but what can be done? We shall move in smaller bodies than we have done, and have a roof each night over our heads to shelter us, though we cannot always expect they will be good ones.

We have had nothing but racing, coursing, dinners and suppers since I wrote last. I was present a few nights ago at a house where I for the first time, saw the bolero well danced. It was at the quarters of an officer of the regiment, who gave a supper on his coming of age. To this supper he had invited his landlord, a sort of animal that is almost a nondescript in England, who lives content on a very small pittance rather than work for more, being in fact too proud to work. He told us he was an half pay ensign in the Portuguese service, on eighteen pence a day, a splendid establishment!! In honour of the occasion he was dressed in a green silk jacket, embroidered with silver and tinsel, a pair of small clothes of the same, with a broad knee band of somewhat tarnished lace, silk stockings that were drawn as tight over a pair of spindle shanks as if they had been drawn up by a pulley, long quartered shoes, and large silver buckles. After supper we got this animal to sing, accompanying himself on his guitar. His voice was not melodious, nor was there anything pleasant in his manner of singing. After his song, he stood up to dance, and in this he acquitted himself capitally. His wife, the remains of a good looking woman, stood up with him. It was certainly the prettiest thing I ever saw off the stage. They danced with so much grace, and the dresses were so picturesque it was quite delightful. I wish I could contrive to set them down on the night of the Christmas gambols, in the hall at Melcombe, with the dresses, guitar, and all their machinery.

I was to have gone to Elvas today, but the intended removal has altered my plan. Sir William Myers and Colonel Lyon[1] went last week on a tour to Seville and Cadiz. They strongly pressed me to accompany them, which many reasons prevented. I am now glad I did not go, as they will be so much hurried, and I should not cut a good figure on a post mule with bells round its neck, the mode in which they proposed to travel. It would besides have cost me more money than I have a right to throw away.

December 10th. We are still without orders. The Guards marched yesterday to Elvas, and the German Legion replaced them at Badajoz. It is conjectured that we shall embark, though it is not given out that it is so. Today it is cloudy and looks like rain.

December 11th. We know nothing more for certain, with regard to the movement of our division. General Cole says we are to be the last. It is reported the sick are to be left at Vila Vicosa; I am sorry to say they do not decrease in number. We are still without any details of the Duke del Parque's action. You will most likely hear it before we shall, in England.

December 12th. I now close my letter without any further information. The army still continues to march, and the Brigade of Guards will be on the north bank of the Tagus on the 18th. It will be the latter end of the week before we move, and we shall be seven days reaching the Tagus by easy marches, the roads being bad and many rivers to ford. Yesterday it rained a little and threatened more, and this morning the white frost was severe. Harrison has joined from Lisbon, he is still lame, and his leg disfigured. Adieu.

Letter 30   Estremoz, 21 December 1809

My dear Madam,

We marched at 12 o'clock on Tuesday last from Olivenza, leaving it not without many good wishes towards its inhabitants,

---

1. Sir James Lyon 24 Foot.

by whom we had been so hospitably entertained for eleven weeks, during which time there has not been a single complaint against a soldier, or a punishment. Notwithstanding the lovely weather, we had lost many people, and the brigade sent nearly one hundred sick to Vila Vicosa before we moved. About 3 o'clock p.m., we forded the Guadiana and entered Portugal, having been nearly six months in Spain. We halted for the night at Iuromenha, a small fortified town, standing above and commanding the ford over which we crossed the river. The accommodations were far from splendid but the people were civil. At the house where I was billeted, they complained heavily of some Spanish officers who had passed through their town about four months before, whom they accused of having all their plates and of having stolen a watch; but allowances must always be made in Portugal for the hatred that exists between the natives of the two countries.

From the citadel, the view down the Guadiana over which it hangs is very fine. The river loses itself in thick dark forests; we saw it about sunset, enriched by the tints of a frosty winter's evening.

On the 20th (Wednesday) we marched at 7 o'clock, just daylight. The first part of the road diversified with gentle hill and dale, tolerably well cultivated, and each brow crowned with a neat white farm house, large forest trees, chiefly ilex and cork, amongst the green corn, which has just made its appearance. As we proceeded the scenery became more wild, the glens deeper and well wooded. At 12 after a march of about eleven miles, we came to Vila Vicosa a place of considerable consequence formerly; there are two good squares, one of which contains the royal hunting seat, now a military hospital. It is by no means a handsome building, of three storeys, full of windows, and has more the air of what it is now used for, or a manufactory, than a royal residence.[1] In the garden are models in wood of all the fortresses of Portugal, probably for the instruction of some of the younger branches of the family, with a variety of box and yew trees cut into grotesque shapes. The tapada or park is a short distance from the town. You enter it at a handsome iron gate commanding a view of the whole park and country for many miles round. It is very well wooded and well stocked with deer, these were formerly three thousand head; they have now however been thinned by the English officers quartered

1. The 'Paco Ducal', the sixteenth century palace of the Braganza family.

here; liberty to shoot, having been seldom refused by the regency. On the whole the park would be considered beautiful in England, the trees being evergreen, with the exception of a few alders planted near the gate, the gay variety of autumnal tint we admire so much is lost; a small mountain stream runs through it. The attempts made to embellish it, we should consider as having a contrary tendency; a row of trees on each side of the road which goes through it. It is said to be four leagues in circumference; it does not appear to be half that size, but I do not think the eye takes in the whole, even from the entrance above mentioned.

I was asked by General Slade to dine.[1] His venison was not good, and his wine was worse. He begged to be kindly remembered to my 'good' father and said that both General Garth[2] and himself were 'enraptured' with the Dorsetshire people, for their attentions to the Princess Amelia.[3] I left him early, being much fatigued not only having walked the whole march, but had been in the park the whole day afterwards. I was billeted on the house Lord Wellington had occupied, and slept in his lordship's bed, with a crimson satin counterpane, as sound as his excellency could have done.

December 21st. As we had only two leagues and a half to go, we did not march till 8 o'clock. Our road was very good, but the day, that was fine at starting, became overcast and we were enveloped in a thick fog. The country was flat and well cultivated and about two miles from Vila Vicosa we passed through Borba, a large well built town, and we understand it has a better and pleasanter society than any country town in Portugal. 12 o'clock brought us to Estremoz; the fog so thick we could not see from one side of the square to the other. In the afternoon it cleared away, and gave us an opportunity of seeing the town. It is large and well built, the Plaĉa Maior or Great Square is very fine. Like all the other towns in Portugal, it is overrun with convents for male and female. There are no less than six within the walls; all immense buildings and now made use of for hospitals. A church is now building entirely of white marble, which will when finished, be very handsome, but the

1. Major General Sir John Slade, Lieutenant Colonel of the 10 Light Dragoons.
2. General Thomas Garth, Colonel of the 1 Royal Dragoons.
3. Amelia was the youngest daughter of King George III; she died in November 1810. Her death is thought to have caused the King to relapse into his final bout of illness.

work on account of the war proceeds very slowly. The friar, who showed it us, told us it would be completed in six years, but under the present circumstances I doubt whether it ever will. White marble is very plentiful here; almost every house is decorated with some, either as door posts, as ornaments round the window, or in the staircases. From a Moorish tower[1] of marble in the citadel, there is a magnificent view, extending over an amazing space, taking in eight or ten other considerable towns; and the surrounding country is well cultivated.

The fortifications of the town which were extensive (but almost everywhere commanded) have been allowed for several years past to go to decay. They serve now to add much to the picturesque appearance of the town and by their dusky hue to contrast with the gay white and green of the houses. There is an extraordinary comfort to be met with here for Portugal, a good inn; it was so neat that I was almost tempted to join a party going to dine there, but I had an excellent dinner ready for us at our billets in the Plaça, and today I dine with General Cole. It is now said we are not to halt at Abrantes, but to proceed to Coimbra, and even further. This would be very pleasant, if we had a continuance of the present fine weather, but at this time of the year we cannot expect it, and after we leave this we must look for indifferent accommodation. The last mail brought me no letters from home; I hope to meet some at Abrantes from whence I shall despatch this letter.

Cano, December 23rd. It rained hard last night which did not improve the first part of the road, leading through narrow lanes. The brigade marched at 8 o'clock, at 10 the rain ceased and the roads became better, and the country more open. At 1 we arrived at this village, which was a much better one than we were led to expect. On the right of the road a chain of hills extended the whole way from Estremoz on the left, and before us lay a country as flat as any part of Essex; apparently a good soil and well cropped, the corn just now making its appearance.

Ervedal, December 24th. We marched at 9 o'clock. The Fusiliers preceded us as we were to separate. They went to Avis and a short march of seven miles brought us to this place, a very small village.

---

1. The thirteenth century 'Torre das Três Coroas' (The tower of three crowns), because three Kings helped in its construction.

Our landlord, an ignorant, officious, old fellow. The whole way was through a flat, well cultivated country without enclosures, but well wooded, large trees, chiefly ever-green oak (ilex) spreading their wide branches over the green corn. They suffer so much from heat in this country that they consider the shade an advantage as it prevents the crop from being burnt up. From the top of the hill I ascended near the village, I could distinguish ten others, some of them apparently considerable. The Serra da Estrela is also in sight, covered with snow, and the weather is fine and frosty. There was a thin coat of ice on the water near the road as we passed this morning, and this evening we were glad to exchange a fine painted room without glass windows, for the kitchen chimney corner, although we were favoured by the company of our landlord, who kept hawking and spitting the whole evening. Fortunately some militia officer supped with him, which relieved us of his company.

Benavila, Christmas day. We had only six miles to march this morning, the weather clear, frosty, and beautiful. Our billet too was an excellent one, having a room with a fireplace in it, a luxury confined to the middle-class people residing in small towns in this province. The better class throughout Portugal prefer charcoal. Our road for the whole distance was over a dreary heath; we passed one small river, but rivers are scarce in this flat part of the Alemtejo, and this is therefore denominated Rio Grande; at present it is but a brook and hardly over a shoe. I gave a Christmas dinner to six people. General Slade had given me half a buck at Vila Vicosa, which I had brought with me. The haunch was roasted, I had a goose, and a plum pudding; indeed we have fared well the whole of this march, and are so well accustomed to this vagrant sort of life that we have always (if we choose it) a good dinner two hours after our arrival. Harrison lives with me. His leg, poor fellow, is sadly out of shape, but he gains strength, and walks better on it every day.

Ponte de Sor, December 26th. Nothing could have been more dreary and desolate than the whole twelve miles from Benavila to this place; the weather continued fine, and compensated for the dreary heath we passed over. About two miles from this town it improves; you descend into a picturesque glen with a pretty Quinta at the bottom of it. The village is considerably larger than either of the two last we have halted at. Why it should have the appellation of ponte, I cannot tell. Over the small river or brook, that runs near

72

the town, there is only a single plank, and they have even a boat to convey people across in floods. It did not seem to be in a very flourishing condition; many houses deserted, as was the one on which we were billeted, one of the most considerable in the town. They complained of the inconvenience of troops marching through. They have had their town full for these last ten days. Our men have during the whole march behaved very well, and there have been no complaints; but to have two or three officers, or eight or ten soldiers put into a house cannot be very pleasant to the owner or occupier, especially as customs are so different, and difficulty of explanation in consequence of not understanding each other, takes place frequently.

Abrantes, 27th and 28th December. We marched into this place exactly six months after we had left its neighbouring camp. The road from Ponte do Soro is much more picturesque than that of the last two days, ascending small hills and descending deep narrow, well-wooded glens; the cork trees were larger than any I had before met with. The distance was twenty miles, crossing one small stream several times. The view of Abrantes from the south is always magnificent, and now the river, covered with a swarm of boats, and lit up by the brilliant sun of a Portuguese winter, was doubly interesting. On our arrival, we learned we are to proceed to Coimbra, and march to-morrow. It is even rumoured we are to go on from thence to Guarda, the exhausted state of the country and the necessity of marching through large towns to cover the troops, makes our route round by Leiria.

I dined yesterday with General Cole; today I am to dine with General Hill, who is to remain here with his division. At General Cole's I met Lieutenant Colonel Alexander Abercromby, a brother of the General's.[1] He is a fine young man, and puts me much in mind of his brother. The town of Abrantes, never very clean, has become more filthy than anything you can imagine. The billet I am now in is by much the dirtiest place I was ever in, and swarming with vermin of every kind and description, and the inhabitants so uncivil that they extinguished their only fire yesterday, lest we should have anything to cook by it.

The works are in a state of great forwardness, and it is already

1. Alexander was the brother of Sir Ralph Abercromby, victor of the Battle of Alexandria in 1801 and who had died of his wounds soon after.

a formidable position. I earnestly hope the weather may continue fine and we shall do better whilst on the march than at rest. I have one grief, my favourite horse is lame. I was offered at Olivenza anything I chose to ask for him, for the commander of the forces, but he had carried me so well through the campaign, and at Talavera, that I could not make up my mind to part with him. Harrison rides my Portuguese horse, so I am on my legs. This I do not mind; walking is good for me, and indeed [in] this fine weather I should always prefer it.

I shall be able to forward another journal from Coimbra, but as a great part of the road we have gone over before, it will lose much of its interest. All this time we think no more of the French than if they were not on the peninsula. As soon as we arrive at our final destination, we shall look out for them. In the end I suppose we shall be obliged to embark, but I think now we shall give them some trouble first.

Letter 31   **Coimbra, 6 January 1810**

My dear Madam,

I received your letter of the 2nd December at Tomar, and yours and Nora's from Deans Leage of the 17th at this place. I rejoice to hear Still passed so well, and hope he may be appointed to the staff in this country, which is not improbable.

General Hill was good enough at Abrantes, to take charge of my letter to you, with the journal of the first part of our march. I believe I told you that at Abrantes we found a route for Coimbra, and at Tomar we got another to carry us on to Guarda, five long marches from this, so that it will be the 11th of this month, before our peregrinations are at an end. We have been fortunate in our weather, having had scarcely any rain, although we have been marching since the 19th of last month. We could hardly have marched half the way in England, at this season of the year, without being well drenched. The Portuguese tell us we may reach Guarda yet, without any. The day looks cloudy, but as it is what they call cold, they say it will not produce rain.

Our route from Abrantes has been nearly the same as last year; you cannot therefore expect much variety. I shall however continue my journal, uninteresting as it may be, as it will serve to complete the march from Olivenza to Guarda. You will observe by looking at the map, that we have made a considerable circuit. Had we crossed the Tagus at Vila Velha, and gone by Castelo Branco, we should have saved half the distance, but supplies of all sorts are so scarce, that we could hardly have been able to subsist on that road, and it was thought easier to bring us to the supplies, than the supplies to us; so if the mountain cannot come to Mohamet, why Mohamet must go to the mountain, and this will serve to explain why we have gone so much out of our road.

December 29th. Marched from Abrantes to Punhente, nine miles. The weather quite warm, more like June than December. The town of Punhente like Abrantes, much dirtier than any person who has never been in Portugal, can conceive. This you perceive the more coming from Spain, or even the Alemtejo, where their streets are comparatively clean, and their houses exceedingly so. Harrison and myself, continue to live together. We are billeted on a house that overlooked the Zezere, the river that joins the Tagus. Just below this place, in the winter (that is after rains) it is considerable; at present it is fordable everywhere, but is very rapid. After rains it rises ten or twelve feet. This, a priest who spoke French and is brother to our landlady, gives as a reason why they have a temporary bridge of boats, in preference to one of stone. He complained that the people are sadly tired of having troops pass through their town. In two years they have seen four armies, one Spanish, one French, and the British twice. Although the officers (he said) generally conducted themselves with propriety, yet servants are frequently careless and do much mischief. He apologised for not being able to furnish us with articles for our table, as the last people billeted there, had broken nearly all the plates and glass in the house.

30th. We marched from Punhente to Tomar twelve miles. Tolerably good road. The last time we went this way, our guide took us a short cut, through the mountain and we were an hour and a half longer in performing the march than we were this time. We missed however the Welsh bridge, and beautiful fall that if you refer to my journal for June, you will observe I was much pleased with.

We found a grand market at Tomar, and the town crowded, it being the headquarters of the Portuguese army. It brought Ireland to my recollection on a similar occasion; the throng, the blue cloaks of the women, and the dirt and filthiness of all.

The regiment was as before at the Convento de Cristo, which I went over again with much pleasure. I had a billet in the town, which was very full, as Lord Wellington was there on his way to Coimbra. He had that morning been seeing some of the Portuguese troops, who are indeed wonderfully improved by the introduction of British officers. But whilst the condition of the soldier has been ameliorated, nothing has as yet been for the officers, who though the worst in Europe, never considered themselves to be so. They have been deprived of the perquisite they had been accustomed to make by plundering their men, and no equivalent has been given them in the room. This, which affects their dearest interests, and the introduction of young foreign officers over their heads, has not reconciled them to the change, and I am afraid will have an effect on the day of trial people in general will not foresee!!

I dined with my old friend General Hamilton and preferred paying this attention to my old Lieutenant-Colonel who is now Inspector General of Portuguese Infantry, to dining with Marshal Beresford where I was invited, and where Lord Wellington (who is now Marshal General, in a coat, the embroidery of which cost five hundred dollars) dined.

31st. A march of thirteen miles brought us to the top of the tremendous, steep and isolated hill on which stands the town of [Vila Nova de] Ourem. The castle here, which is the most perfect Moorish work in Portugal, is very well worth seeing, a gallery on projecting, small, buttresses, which runs round each tower of an octagon form, is different from any I have seen.[1] The view from the hill is extensive and much diversified. A large forest of pines, just under the town forms a contrast with the olives, which are nearly black now with the frosts we have had. At the house on which I was billeted a Portuguese officer was on a visit, who spoke a little English. He made apologies from the master of the house for not waiting on me, on account of his great age; he was upwards of ninety, I can conceive the people of Ourem attaining any age, the air is so pure.

Sir William Myers dined with us. He had just overtaken us, in his return from his tour to Cadiz. He came back much delighted at what he had seen. They suffered however so much trouble, fatigue and inconvenience, and it was so much more expensive than they

1. The fifteenth century castle is still very impressive.

had calculated on, that I am not sorry they did not persuade me to accompany them. Before we marched in the morning I looked into one of the churches which was very plain and handsome, without that profusion of gilding that spoils the religious edifices in this country in general; the altar piece appeared a tolerably good painting.

January 1st 1810. Fourteen miles of very bad road brought us on New Year's day to Leiria. The old doctor on whom I had been before quartered exerted himself, to get me to his house again. The magistrates however, very properly refused to remove some Portuguese officers who were quartered on him, to make room for me. He was very glad to see me, and freely offered me whatever his house afforded. The town is much altered since we were here last year. It was then crowded with military and the peasants from the country were shy of making their appearance. Now the market place is crowded with people; every article of life is to be sold, exceedingly cheap, and everything looks like peace and happiness. The quantity of gold ornaments worn by the peasantry is striking. Not a woman who comes into the town to sell eggs, but has two gold necklaces, (the one of gold beads as large as small peas) with gold or silver ear-rings, and each man has his shirt buttoned at the collar with gold studs, and these ornaments have generally descended from father to son, from mother to daughter for several generations.

2nd January. Halt at Leiria. Retraced all my old walks; and I showed Harrison all the lions; the castle looked as usual, beautiful; the cathedral, the neatest we have seen in <u>Portugal</u>, in Spain, those at Coria and Plasencia are superior.

3rd January. Marched to Pombal, which looked as cheery as ever. In the church we saw the coffin of the great Marquess of Pombal; he is embalmed and kept above ground under lock and key. Some of the party were anxious to have the coffin opened. I had no such wish. If ever the French come here, they will serve him as they did the Saint at Jarecejo, whom they took out of the ground and set him up as a sentry at the church door.

January 4th. Marched to Condeixa. The roads are now considerably better than when we last passed them; having been no rain as yet this winter, it made a difference of nearly two hours in each of the last two day's march. This and the coolness of the weather, enables us to get on famously, and some little help is necessary to our poor fellows, who have now a blanket as well as a great coat to carry; three days bread, sixty rounds of ammunition; and when besides all this you know they have not slept on a bed these nine months, you will be inclined to believe a soldier's life is no luxury on service. They however laugh and joke and don't appear to feel it. They are in high favour with me at present, they have conducted themselves so well during the whole march; no pilfering or petty larceny, of course no necessity for punishment. My former landlord at this place was very anxious again to accommodate me, but I did not get his billet. I dined with General Cole and passed a pleasant day.

January 5th. We arrived here by eleven o'clock and I walked all over the town to show it to Harrison. I was asked to dine at Lord Wellington's where I found a large party. There were two ladies of the party, the Vicomtesse Alberche, and her sister, the former a very fine woman dressed quite in the English style with a profusion of diamonds. She talked a great deal in French; she has been at many foreign courts; I am not certain whether her husband did not hold a diplomatic situation in London. Although her dress was English, her manners were French; she ate voraciously, off the same plate, put her knife into the salt cellar &c. &c., the sister, who was very plain, played quite a second part. Her husband is now a Lieutenant in one of the regiments here, and a very old man. We were served off plate, the property of the bishop at whose palace Lord Wellington lives. The dinner was cold and ill served; his lordship cares little about his table, and although I made no doubt he lives expensively, he lives badly. I dine today at Marshal Beresford's, where I shall get a better dinner, and perhaps a pleasanter day. The tables of all commanders of the forces are formal. You will be glad to hear that my favourite horse, that in my last letter, I mentioned as being lame, has recovered. He had a thorn in his shoulder. It has worked out, and he is quite well again. We expect Campbell out immediately, and he will resume the command of our brigade. I am not dis-satisfied with Cole, who is a pleasant, sensible, agreeable man. Campbell is however the man for action. I have now brought my long letter to a close. You shall hear from me again from Guarda where, if the rains set in, I shall have nothing else to do but write. We hear it is the coldest place in Portugal, situated amidst the wildest mountains. It is a query how long Bonaparte will allow us to remain there. Altogether this march has been the pleasantest

78

yet made in this country. There has been great variety, and we have been excellently well supplied in every respect. You will find it hard to believe that a march of nearly one hundred and eighty miles in the months of December and January can be pleasant. We have I am afraid the worst part, eighty-four miles, to come; the roads are represented as bad; marches are long, and accommodation worse than any we have lately been accustomed to experience.

Letter 32   Guarda, 13 January 1810

My dear Madam,

I am now writing to you from the midst of the clouds, enveloped in a snow storm, and although we have been in this place forty-eight hours, I cannot attempt to describe it, as the fog has been so dense, I have never been able to see from one side of the narrow streets to the other. How fortunate we ought to consider ourselves that the bad weather did not set in before we completed our march, but allowed us to get into settled quarters before it commenced. Our history since we left Coimbra has been as follows. My last letter was dated on the 6th on which day I dined with Marshal Beresford, and although not served on plate, or treated with the society of a countess, the day was less formal and much pleasanter than the preceding one. I sat next a Colonel Campbell who has accepted a command in the Portuguese service, and is a brigadier.[1] He pressed me much to stay the next day, and dine with him to meet Lord Wellington which I was afterwards glad I had refused, the next day's march being so long, and the road so difficult to find. We marched on the 7th at half past seven; a most lovely morning. The first two miles were over a good paved road and through a perfect garden nearly the whole way; over hung with orange and lemon trees loaded, <u>over-loaded</u> with fruit. Amongst other country houses or Quintas, one of the most pleasantly situated and best, belongs to the Convent of Santa Cruz of Coimbra. These gentlemen well understand where best to place themselves. Shortly after, we crossed a small river which was everywhere fordable, but was furnished with a small temporary bridge for our accommodation, and began to ascend a considerable and very steep mountain. The

1. Almost certainly Brigadier General A. Campbell commanding the Independent Portuguese Brigade of 6 and 18 Line and 6 Cacadores.

view from the summit amply repaid the trouble of the ascent and the badness of the road, which was in some places so narrow, that only one man could pass, and so steep that some of the baggage mules losing their footing, were rolled nearly to the bottom. On one side we saw the city of Coimbra with its fertile plains, washed by the Mondego; as far as the sea at Figueras; on another a rocky, well wooded glade through which ran the torrent we had just passed, and before us mountain piled on mountain, till the view terminated in the Serra da Estrela, covered with snow. These mountains appeared well inhabited and the spires of churches and convents peeping through the dusky foliage of the olive tree completed the picture. I have seen no view so extensive since I have been on Snowdon. The descent was equally steep. At the foot was a considerable village, and very large convent of nuns. At their request we passed through the courtyard, as they wished to see the troops and hear the music. They showered oranges on the men, and sent out cakes and sweetmeats to the officers. They appeared about fifty in number. As the grating of the windows was large, we had a good view of their persons, but none appeared handsome. After leaving this village the road was excessively bad, which retarded our march. About noon we crossed the Ceira, rather a considerable river, and like the Dee in many places. About sunset we had another mountain to pass, on the summit of which night overtook us, and we stumbled about for one hour in the dark, and after crossing the Alva, a larger river than the last, we found ourselves in the wretched village of Ponte de Mucela, glad enough to get in anywhere and after our beefsteak was cooked, and we had taken our glass of wine, retired to rest in a room so dark, so dingy, and so filthy, that coming as we did from Olivenza, and the clean cottages in the Alemtejo, did not go down at all [well]. We marched at seven o'clock on the morning of the 8th, and met the other regiments at 8, about a league on the road. They had been as badly accommodated as ourselves. The 11th Regiment did not get to their quarters till 9 o'clock. The roads for this day's march were considerably better. We crossed large heaths, and some cultivated valleys; the Serra da Estrela bounded the prospect.

You perceived that, as you were constantly ascending, the features and productions of the country altered. Oranges disappeared and were succeeded by chestnuts, which at any other time but just in the depth of winter, would have looked as well. The grape instead of being cultivated in large vineyards, began to be trained 'en espalier', and to surround small fields, much like the divisions of land in Wales.

The headquarters were at Lourosa, a village on the road. We went off to the left and were distributed in the two little hamlets of Valvilla, and Valongo. The inhabitants though poor were hospitable; whatever they had they freely disposed of. They never had any troops pass through their retreats before.

I was billeted on the Curé who had a small well cultivated farm about him. The system of irrigation is much practised here and appears to have been of considerable standing. They have excellent grass and hay, and the land intended for Indian corn or maize, was almost covered with water. Our host gave us some apples and grapes, so sour that they would not have been considered eatable in England. Even in this retired spot he was anxious to be made acquainted with the events that were passing in the great world, and seemed to take a pride in showing that he took in the 'Gazetta di Lisbon', as considering it a tie between the world and himself. He was not an old man, and appeared as if he contributed by his own manual labour towards the cultivation of his own lands. There had been a fair at Lourosa, which had been attended by the whole country, and which gave liveliness to the scene. Some of the young men although not absolutely intoxicated had been drinking as much wine as made them gay. One of them who undertook to show me from the Curé's to the village, apologised to me for having done so, or I should not perhaps have perceived it. The climate of these mountains must be their excuse, as it assimilates them more to the northern nations; it is a practise I never before noticed in Portugal. The distance we marched this day, must have been twenty miles.

January 9th. The road was not so good as the day before, and we passed through several very poor looking villages; they are now all built of large blocks of granite, and not being white-washed, and furnished but scantily, with tin window shutters instead of glass, neither cleaned nor painted, have a gloomy appearance. The practise of putting down heath or straw to retain the wet and to make manure causes these villages to be very dirty. Crowds collected in every one of them to see the troops pass, and several came from villages out of the road. There fell a little rain this day, the first we have had since we left Estremoz, that made the road worse than it otherwise would have been, and very slippery. The

81

country is well wooded, chiefly oak, and chestnut. The pinaster[1] begins to be planted near the villages for fuel. We drew nearer the Serra da Estrela, and tomorrow shall begin to pass round their base.

The distance from Valongo to Pinhancos where we halted, we computed at eighteen miles, the wet prevented our going about much after our arrival. The town was gloomy and the houses uncomfortable and dirty. The style of room here has two beds in recesses, or sort of cupboard, without a window. Our landlord, a captain of militia, is absent with his regiment. His lady supplied his place, was very dirty, and talked a great deal, without being half understood, but that she did not seem to care about.

January 10th. As we advanced on this day's march the country became more sterile, and but scantily wooded; the road was bad, we passed several streams on good strong stone bridges and it was dark by the time we reached Celorico [da Beira]. I dined with General Lightburne,[2] who was here with his brigade, and to do him justice he gave us the worst dinner I ever sat down to. The town was so crowded, that I was put into a house occupied by Colonel King of the 5th Regiment[3]; I however saw nothing of him, but the landlord gave me a very comfortable bed. For the town of Celorico I can say but little as it was dark before we were dismissed, and we marched soon after daylight, the next morning. It stands high, and has the remains of an old castle in the centre.

January 11th. Our road, which was better than we had been led to expect, wound round a barren hill into a most beautiful valley, through which runs the Mondego, of a much smaller size than we have hitherto seen. About six miles from Celorico we crossed it on good firm stepping stones; it is very clear and rapid. There is a bridge, but it makes the distance greater. Soon after passing the river we began to ascend the mountain, by a good, wide paved road, winding like a corkscrew. The ascent is about four miles. We had heard of nothing during our march but the cold of Guarda, and directly we attained the summit of the hill, we found a very piercing wind, and a sensible difference of climate.

1. Species of fir tree.
2. Major General Safford Lightburne, 53rd Foot had been on the Staff in Ireland. He now commanded a Brigade in the 3rd Division, consisting of 2/5th, 2/83rd and three Companies of 5/60th.
3. Lieutenant Colonel Henry King.

At 2 o'clock we arrived at Guarda; our men are quartered in the most dreary convent I ever saw. Over the gate, St Francis with a skull in his hand denotes the misery to be expected within. I am fortunately billeted on a civil old canon by the name of Silva di Rua, who is schoolmaster on the establishment of the cathedral.

Ever since we came in, and it is now the 15th, it has been snowing more or less, and it is in some places five and six feet deep; we have been besides completely enveloped in clouds, so that I cannot attempt to give you a description of the city, but shall reserve it for another time, and bid you adieu, perished with cold, as there is not a fire place in the town, and the only mode of warming the room is by a pan of charcoal, which gave me such a headache yesterday, that I shall not be in haste to attempt it again.

Letter 33   Guarda, 3 February 1810

My dear Madam,

I received your letter of the 25th ultimo, and Tryon's and Mary's of the same date, the day before yesterday. I cannot surmise how my name got into The Globe;[1] my correspondence extends no further than yourselves, and occasionally General William Wynyard,[2] who is not likely to make my name public, unless indeed some of the people at the Horse Guards have got hold of my note.

This letter leaves us in the same situation as the last. On our advance to this place the French retired, and we understand are now all gone to the southward. A small force is at Salamanca and there is nothing nearer; various are the reports in circulation, but few to be depended upon, for these last two days. We have heard that they have forced the passes of Sierra Morena, but we are not inclined to credit it. I believe I have frequently told you how much credit the people of the peninsula attach to the most absurd reports provided they are favourable to their cause. An English officer dined here last week at the table of the Duke del Parque, where the whole conversation turned on an account of a revolution said to have broken out in France, headed by Talleyrand, Massena, and

1. *The Globe and Traveller* published in London.
2. General William Wynyard was the father of George's Aunt Sarah; she was married to the Reverend William Bingham.

Josephine, and the Spaniards were boasting of what feats they were to perform in France, and of the manner in which they would retaliate on that country the evils their own had suffered from Bonaparte. This anecdote you may depend on as authentic.

My last letter was written in a snow storm. The snow has not as yet left us, having been seventeen or eighteen days on the ground, which length of time I hardly recollect even in England. The weather was for some time uncommonly severe. For several successive nights the water froze to a solid mass in the rooms; for these last few the weather has been finer, the sun has dissolved the snow in the valleys, although it as yet remains here. The temperature of the valleys and the town is very different. All the people who are rich enough to afford it retire to the banks of the Mondego in the winter, and return to Guarda for the heat of the summer. The houses in the town having no fireplaces are not desirable winter habitations, a pan of charcoal being but a sorry substitute, and the rooms (being without carpets, curtains, ceiling or glass windows) afford no comforts in this severe climate.

The town, or as I should say the city of Guarda, is of great antiquity, and has been enclosed with walls, and defended by a castle. The situation is strong, but the fortifications which were never modern, have gone to decay. It is said to be (by the Portuguese) 'multo fria, multo fasta, multo fia,' very cold, very abundant, and very ugly', and it certainly well answers to all these terms. The streets are narrow, and the town being four days out of the seven, either in or above the clouds, you can scarcely find your way through them. The inhabitants either from constantly sitting over charcoal or for want of pure air are plainer than any in Portugal. As the valleys about the town are very fertile, the town cannot be but abundantly supplied. Although every town in this country is over run with clergy, this is particularly so; the population is small and there are at least one hundred and fifty. The cathedral supports an establishment of thirty canons, besides the same number of different denominations; this is rather too much. The cathedral is a rather handsome gothic structure, the altar-piece is in alto-relief, but the figures being gilt on a white ground, the whole has a paltry effect. It has two organs, the large one, though out of repair, is exceedingly fine in tone. It is supported by two large grotesque heads with their tongues lolling out, and which their bad taste has painted in colours. The principal parish church is a handsome modern structure,[1] very gaudy in the inside, as most of the Portuguese churches are, exactly resembling the last scene of a pantomime, with pillars of all colours.

The inmates of the nunnery are twenty-three in number besides the abbess. They are said not to have the best of reputations; I believe their inclinations may not be very pure, but the gratings and bars with which they are secured, must prevent their having any intercourse with the world. They are most of them plain and old, and there is not one that would pass for good looking in England; however two of them, who are rather plump, pass for beauties at Guarda. Religion is not carried on with that outward decency that it was at Olivenza, where the clergy were few in number, and respectable in their manner and appearance. I was present, a few days since at the funeral of a young lady. Thirty-three priests sang the requiem over the body, which was well dressed and as is the custom of the country, in an open coffin, ornamented with purple silk and gold lace. For this they each received three shillings and a wax taper; no one of them (the weather being cold) remained to see her put into a vault, but left her to two ruffian sextons, who probably stripped her of her dress and artificial flowers before they put her down.

I have taken advantage of the fine, cold, clear weather which there is to be found in the neighbourhood though not in the city. I descend from the clouds and extend my walks to several miles around. I set off every day, with my staff in my hand, as if I was at home. The scenery in the valleys is beautiful, particularly in the Val de Mondego. I hope to show you on my return, some pen sketches, which will be sufficient to prove how well worth attention this part of Portugal is to the lovers of picturesque scenery. The Mondego, which is here a rapid, clear stream, dashes through a rocky channel. The hills or rather mountains on each side are extremely well wooded, and cultivated, indeed industry is carried to a much greater length in this retired valley than in the more favourable and fertile plains. This is the season for gathering in the olives for making the oil, and the girls who collect them sing so beautiful in parts, that it is quite delightful.

The bishop's palace in this town is like a large barn, and ill contrived, being all passages. The rooms are gloomy and lined with

1. The Igreja da Misericordia.

tapestry, with a few daubs of paintings of former bishops on the walls, with a raised dais and chair of state of moth-eaten velvet in every room. It is the coldest house I was ever in. General Cole lives at it, and I am frequently there.

The Portuguese seem to have but little idea of social intercourse. I will detail to you the life of my landlord, a dignitary of the church as a specimen. He gets up at six o'clock and walks about in his room about an hour, wrapped up in his cloak. At seven he takes some tea, and a little bit of fat pork, after which, he sits over a pan of charcoal rationally amusing himself with picking out of it any piece that smokes, calling it Bonaparte, ladron, and plunging it deeper into the fire. At ten o'clock he eats a little bit of bread and cheese and sometimes a broil, with a little wine. This keeps him till noon, when he takes a little snack and goes to bed, till nearly three, when he has a hot dinner served on a chair, with a napkin tucked under his chin. He has then another sleep till about five, when he takes coffee, and two or three people (generally ecclesiastics) drop in for an hour or two. At nine he has his supper, which carries him through the remainder of the night. As he drinks freely at all these latter meals, he contrives to get through about three bottles of light wine, in the twenty-four hours. He sometimes officiates in the church, which is just across the street, but this is a great exertion, and always calls for additional aliment. He does occasionally read that instructive and edifying work 'The Lisbon Court Calendar and Almanack' (his is for the year 1807) and can tell how all the nobility are disposed of, whether carried to France, or emigrated to Brazil. I believe I told you that Lord and Lady Shuldam lived here some time since, when on their travels (I fancy the only English travellers that ever penetrated so far) and that they had rewarded him for his hospitality by giving him a gold repeater, which he is very proud of, and shows to everybody.

This is but a poor account of the Portuguese clergy. I hope this letter will find John at home.[1] Adieu.

1. His brother John was a Captain in the Royal Navy; he had been captured by French privateers off Cephalonia in 1807 and as a prisoner was held at Verdun until the end of the war. I must thank Liza Verity of the National Maritime Museum, Greenwich, for this information.

Sir George Ridout Bingham in the uniform of colonel of the Rifle Brigade.
(Image Ref: Eg 3715f19 by kind permission of the British Library)

The 53rd at Talavera by Richard Simpkins. (by kind permission of Lieutenent Colonel P. J. Wykeham, RHQ The Light Infantry)

Battle of Salamanca by Richard Simpkins.

Top: View of Abrantes from the Tagus by Major Leith Hay. (from Views of Spain, drawn on campaign, published by Lizars of London 1830)
Centre: The Battle of Vittoria by Major Leith Hay. (from Views of Spain, drawn on campaign, published by Lizars of London 1830)
Bottom: The British encampment before Pamplona by Major Leith Hay. (from Views of Spain, drawn on Campaign, published by Lizars of London 1830)

The Battle of Sorauren 28-30 July 1813.

St Helena by G. H. Bellasis. (from Views of St Helena, Tyler, London 1815 by kind permission of Barry Weaver)

Jamestown harbour St Helena 1815 by G. H. Bellasis. (from Views of St Helena, Tyler, London 1815 by kind permission of Barry Weaver)

Plantation House St Helena 1815 by G. H Bellasis. (from Views of St Helena, Tyler, London 1815 by kind permission of Barry Weaver)

The garrison of Jamestown St Helena on parade 1815 by G. H. Bellasis. (from Views of St Helena, Tyler, London 1815 by kind permission of Barry Weaver)

Longwood House circa 1815.

Longwood House today.

Napoleon's bed at Longwood.

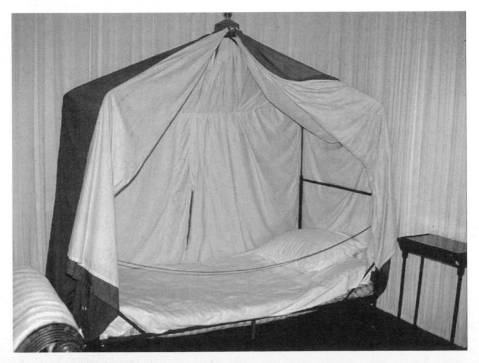

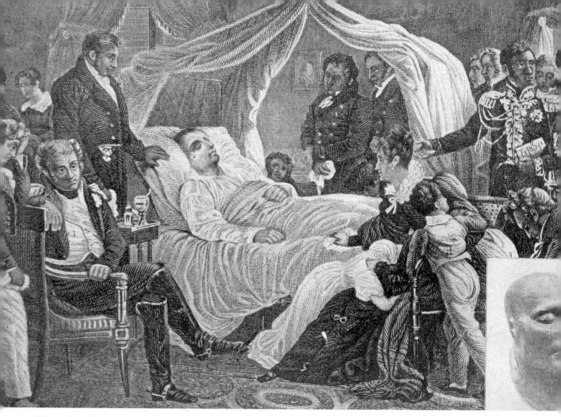

The death of Napoleon, with a view of his death mask inset.

Napoleon's tomb on St Helena.

Letter 34   Guarda, 10 February 1810

My dear Madam,

I received your last letter &c. Since I last wrote the frost has left and the snow is almost gone, and we have had even here one or two fair days. On all the rest the fog has been so thick that we have been able to see nothing. To prove to you the luxury in which we live I must tell you that last week I gave a grand dinner to the general and his staff. Eight was the number we sat down. I had hare soup, a roasted turkey; two courses; I assure you it 'went off very well', as they say in Dorsetshire. On one fine day last week I rambled further into the Val de Mondego than I have hitherto been, and stumbled on a most romantic glen, through which the Rio Alva forces its way into the Mondego, through a narrow cleft in the rocks, and tumbles down into the larger stream in a variety of picturesque cascades near the Ponte de Mucela. At this place the Mondego is much contracted, as well as the valley through which it runs. It is extremely well wooded with oak, and chestnut. I promise myself great pleasure if we remain till the budding of the leaf.

No one seems to know or care anything about the French, and their movements are less canvassed than with you at home.

The Spanish Army are said to be gone to the southward. It matters little where they are. Adieu.

Letter 35   Guarda, 24 February 1810

My dear Madam,

Since I wrote to you on the 10th we have had a partial movement in our brigade. The light infantry companies have moved to villages in front, near the banks of the Coa, a river that deserves some consideration in a military point of view, from the steep rocky channel through which it runs; it is about seventeen or eighteen miles from this. I accompanied the light infantry of our regiment to Rochoso, the village they are to occupy. After descending the steep hill on which Guarda stands, the country undulates in gentle hill and dale. It does not appear to be particularly fertile; the soil in most parts a glittering sort of sand. The chief produce is rye; it is I believe too poor and dry for Indian corn. The quarters at Rochoso were not particularly inviting, but the climate is warm and pleasanter than our own. At this place we had the ground covered with snow on the seventeenth, and some hard frosts since that time. Today the weather is milder and we hope the severe part of the winter is over. If we were to take the field, this cold weather would soon reduce our numbers; as it is, I have been thinking of asking the general to allow us to quarter the regiment in the villages in the Val de Mondego, for a change of air, and climate; for we do not get at all so stout as I could wish. I am speaking of the soldiers who are but miserably off in the cold, dreary convent in which they are quartered; where they all sleep in a long corridor over the cloisters, which although boarded, yet not being ceiled beneath, is worse than any loft. We have never been able to collect straw sufficient for them, so that these cold boards are not likely to recover them after the fatigues of the last campaign. In fact our numbers do not increase, and we send more men to the rear than we receive from the hospitals, for whenever any man is taken ill he is immediately sent on one of the mules that bring up provisions, either to Celorico or to Viseu, still further in the rear. Thus though our numbers may be lessened, we are always in readiness to move, without encumbrance. We hear but little about the French, who are supposed to be collecting at Salamanca, which has occasioned the light infantry being sent to the front. Adieu.

Letter 36   Lajeosa [do Mondego], 10 March 1810

My dear Madam,

The movement I mentioned to you in my last, I meant to propose to the general, has taken place, and we have shifted our quarters to this and the neighbouring villages, and the health of the men has considerably improved by the change. We came here the 1st of the month, and occupy Porto de Carne, Val Cortes, and this place, all situated in the Val de Mondego, though not immediately on the banks of that river. At first the weather was delightful, like May in England; it has however since that been so wet and stormy that there has been but little temptation to explore the beauties (which are many) of this neighbourhood.

I am quartered in an excellent stone house belonging to the fidalgo of the village, a plain, honest, good sort of country gentleman. He himself lives in the offices from preference (a

Portuguese always appearing at a loss in large and clean rooms) and generally takes refuge in the kitchen. He must have a good opinion of my honesty, as he gave me a massive silver ewer and basin, amongst the furniture of the rooms he allotted to me. He has a wife, and one only daughter, rather a pretty girl, but he is very shy of allowing her to communicate with us. Four or five days after we came here, he gave us a regular invitation to dinner, that is to say, to four officers besides myself. I thought his repast would never have been over; there were seven regular courses, and in the last appeared a large hog roasted whole, and there was plenty of game, a kid roasted, and laid on its side, that looked exactly like a greyhound. Several dishes were very palatable, especially the sweet things. The wine, which was as every thing else, the produce of his own estate, was very pleasant though in England it would have been considered light. We made a shift to converse, though but imperfectly, in our indifferent Portuguese. Unfortunately it blew a gale, and the rain poured down in torrents, so the shutters were obliged to be kept shut, and the only light was from the bad panes of glass, above the tin shutters. The room had once been whitewashed, and a heavy carved oak ceiling, made the whole dreadfully gloomy. Mine host's name is José Mendez, and he holds the post of Capitâo Mor, which answers to our Deputy Lieutenant of Counties; as they are charged with the calling out of militia, and ordenanca, as well as providing men for the line, which is all done by conscription. All the necessaries of life are so plentiful and cheap, that I can afford to keep a table, and have some two or three officers to dine with me every day. The soldiers are much better pleased with their quarters than at Guarda. They are billeted by twos and fours on the farms and cottages, and as they have behaved very well the inhabitants are quite attached to them. They help their landlords in their farms and gardens, and as we oblige them to keep their quarters neat, the houses have never been so clean. They begin to understand the language, and have nothing but the ear to depend on and mixing more with the inhabitants; they are more apt scholars (especially in pronunciation) than the officers. There are still reports of reinforcements arriving to the French in front, but we pay no great attention to them. Adieu.

Letter 37   **Lajeosa, 22 March 1810**

My dear Sir,

We moved from Guarda to this and adjacent villages about three weeks ago, and have been living here in great peace and quietness. We are at the foot of the range of mountains called the Serra da Estrela, on the banks of the Mondego. The valley we inhabit is now in high beauty, as it is full of fruit trees in blossom. These fruit trees are not confined to the gardens, but dispersed everywhere about the fields and vineyard in the prettiest manner possible. I understand this is likely to find you at Weymouth. I wish it may be our luck to join you there this autumn, after the campaign is over, which I am afraid cannot last long. Junot has arrived at Salamanca with 13,000 men; they had 9,000 there before, and I suppose after the next reinforcement arrives the ball will open. I wish we were stronger. We begin this campaign with 400 men; we brought out to this country 700, but I hope we shall get some more up before we take the field. Our casualties since we landed are 125 dead, six killed in action, thirty taken by the French at Talavera, and Plasencia, who were left either sick or wounded; and we have upwards of a hundred now in different hospitals in the rear of the army. Those we have with us are more healthy than we should be at home, and as for myself I never enjoyed better health in my life. Give my love &c.

Chapter Three

The Campaigns of 1810–12

Unfortunately the parcel of letters covering the period March 1810 to January 1812, are missing. The letters, therefore, resume in early 1812. During the missing period much had happened to Wellington's army (Wellesley had become Viscount Wellington for his victory at Talavera), but it is fortunately a period in which George and the 2/53rd were little more than spectators and so little information of vital importance can have been lost.

Forced to fall back in the face of overwhelming numbers following the loss of the frontier fortresses of Almeida and Ciudad Rodrigo, Wellington chose to stand at the Battle of Busaco on 27 September 1810 where Campbell's Brigade held the extreme northern tip of the ridge and saw no action at all. The army then retired towards Lisbon until they, like the French, discovered Wellington's secret. A chain of defensive forts and redoubts running from the Tagus to the coast, known as the Lines of Torres Vedras had been surreptitiously prepared and were only discovered by Marshal Massena when he was brought up in front of them. The British army settled comfortably within the lines, whilst the French stubbornly refused to retreat and slowly starved in a land largely denuded of foodstuffs by the Portuguese population, as they were herded into the lines.

In October 1810, Campbell's Brigade, including the 2/53rd was transferred to the newly organized 6th Division; Campbell was to lead the division and Major General Hulse would command the brigade. The 53rd's old partners, the 2/7th including George's great friend Myers, were removed from the brigade to form a 'Fusilier Brigade' with the 1/7th and 1/23rd.

In mid November, the French retired to Santarem, the British

91

following at a respectable distance. Remarkably Massena and his troops hung on here until March 1811 before finally being forced to retire to Salamanca. Wellington blockaded Almeida and Marshal Beresford was tasked with besieging Badajoz in the south, which had recently fallen to the French.

In March 1811 a second brigade had been added to the 6th Division, consisting of 2nd and 1/36th Regiments; commanded by Burne of 1/36th and was joined by the 1/32nd in the July.

The 2/53rd were present at the Battle of Fuentes d'Onoro on 3–5 May 1811, when Massena attempted to break the blockade of Almeida, but their casualty toll of three wounded clearly indicates little involvement in the combat. Despite Massena's failure, the French garrison of Almeida managed to escape during the night.

Beresford was forced to call in his besieging troops at Badajoz to face a relieving force commanded by Soult which led to a very bloody encounter at Albuera on 16 May 1811, with no clear winner. The Fusilier Brigade was severely tested and George's friend Myers died of his wounds the following day.

1812 was a year of dramatic events. Having been cantoned near Trancoso through the early winter, the 2/53rd was suddenly roused from their rest in early January to cover Wellington's surprise siege of the fortress of Ciudad Rodrigo. The capture of this fortress, closely followed by that of Badajoz, gave Wellington the upper hand. A stunning victory at the Battle of Salamanca led to the temporary liberation of Madrid and the abandonment of southern Spain by the French. However, the siege of the castle of Burgos was a debacle and the year ended with bitter disappointment as the army trudged back to Portugal in appalling conditions.

Letter 38   **Pena Verde, 13 January 1812**

My dear Madam,

Tomorrow we start for the frontiers again, and shall be once more engaged in the battle of war, for we heard yesterday that [Ciudad] Rodrigo has actually been invested, and that a brilliant success has crowned our first efforts, an out work on the north side having been carried by Colonel Colbourne and the 52nd, with little loss;[1] and

---

1. Colbourne led ten companies of the Light Brigade against the Redoubt Renaud which they succeeded to capture by *coup de main*.

the work was begun on the point thus carried on the night of the 8th. The weather is fine, but cold and it will be severe work in the trenches if that should come to our share. Our route, in the first instance is to Junca, near Almeida, and we are not hurried, we take four days march. I shot my poor black horse for the glanders, on the 7th, and two mules have shared the same fate. Fortunately I can walk, and of late have taken so much exercise of that description, that the marches will be only pleasure. I shall regret at this time of the year my excellent billet, and I was in hopes never to have seen Coa and Agueda again. My servant has not had the ague for some days; I shall be fortunate if he can stand this early campaign. I shall however have no one to look after but myself, Moysey and Bowles[1] being far too far on their way home to think of moving up again.

The old man of the house in which I am billeted, says he will pray to St Antonio, for my success. I wish the season had been a little further advanced, before we had taken the field; another month in winter quarters would have increased our numbers. I have very little to write about, and on the eve of a march have many things to arrange, you must therefore be content with this short letter and wishing you all prosperity and happiness I remain & c.

Letter 39   Junca, near Almeida, 18 January 1812

My last letter was written just as we were going to march, from Pena Verde. Thus far we have been fortunate in our weather which has been cold and frosty, indeed much more so than I have ever known it in this country. The ice has been so hard as to bear even cars on it. The first day's march (the 14th) was to Freches, and at that place we heard the intelligence of the successful commencement of the siege, confirmed. On the 15th, we marched to a small village called Bouca Cova, near the town of Alverca [da Beira], into which I walked after the men were billeted, and saw the 14th and 16th [Light] Dragoons there. The day following was miserably cold, it was a thick fog that froze as it fell, and covered hats, hair &c., with ice. Our route was to Vascoveiro. On our arrival we found the village was not large enough to hold the 11th and 53rd, so we returned to Aldea de Lorenzo, from whence (to gain

1. To date I have been unable to trace these people; they are not in the Army List, nor in the Regimental Returns.

information, I walked into Pinhel, where I met General Slade. From him I learned the siege was going on very well, and hitherto with small loss on our part, and two fortified convents had been taken just under the walls.[1] That on the 14th, twenty-two 24 pounders had opened on the defences, and had soon silenced the fire of the town. That the breaching battery was expected to open on the 17th, after which it was not thought the town could hold out twenty-four hours. He also said Marmont[2] was rapidly assembling his army to advance to its relief, but was not expected to be able to bring up their force before the 22nd, or 23rd, of the month, which would be too late to save Rodrigo. On my return to my village, I found my accommodation not very good, but I had a letter from you, and the newspapers to a late date to read; and poor Mansel[3] by this same packet heard of the death of his mother, Lady Mansel. Yesterday (17th) we marched at the usual hour with the fog as thick as the day before, which however cleared away about eleven o'clock, and we crossed the Coa, at the bridge of Almeida and arrived here about two, after which I walked into Almeida with General Hulse.[4] They are getting on fast with the works of the place, and have guns mounted and platforms laid at all the embrasures. This morning we heard plainly, the firing at Rodrigo, and I walked to the hill above Sao Pedro [de Rio Seco], from whence I could see (although at a distance of upwards of three leagues) the firing of our batteries, with now and then a shell from the town. A person I met, coming from thence, represents the breach as large, and that there is little doubt the town will be in our possession before tomorrow night.

The scene was highly animating and picturesque; I stood on the

1. The convents of Santa Cruz and San Francisco had been converted into veritable redoubts by the French. It was necessary to capture these outposts as a preliminary to an assault as they flanked the approaches to the breaches in the walls of Ciudad Rodrigo.
2. Marshal August Frederic Louis Viesse de Marmont, Duc de Ragusa had become commander of the French Army of Portugal. He proved a formidable opponent for Wellington.
3. Major John Mansel had been serving with the first battalion 53rd in India 1807–10. Returning to Europe he joined the 2nd battalion in Spain, acting as second-in-command to George Bingham.
4. Major General Hulse commanded Campbell's ex Brigade now in the 6th Division, comprising 1/11th; 2/53rd; 1/61st and a company of 5/60th. He died on 7 September 1812.

plains of Fuentes d'Onoro, the distant mountains covered with snow, the smoke of the cannonade, with the bustle of the road in the foreground, covered with military stores, Spanish and Portuguese peasants, made it very interesting. We march tomorrow to Albergueria [de Arganan], four leagues; good road, and this movement looks as if the French are expected by Puerto de Banos, but they will find it difficult, if not impossible to traverse those mountains, that are several feet deep in snow, with an army, said to be badly clothed and ill-provided with provisions, and means of transport; and when he does come, it is doubtful if he will be in force sufficient to fight Lord Wellington, who has performed this business as far as it goes, in a masterly manner.

This bitter cold weather has brought on my servant's ague again; what a dreadful disorder it is. My house is so crazy, that I can scarcely keep my candle alight, I believe I shall soon be obliged to retire to my bear skin bed, to warm myself. I am shivering over about a warming-pan full of wood ashes that just serves to remind us what a good thing a comfortable fire would be just now. If we have to fight a general action, pray pity us in the fields at this time of the year, without tents or baggage. I trust in God for health, and spirits to carry me through this arduous trial, and I join my earnest prayer to yours that we may soon meet in peace and safety, to talk over all these things. It is so cold I can write no more. On Monday, if I can, I will finish this letter, when I hope I shall be able to announce the fall of Rodrigo, till then, adieu.

Letter 40   Albergueria, 20 January 1812

We marched yesterday at day break. A bitter cold day; after seven hours march, very good road, we arrived at this place. We saw Rodrigo great part of the way; the fire from our batteries was very heavy, at about half past seven o'clock in the evening it was heavier than ever, and then suddenly stopped; and this morning, we hear it was carried by assault at that time by the Light Division.[1] We are very anxious to hear particulars. We are completely (since General Campbell went away) in the background, and unless our new

---

1. There were actually two breaches assaulted at the same time; the main breach was attacked by the 3rd Division and the lesser breach was attacked by the Light Division; both were successful.

General of Division (Clinton[1]) has more head than our present commander General Burne[2] we are likely to be so. Nothing short of a general action can bring us forward, but I trust in God, who orders all these things for the best, who appoints those he chooses to command, and elevates them above their fellows in the proud distinction of their country's service. Forage is become more and more scarce, and I was obliged to pay two dollars for as much bran as would feed my animals last night, and this morn. There is neither corn, straw or grass, to be had, and if you do not buy at any rate what you can find, you are likely to lose your beasts, which is but bad economy. I am very anxious to see what is next to be done.

Whether we shall advance on Salamanca, or move towards Badajoz, we cannot be anywhere worse off than we are here, except we were in bivouac, which at this time of the year would not be pleasant. I have spun out this letter to a great length, I now hasten to conclude it, hoping I may be able to send it some time in the course of the day, that it may get to England with the despatches; so adieu.

Letter 41   **Albergueria, 27 January 1812**

My dear Madam,

I went on Saturday into Ciudad Rodrigo. Notwithstanding the starving state of my cattle, I thought it would have been a pity to have been within eighteen miles, without taking advantage of it. It was as cold a day as I was ever out in. On our arrival in the town we were much struck with the dead silence that reigned in it, there was neither officer or soldier or scarcely an inhabitant to be seen in the streets. Presently we heard at some distance a long drum, as of a military funeral in the direction of the breach. We ascended the walls and were struck by the funeral procession of poor General Craufurd (of whose death we had not heard, although it was known he was severely wounded) winding down into the ditch below. Lord Wellington followed as chief mourner and appeared

1. Lieutenant General Sir Henry Clinton took command of the 6th Division on 9 February 1812. George was obviously aware of this change in advance.
2. When Campbell left for his post in India in November 1811 Burne temporarily took command of the division and George Bingham command of the brigade until Clinton was appointed.

much affected; he was attended by Marshal Beresford, the Spanish General Castanos,[1] and almost every other general officer of the army. He was interred at the foot of the breach, at which he so gallantly fell. The whole was calculated to make a deep and lasting impression; there are many circumstances which make a common military funeral striking, but this was particularly so, and there were more tears shed on this occasion, than at funerals in general. Although Craufurd was not liked in his division, there was scarcely a dry eye amongst them, either officer or soldier; all seemed absorbed in grief for the man whose gallantry they had so lately witnessed, and whose danger they had on that very spot so lately shared.

After the funeral there was a sort of military leveé, that is to say, Lord Wellington stood at one of the gates in the sun, and we all paid our compliments to him. He was for the first time dressed in the new uniform, feathered hat and such.[2]

Ciudad Rodrigo, before the first siege in 1810 (by the French), must have been a beautiful place. The esplanade between the town and the suburb, was planted with trees, and embellished with seats and fountains. The convents were handsome, and are now nothing but a heap of ruins. The first siege had completely ruined the town, the destruction was not so much added to by us, as during the last siege. We threw no shells, except <u>that</u> the night after[3] the storm. The weather being very cold our people in making fires burnt two or three of the ruined houses, and the town was completely plundered, not very creditable to us, but perhaps in a night attack difficult to prevent. It is said, however that General Craufurd promised it to our men, to encourage them, but certainly this need not have been done. Sir Samuel Auchmuty carried Monte Video without it, and it must be surely most disgraceful to plunder our allies. The inhabitants had notice from the Spanish government

1. General Franciso Xavier Castanos, Duke of Bailen commanded the Spanish Armies of Galicia and Extremadura at this time.
2. Wellington had been a full General since 31 July 1811, so this comment cannot refer to his new General's uniform. The uniform regulations for every aspect of the British Army were revised in 1812, although it would normally be a very long time before those on service in Spain would see the new uniforms. Presumably Wellington was able to secure the revised uniform from his tailors more quickly.
3. The text has been checked and is correct, but presumably this is a mistake and should read 'the night <u>before</u> the storm'.

that they were to quit the town, and were never prevented by the French. A great number had done so; those that remained suffered I am afraid severely. When you once let soldiers loose it matters little to them, to whom the property they lay their hands on belongs. I passed the day with Dudley Lieutenant Colonel,[1] formerly with me in the 82nd, and who now commands a battalion of cacadores.

The report now is, that we shall fall back on our supplies, even as far as Coimbra or Abrantes, but all Lord Wellington's movements are so secret, that there is no guessing what we are likely to do. It appears to me probable, that the campaign of 1812 will be more active than any we have yet undertaken. I pray God may grant me health and spirits to go through with it, and that at the conclusion, I may return to you with credit. It will be (I believe) the last the 53rd, will be enabled to undertake; we have scarcely four hundred men now present with us. The 5th Division have repaired the works at Rodrigo, with great celerity, and have even added new works, which makes the place stronger than it was before. It will be garrisoned by Don Carlos d'Espagne,[2] and his corps, and with Almeida will cover the frontiers very well, for this summer, and allow us to act in other parts of the peninsula. This will be a treat to us, as we are all heartily tired of the everlasting Coa and Agueda, and forage is so scarce that if we remain here a fortnight our cattle will never leave it at all. I forgot to mention one thing I saw yesterday at Rodrigo, which struck me very much; a fountain completely frozen, the water which should have flowed from a sort of table, had been arrested by the frost, and hung in large icicles, as clear as glass, and when I saw it, was coloured by the rising sun; after this pray don't talk of the mildness of the climate. I wrote a long letter by the last packet, so pray excuse a short one now. Adieu.

Letter 42   **Granjal, 10 February 1812**

My dear Madam,

Here we are once again in winter quarters, behind the Coa; how long we are to rest, or what we are to do, no one of us ventures to

---

1. Sir Dudley St Leger Hill was appointed as a Lieutenant Colonel in the Portuguese service in 1812, he commanded the 8 Cacadores.
2. General Carlos José d' Espagne commanded a brigade in the army of Castanos. He was hurriedly moved into Ciudad Rodrigo to ensure a Spanish garrison.

conjecture. I write to you the day after I went into Rodrigo. Marmont had just on that day assembled his army at Salamanca. From thence he pushed forward a strong reconnaissance, but finding the place had fallen, and was rapidly repairing, (in fact it was safe from assault the 27th) he dispersed his army for the sake of subsistence, and sat himself down with the loss. The place was taken in twelve days and it had held out against the very superior strength of the French, under Massena upwards of two months, so that this enterprise will add much to the credit of Lord Wellington, at home.

The separation of Marmont's force enabled us to break up which we did on the 31st, marching by regiment, for better accommodation. The first day we went to the Quinta de Brenda, a miserable hamlet, with hardly a roof left to the wretched cottages that composed it. The weather was fine though cold, but at night the rain was so heavy, that all the fords over the Coa were rendered impassable, and to get to Safurdao, we were obliged to go round by the bridge of Moteiros. This was the 1st of January; on the 2nd, it did not rain, but blew tremendously, and the whole country was inundated. We passed through Freixedas, and got to Domingo Cha about 1 o'clock; this was but a few houses which did but just afford us cover, and appeared as if in finer weather it might have been pretty, amongst rocks and vineyards. The 3rd, was a dreadfully wet day, and put us in mind of our march to Sobral in 1809. Every brook was up to the soldiers' middle, and we had to ford one of these every mile. We arrived at 1 o'clock, at one of the most wretched miserable villages called Benevende, where we could scarcely muster fuel enough to dry ourselves. The following day (4th) brought us here, our present destination. It is not an unpleasant village, though I have got a sulky, inhospitable landlord, with a house full of fleas. And the country about is well wooded, picturesque and diversified. The head quarters of the brigade are at Sernancelhe, about two miles from this. Since our arrival the weather has been fair, and I have visited not only the villages in which the brigade are stationed, but several others, and have employed myself in constructing a map of the quarters of the division. There is a convent, containing about half a dozen miserable, wretched, dirty old nuns near Sernancelhe; it is called Monastero de Ribeira, and there is a country house called the Quinta de Rap, near it long since deserted and nearly in ruins.

Saturday I walked to see the officers of the 61st Regiment, who are about five miles from this. The village or rather town is called Nostra Senhora de Lapa (Our Lady of the Den). Under the high altar of the church there is a cave in the rock, on which it is built, and a skin of an animal of the alligator species is hung from the roof of the choir. The tradition runs, that this beast lived in the den under the altar, and used to devour the people in the neighbourhood, which was destroyed by the Virgin at the intercession of some monks, who resided near, and the church was built on the spot to commemorate this deliverance. The church is very neat, and the town itself has never had troops in it before, consequently is in good condition. These places are so buried in the hills, so far from any communication, and the roads are so bad that they have been until now quite overlooked in the operations of the war, and have escaped; to which their poverty has doubtless contributed. I am sorry to say, since we arrived here our men have not behaved in a manner to give me satisfaction. I have had nothing but complaints of plunder, and insubordination; some of these may be unfounded, the Portuguese peasantry being always ready to cry out before they are hurt; but a wet march always engenders irregularity and disorder. I shall write again soon, so adieu for the present.

Letter 43   Sernancelhe, 18 February 1812

My dear Madam,

We removed to this place on Sunday; the 11th Regiment having been sent to Coimbra, to get their clothing, but we are not likely to remain long in our new quarters, as reports of our march to the south for the investment of Badajoz, gain ground. It is not to be supposed Marshal Soult will allow that important point to be carried without making more effectual efforts to relieve it, than Marmont did for Rodrigo, and we shall have a second Battle of Albuera, which (as we shall be differently commanded) will be very different in the result;[1] but all these things time will show. Our new

1. The Battle of Albuera was fought on 16 May 1811. Marshal Soult advanced to relieve the fortress of Badajoz which was besieged by forces under Marshal Beresford. The battle was nearly lost by Beresford but he was saved by General Cole, who brought up his division without orders and repulsed the French.

General of Division, H. Clinton, has made his appearance here, and has already made his inspections. He saw us on Monday; he was very well satisfied, and was pleased to say he had never seen in any situation, either at home or abroad a battalion in higher order; he looks very sharply and narrowly into everything, and though strict is not violent, so in this is quite the reverse of General Campbell. I believe I am much indebted to Hulse for his previous report. This village stands high, and is a better and in a much pleasanter situation than Granjal, our last quarter. There is in it a dilapidated old house belonging to the Counts de Lapa; in prowling over it this morning I discovered in a corner, covered with dust, and amongst some old lumber, two beautiful mosaic tables, the ground of black marble with a wreath of flowers for the border, and a hoopoe in the centre of one, exceedingly well executed, and another bird on the second. They were offered to me by the man who had the charge of the Count's concerns, whilst he is in Brazil; and I should have much liked to have accepted his offer, and have sent them down the Douro to Oporto, from whence I could have got them to Poole. They would have looked very well at Deans Leage some day or other, but they were too heavy to carry on mules, if I could get them, and a wheeled carriage is out of the question. Since I began my letter, the route has arrived to march the day after tomorrow, a long notice for us. The days marches are short, and the route is as far as Nisa, so the siege of Badajoz, may be set down as certain. Till we arrive we cannot tell whether we shall be employed in the trenches, or the covering army. We are all delighted at the idea of an active and bustling campaign. Adieu.

Letter 44   Caria, 26 February 1812

My dear Madam,

Our destination we all believe is Badajoz, and we are proceeding by very easy stages to allow the stores to be there as soon as we are. Hitherto the weather has been delightful, and I have walked every step of the way. Our first day was to Trancoso, which has been a good town; is situated as most of the towns in Portugal are, very

---

Although classed as a British victory it was more of a stalemate with severe losses on both sides; it is obvious that the officers of the British Army did not see it as a victory either.

high. The old wall and battlements are very complete, but the buildings, (from having been in the hands of the French, and standing in the direct road from the point on the Douro where the stores for our army are landed and Almeida) much dilapidated; it suffers too not having any wood near it. When a soldier comes in from a wet march and hungry it is difficult to resist the temptation of taking part of an uninhabited house, to boil his kettle with. A nunnery takes up nearly half the town, seven nuns have returned to it out of thirty who quitted it when the French advanced, two years ago. If report says true, the rules of a monastic life are not very rigidly enforced, and the doors are open after dark, to such people as choose to pay, not I believe for peeping only.

We arrived on the 21st at Minhocal a small village east of Celorico. This has also been pulled to pieces in every possible manner. The room I slept in had only one shutter, the other had been made fuel of. On the 23rd, we marched to Porto [da Carne], our old quarter in the Val de Mondego. This village had not suffered at all not having been a thoroughfare. The inhabitants were quite delighted to see their old acquaintance. The two Quintas near the village, in one of which I had passed so many pleasant days with General Campbell had been burnt by the French in 1810. I dined at the Ponte de Faia with General Clinton, who had established his quarters there. The gardens were all out of order and the place so different from what it was during my long residence. Dona Marguerita and her daughter were not at home, but had retired to some more tranquil part of the country. The old house dog Rusco, was the only inhabitant that recognised me. On the 23rd, the whole division assembled at Guarda. General Clinton was at my old quarter, with the old canon who has not eat himself into an apoplexy; and it certainly is the best house in the town. On the 24th, the division separated again, and I was quartered at Vela with the 53rd, and occupied the house Marshal Ney lived at when he was in this part of the country. The garden was in good order, ornamented with fountains and quite delightful; the orange was in full fruit. More attention had been paid by former residents to the garden than to the house which was old, dirty, and inconvenient. It had the figure of a man in stone as a chimney, the smoke issuing from his mouth. Nobody but a Portuguese would have thought of such a device. The present occupant, a fine young man, lieutenant colonel of the Guarda militia, was exceedingly civil, and attentive, and I spent a very pleasant evening with him. From Vela this place is about twelve miles, and although it rained when we came in, I could not help walking to see the old mill I lived in when here last year. For the ten days we bivouacked near this place, no one had attempted to take up my quarters, for I found the cover of a newspaper with my direction on it, laying about. Today we halt, as we are closing on the divisions in our front, and tomorrow some regiments of the division will be at Alpedrinha, the pleasant quarter from which I wrote to you several times last summer. We are to reach Nisa, on the other side of the Tagus on the 3rd of March, and our route goes no farther, but we expect to break ground before Badajoz, in the course of that week. I hope we may be fortunate in our weather in the trenches, although we cannot expect it will prove a matter of so short a duration as the siege of Rodrigo, I think it probable the beginning of April will see it in our hands, although perhaps we may have to fight a general action for it. The two French armies, which it would be necessary to unite, in order to raise the siege, extend from Benevente to Seville, and we shall be too strong for either of them if they do not form a junction. Adieu.

Letter 45   Estremoz, 8 March 1812

My dear Madam,

We have not only arrived in a new world, but we have changed climate as well as everything else, since we left the north. Not only are the hedges in blossom, but the flowers are out, the rye is in ear, in this part of the country, but the birds are singing and we enjoy as much the appearance of spring as you will do two months hence in England, a month perhaps after this reaches you. I am settled (I am afraid for a short time only) in the cleanest house I was ever in since I have been in Portugal; it would be reckoned so even at home, and in Ireland it would be visited as a sight. Every article of vegetables and fruit are in abundance here; our stay to partake of these luxuries will however be short, not later I think than Wednesday or Thursday next, and then with the experience we have obtained at Rodrigo, we shall see if we can make a better hand of Badajoz than we did last year. Every preparation has been made on a giant scale, and considerable magazines are and have been forming, as if the capture of Badajoz was not to be the final end of our operations in the South. The divisions (except the 5th, which is at least for the

103

present left in the north[1]) are all closed up and three days after we are put in motion, Badajoz will be invested.

Soult is at Llerena, having lately taken all his foreign troops out of Badajoz, and having introduced French in their stead. I am not certain whether we shall not be able to fight the whole force the French can bring against us, even if they can collect from the various quarters time enough to raise the siege, and it is certain their resources will not enable them to keep so large a force for any length of time assembled, so you see all things look like an active campaign. I will not enter into the details of our march, as we have been over the ground so often before. It is enough to say that after I wrote to you from Caria, on the 26th of last month, we marched on the 27th to Lardosa, on the 29th to Castelo Branco, on the 1st of March to Sarnadas (making two days to the Tagus which formerly was one), on the 2nd to Nisa, on the 3rd at Crato, 4th Alter do Chao, 5th at Fronteira, a very good town, and 6th to this place. We were very fortunate in our weather, not one wet day out of sixteen. Our new General (Clinton) is the most particular man I ever met with. He troubles both himself and us (I think) to very little purpose; the files are counted every day on the march, and he expects distances to be kept exactly as on a field day. You must observe that this part of my letter is intended for my father, who understands these things. On the whole Clinton has been very civil to me, and tells me that considering the comparative state (not intended for a great compliment) in which he finds the 53rd Regiment, that he shall report us to Lord Wellington, and ask him to give us more men, a request it would puzzle his lordship to accede to. I have just sent in to him a sort of remonstrance, against British officers in the Portuguese service being put over our heads. The order at present stands, that British and Portuguese officer shall command according to their respective ranks and dates of their commissions in the service to which they may belong. A British officer on entering the Portuguese service immediately gets a step of rank in that service superior to that he holds in his own. Thus a lieutenant colonel of one day's standing becomes a colonel in this army. Whilst the number was not very

1. The 5th Division remained for a while in the north, presumably until Wellington was sure that Ciudad Rodrigo was fully secured and supplied. Northern Portugal was then left with only Portuguese militia to defend it from incursions by Marmont.

great I said nothing about it, but by a late promotion those officers who were captains three years ago, when I landed in this country, having been first made Majors on entering the Portuguese service, have been made lieutenant colonels in our service, and are consequently colonels in the Portuguese service, and serve as such with us, under whose command I am likely to be, and am liable by the existing regulations to serve. One of these colonels was a captain in my own battalion, when we landed in the Tagus. In this memorial I have pointed out that the rank is worth but little, unless it entitles to command, and command less, except on actual service; that if my juniors thus step over my head in this army, it will be no satisfaction to me, that I should be again entitled to my command when the army returned to England; that it is more than probable that ere I can get the next step by the usual routine of promotion, most of these officers who came into the service after I was a field officer in it, will have passed over my head. I have not however at this moment pressed this memorial being laid before the commander of the forces as it might cause him embarrassment, but I have given it to Hulse (who is clearly of my opinion) to show Clinton and hear what he says to it. I do not at all consider myself so dependent on the service as to suffer without complaining. On one point I am decided; I never will serve under Harvey[1] the officer of the 53rd I alluded to above, who is now a lieutenant colonel in the Portuguese service, and will, unless our case is taken into consideration, be a colonel in that service long before I become one in ours. Granting us temporary and local rank, whilst the army is in this country would obviate, I should think, without inconvenience, the evil complained of.

Another of my mules was yesterday, shot for the glanders. I do not expect to save one of my original stock; two only are now left. Adieu.

Letter 46   Estremoz, 13 March 1812

My dear Madam,

We are on the wing again tomorrow, so I write now, as I know not when I may have an opportunity. I have replaced the loss I have

1. Captain Robert John Harvey, 53 Foot was transferred to the Portuguese army as a major on 25 June 1811. He did gain, as Bingham feared, a brevet lieutenant colonelcy in 1813.

sustained by the glanders, by a new horse of the country, and a good mule; they arrived from Lisbon yesterday, so that I am now perfectly ready to take the field, and I do not care how soon we do so, for our new General Clinton, allows us no rest, and keeps teasing us with squad drills, and first principles, and harasses both officers and soldiers, who think these short intervals of repose were intended as holidays from all such nonsense. In the course of this week a mail has arrived from England in the short space of seven days, the quickest passage we have ever known; by it the intelligence has arrived of our commander being created an earl. I suppose if he takes Badajoz they will make him a Marquess. I have described this place to you during my winter march of 1809, so that I have nothing now to add on the subject. It is all life and animation now, but it must be a good town at all times, and stands in a fertile country, producing corn, wine and oil, and all the comforts and conveniences of life.

The marble church in the great square has made no progress and indeed these are not times in which either churches or convents are likely to flourish.

Our route is to Elvas, which has been head quarters since the 9th, and we are as yet ignorant whether we shall be employed in the besieging or covering army. I will write again whenever it is ascertained, as I know it will be a subject of anxiety to you. Adieu.

Letter 47   **Elvas, 15 [March 1812]**

I open my letter to tell you that our lot is decided, and that we start tomorrow, with the covering army, under the command of Sir Thomas Graham.[1] The army is disposed of as follows, the 4th and Light Divisions open the siege, and are to be joined by the 5th, who are now on their march from the north; the 1st, 6th, and 7th Divisions as I said before, under command of Graham, are to observe Soult's motions to the south, whilst Hill with the 2nd and Hamilton's Portuguese divisions are at Merida to look after any force Marmont may detach to join the Duke of Dalmatia [Soult].

---

1. Lieutenant General Sir Thomas Graham, the victor of the Battle of Barrosa in 1811, was now serving as second-in-command to Wellington. He was soon forced to return home for treatment to an eye problem. He eventually became Lord Lynedoch.

The preparations for the siege are on the most extended scale, and tomorrow we all pass the Guadiana, on a bridge of boats to be laid down tonight, four miles below the town. We marched yesterday at 10 o'clock, to Borba, an excellent town, and much celebrated in this part of the country for good wines. There are in and about the place many Quintas, with gardens and fountains. Our billets were superb. I was in a house with a room of large dimensions and hung with curious old gilt stamped leather, and a bed so fine I scarcely knew how to lie in it. Today we are in bivouac. The three divisions that form the covering army in contiguous columns of battalions, in the olive groves near the town. The divisions that form the besieging army are in the town. Just above our encampment rises the fort La Lippe, a model of modern fortification, and so high that nothing can touch it, but shells. Below us we have the vast plain to the Guadiana, at this season greener and more fertile than we had ever seen it look. We can see Badajoz, Olivenza and many other towns and villages lying as it were in a map, under our feet. We are all joy and expectation, and we only want another commander for our division to make us the happiest fellows in the world. So once more, adieu.

Letter 48   **Almendralejo, 23 March 1812**

My dear Madam,

Our adventures since we left Elvas have been as follows. On the 16th, at daylight the whole five divisions moved in one column across the plain, towards the Guadiana; the cavalry formed the advance guard, the divisions destined for the siege led, and after we had crossed the river which we did about noon by the bridge of boats laid down in the night, they turned to the left, whilst the covering army moved to the eastward, and just before 5 in the afternoon we arrived at our bivouac near Valverde [de Leganes]. The march was long and the last part of it tedious; we calculated the distance at eighteen miles, for some time was taken in passing the bridge, it not being thought advisable that too many men should be on it at the same time. This is the first regular pontoon bridge we have put down. The boats on pontoons are of tin, very light and portable, and carried on wheels. When launched into the water they are moored head and stern by anchors. Sleepers and platforms are then laid over them. They are in charge and managed by some of the Portuguese Marine Corps.[1] It does seem extraordinary, that we have no establishment of the kind in our service, for it becomes impossible to carry on the most common military operations without them. The day was dark and gloomy, with frequent hailstorms, giving intimation that the bad weather was about to set in. On the 17th, we marched at 7, passed over the ground on which the Battle of Albuera was fought last year; and about 4 in the afternoon arrived at the ground we were to occupy near Santa Marta. A small corps of the enemy quitted the village about two hours before we had completed our march. We computed the distance twenty-two miles over an open and un-interesting country, nearly flat; for the position at Albuera (if position it could be called) is on gently undulating and hardly to be called hilly ground, the only features are the mountains of the Sierra Morena that at some distance bound the prospect to the south, but even these are not very striking. The bad weather we had antici-pated came down upon us, in pitiless fury soon after midnight. In ten minutes not a tent of any kind was standing and the roaring of the thunder echoing the cannonade at Badajoz, which we plainly heard made the night quite terrific. At eight on the morning of the 18th, we crawled off our ground like drowned rats, and at noon got under cover in a town called La Morera; what a comfort!! And such a contrast!! For though it was little more than shelter that was then afforded us (as we were much crowded) yet the houses were much cleaner, and more comfortable than those we have been accustomed to in the north of Portugal. From the lower and middling class of people we experienced hospitality and kindness, not so extended or so open-hearted and cordial, as from the Portuguese when we first arrived in their country. They seem to feel they are conferring an obligation on you, in permitting you to drive the French out of their country for them.

We heard the whole day the firing at Badajoz, which was very heavy. A number of reports were in circulation, and 'twas said a

1. Bingham would appear to be mistaken. Referring to Jones' *Sieges in Spain*, it would appear that Wellington had ordered a pontoon train formed and one arrived at Lisbon from Britain in June 1811. The pontoon train was commanded by engineer officers and manned with a small number of Royal Military Artificers, sixty infantry and twelve Portuguese seamen. It is presumably the latter that main-tained the bridge once laid and which Bingham saw. I must thank Rod MacArthur for this information.

corps of Drouet's[1] was likely to be cut off. We marched at five after having been an hour under arms in the dark. At noon we arrived at Zafra, an excellent town which afforded ample room for the whole of us. After we came in it began to rain, which cleared the streets of the population that had turned out to look at the strangers. The French had left the place the day before. Our slight knowledge of the Portuguese language is of little use in this country, and we must learn Spanish to enable us to get on with the inhabitants; but supplies and forage are plenty, and the houses are so good and so clean, that we begin to think the 2nd Division, who have been so long on this side of the Guadiana, must have had much the best of it. The morning of the 20th was wet, and we did not move till ten o'clock, and then only went six miles to another good town, Fuente del Maestre, where we were as well accommodated as at Zafra. I went to a ball in the evening given at Colonel Bradford's[2] quarters. Many well looking dark girls, tolerably free in their manners, and as well acquainted with us as if we had been as many months, as we had been hours in the place. They danced both English and Spanish country dances, and gave us several boleros. The 21st we came on to this place, only ten miles distant; it is a larger town than either of the two last we have been in; but having been constantly occupied by the troops of either nation, is more dilapidated. It stands in naked majesty without a tree, or even shrub near it, on an immense plain without sufficient undulation of ground to hide either man or horse, on quitting or coming towards it, and you lose sight of them as of a ship at sea in the distance. There is a large church, and high tower of flaming red brick, which does not add to the beauty of its appearance. The wet weather continues, and we hug ourselves on being under cover and not in the trenches. Wet weather damps military ardour exceedingly. I have a room sufficiently large to walk and take exercise in, with a fine glass chandelier hanging in the centre of it, rather a contrast to our lodging on the heath near Santa Marta. The Spaniards of this town just seem to tolerate us in hopes that

1. At this time General de Division Jean-Baptiste Drouet, Comte d'Erlon, commanded the 5th Division in Soult's Army of the South.
2. Colonel Sir Thomas Bradford of the 82 Regiment was Assistant Adjutant General at this time. In June 1813 he was made a major general in the Portuguese Army where he commanded a brigade.

the capture of Badajoz, may remove the seat of war farther from their dwellings. Amongst the men a feeling of jealousy exists towards the French, and the ladies at Fuente de Maestre publicly said, 'we like you better than our own people, but we must confess we like the French better than you'; a proof of extended liberality of sentiment was exhibited yesterday, when they gave up one of their churches to us to celebrate divine service in. A good many of the people of the town, and many of the clergy from motives of curiosity attended, and were pleased with the silent attention of the soldiers; they have been taught to believe that heretics have no religion, deny both God and Christ, and appear astonished when any of us seem to understand scripture history, when they are showing us paintings in their churches.

We hear an outwork at Badajoz was carried yesterday, in great style[1]; a happy omen of the auspicious termination of the siege. The weather has been sadly against it, the ground will not work. I long to go over to see the progress, but we are so liable to be called on that I dare not venture beyond the sound of the bugle. Adieu, I shall write again soon.

Letter 49   Almendralejo, 4 April 1812

My dear Madam,

The day after I last wrote Soult's movements spoilt General Clinton's squad drills (which no one person in the division was sorry to find interrupted) and we were put in motion again towards the Sierra Morena, in the direction of the great road that leads from Badajoz to Seville. We marched (without any previous notice) on the morning of the 25th, at seven o'clock, and reached our ground near Usagre, at half past five. Here we joined the other two divisions composing the covering army, and nearly the whole of our cavalry. We had no time to see anything of the town, for we got under arms again at eleven o'clock at night, for the purpose of surprising a corps of the enemy at Llerena; it was a bright moonlight night, and as the road was good it was pleasanter marching than in the day time. We arrived at our destination just before the day began to dawn, and had we pushed on, we might have caught the French before they

1. This refers to the capture of what is commonly called Fort Picurina (actually a detached bastion) on the night of 25 March 1812.

could have cleared the town. Unfortunately we halted, and our commander General Graham went forward with a cloud of staff, to reconnoitre, and an escort of dragoons. On approaching Llerena, they were fired on by a French picquet stationed on the road, and came galloping back on the column. The 7th Division was in front; an alarm was given, that the enemy's cavalry were coming down. The leading regiment opened a fire on our own people; it was fortunate that no greater mischief was done; an assistant surgeon who had no business there was wounded, some horses were killed, and grooms and led horses were dispersed in every direction. The fire alarmed the enemy, and quickened their movements, they were apprised that we were in their neighbourhood, and we were deprived of the fruit of our exertions. As the day began to open and objects somewhat distinguishable, a stone wall was taken for the enemy's line, and a fire opened on it. This mistake was rectified as it became more light, but not till after some surprise had been excited amongst the knowing ones, at the uncommon steadiness of the line opposed to us. The troops in general were too much fatigued for any further exertion and the cavalry and light infantry having followed the enemy, we were put into the town, which was an excellent one. The inhabitants were not occupied by the movements of the hostile armies, or of the change from the troops of one nation, who had left their dwellings in the morning, to be replaced by the troops of another nation, who were all settled in their quarters before noon, but by the splendid processions and rites of passion week; it was Holy Thursday, and the circumstances that attended our Lord in the garden, previous to his apprehension were represented by figures either in wax or wood, in all the principal churches, and nearly the whole of the population in deep mourning were prostrate before the altars, bewailing their sins, and totally heedless of the events passing around them. The lights were nearly all extinguished, the churches hung with black, no organ sounded, the priest whispered the prayers to himself, in an inaudible tone of voice, and not a sound was to be heard but the sobs of the devotees, and the footsteps of those soldiers, whom curiosity brought in to witness what was passing. I had a pleasant billet, and very civil people in it, and having seen whatever was worthy of notice in the town I retired to rest in a good chamber and an excellent clean bed. From this most comfortable situation I was roused before ten o'clock by the brigade major, who came to acquaint me that it was

111

my turn of duty, and that the 6th Division was to furnish the picquets, for the security of the town. I reluctantly (as you may suppose) arose, and having posted my picquets and made myself in some measure acquainted with the ground, I dozed away the remainder of the night by the side of the dusty road. On the 27th, we quitted Llerena (I should have been glad to have seen the Good Friday there) and the 6th Division with one brigade of the 7th marched to Lyra, a wretched place, and quite a contrast to the town we had quitted in the morning. On the 28th, we marched again and having separated from the brigade of the 7th Division, we took the route to Berlanga; the officers who went forward with the Quarter Master General, to take up quarters, heard fortunately just before they entered the town, that the enemy were in it. The cavalry who were in front skirmished with the enemy, who were not in force, and gave us up the town, retiring on Azuaga one league and a half distant, we bivouacked near Berlanga, and at four on the morning of the 29th, followed the enemy to Azuaga. They left that place on our approach, and began to ascend the Sierra, which comes near the town, leaving a rear guard to skirmish with our light infantry. We occupied the town or rather village, and remained quiet the whole of that and the following day. At sunset on the 30th, the infantry with the exception of the 53rd Regiment fell back on Berlanga; we took the picquets and remained till daylight the following morning, when we left Azuaga, and joined the division on our old ground near Berlanga. We found General Clinton had been giving the officers of the division a lecture on out-post duty which he declared they knew nothing about, and he placed the picquets himself. When I joined soon after daylight in the morning from the front I marched the regiment into the lines without having passed a single picquet or even sentinel; so much for our new general, who is by much the most tiresome person I ever served under. The weather for these last three days has been cold and wet, and we longed for another day's halt, but we were not so fortunate. On the first of April we joined the other two divisions at Usagre; on the second we came to Ribera [del Fresno], and yesterday we returned to this place. There is a report in circulation that Badajoz was carried by assault last night, and as we hear no firing we are inclined to credit it. I have written this letter that it may go with the despatches. Adieu, I can form no conjecture as to where and from whence I shall be able to write again, but I shall lose no opportunity. Adieu.

My dear Madam,

I was rather premature in announcing to you in my last of the fourth of this month, the fall of Badajoz. That place was not taken till the sixth; our loss in the capture has been very great, and has fallen principally on the officers. To avoid a general action with Soult, which would have disturbed the operations of the siege, and probably have been as severe on the army as the storming the place turned out to be, Lord Wellington determined to carry it by a coup de main, before the descent to the ditch was facilitated by blowing in the counterscarp. The breaches were never forced and so various were the methods they resorted to, to render the access difficult, if not impracticable. I hope to be able to go over there, and then I shall be able to form a better judgement; but if the present report is confirmed that we are to follow Soult to Seville, I shall not have an opportunity. It is said Ballesteros[1] is in that city, but the Spaniards propagate so many reports, as if willing to deceive their friends, as well as their enemies, that there is no knowing what to believe.

To return however to our own movements; we remained two whole days at Almendralejo, and General Clinton had begun to make us all sick by talking of squad drills, when on Sunday the fifth, a sudden order arrived for us to march. On leaving the town the brigades separated, and we went to Solana [de los Barros], a small village in the direction of Badajoz. When we arrived there we heard again the cannonade, proving to us how unfounded the reports of the capture of the place were. We marched late and the day was very hot; we must now soon expect to suffer from the heat of this ardent climate. We did not march, the sixth, till noon. The firing at Badajoz was incessant, and on the march we frequently saw the columns of smoke ascending from the batteries. At six in the afternoon we joined the remainder of our own division, and the 1st and the 7th, in the wood in front of the position of La Albuera. The firing which

1. General Francisco Ballesteros had advanced his army to within twenty miles of Seville, and then inexplicably turned away; in the October of this year he would launch a coup against the Central Junta, which failed. He was incarcerated in North Africa.

had been more than usually heavy all the afternoon, became tremendous as the night set in, and ceased entirely about midnight, which assured us that the place was ours, as had the assault failed the firing would have continued, and our anxiety became quite painful to hear the details; to know who had fallen, who had escaped, which of our friends had met a glorious death, which had survived the terrors of this dreadful evening. Before the day broke, messengers with orders had arrived with very indistinct accounts, and we continued to pick up, little by little, throughout the following day accounts (frequently contradictory) of what had taken place. Our bivouac would not have been unpleasant, had it not been occupied by troops so often before. On the eighth, our attention, which had been riveted on what had happened or was passing in the town, was called to our front. Soult's advance was said to be at Santa Marta, the cavalry in front were reinforced, the light infantry were sent out in advance; and the 5th Division came near to us in the night. From them we obtained fresh details of the loss we had sustained, and of the disgraceful scenes that were continued to be perpetrated at Badajoz, and which could not be justified, even if the town had been an enemy's town, and the inhabitants had entered warmly into the defence of it; but the population were our allies, and the only mercy shown was to the garrison, who had defended the town and who were doomed by the laws of war to destruction, for the loss their obstinate defence had caused us. I do not deprecate the clemency shown them; it would have been glorious if the unoffending inhabitants had not suffered in their stead. Much as the glory has been to those who achieved the conquest, that glory has been tarnished by their subsequent conduct, and I do not envy them the credit they have obtained; as I conceive they have fixed a stigma on our arms, which time will never efface, and when history records their bravery to posterity, it will be sullied by the tales of murder, plunder and rapine, which followed it. It was considered that Soult would not persevere in his advance, as soon as he should have ascertained the fall of the town, and so it turned out. On the ninth our corps broke up, and we marched with our division to this place, where we are now halting in anxious expectation of what may be our next destination. An officer who has arrived from the town this afternoon, rates our loss in the storm (only) at 4,700 killed and wounded; we think he

114

must exaggerate.[1] He also brings an account that Marmont is at Castelo Branco. As soon as we know what is to become of us, you shall hear again. Adieu.

Letter 51   Portalegre, 18 April 1812

My dear Madam,

We have had nothing but marching lately, and that in very wet, bad weather. I went round by Badajoz with General Hulse to see the wonderful defences of the French, which no other troops in the world but our own could have surmounted. Our loss you will see by the Gazette was large and fell particularly on commanding officers of brigades and regiments, almost all of whom were wounded. Several people have received two, three, and even more musket wounds, and brigades came out of action under the command of captains and the 4th Division under that of a lieutenant colonel.

I understand all second battalions in this country are ordered home; the loss the army has sustained in point of numbers at Badajoz will prevent this order being immediately complied with. General Clinton has so completely sickened me of this service that I ardently wish it may be so. He has no consideration for the soldier or indeed for any one else; he does everything by the book, the end of which will be, he will have his <u>division</u> in the book; it will be the hospital book. No one can please him and indeed I have given up all attempts to do so; we are besides always destined to be in the background, having nothing but severe marching, and none of the credit. There is no chance to me of promotion, I see (either by means of the Portuguese service, or by being aide de camp to the King) men whom I cannot bring myself to think have greater pretensions than myself, put over my head. Perhaps a short visit to England, and change of scene might restore me, but at present I own I am horribly out of humour with the service.

1. The losses were slightly exaggerated, but unfortunately were still grievous. Oman Volume 5 pages 594–5 states the losses actually sustained in the storming of Badajoz as sixty-two officers and 744 men killed; 251 officers and 2,604 men wounded and fifty-two men missing; totalling 3,713 casualties. Including losses previously incurred in the siege operations the total killed and wounded stands at 4,670.

I cannot tell you what has happened on the northern frontier of Portugal whilst we have been here in the south. I am willing to hope Rodrigo and Almeida are out of danger. I believe Marmont's movements in that quarter[1] has disconcerted Lord Wellington's plan, which was to have advanced (as it is currently reported in the army) on Soult after the fall of Badajoz, and obliged him to raise the siege of Cadiz. Our cavalry gained some advantage over his rear guard, and had a smart affair near Llerena, but if we cannot proceed during the next three months with offensive operations my hopes will be considerably damped; time will show. We hope to stay here a day or two at least to recruit. I am tired of marching an hour before day break every day, it is quite a holiday to lay in bed till six o'clock. The weather has been very wet, heavy thunder showers; and the roads from the constant march of troops, a good deal cut up. In general we have been under cover, but were out in one very wet and stormy night, en bivouac. Our quarters have been crowded; we had twenty nine battalions in this place last night, and the night before seventeen in the small town of Arronches. I hope I may not be too late for the packet this week. Adieu.

Letter 52   Escalos de Baixo, 27 April 1812

My dear Madam,

I wrote to you last from Portalegre on the 18th, since which we have been constantly marching, and over the same ground we have traversed so often before. Marmont not being provided with a battering train to enable him to undertake the siege of either Rodrigo, or Almeida, and not liking to attempt them by assault, pushed on to Castelo Branco. General Victor Alten[2] who was there with a brigade of hussars of the [King's] German Legion retired across the Tagus at Vila Velha, and took up the bridge. This move-

1. Marmont, in the absence of Wellington, (lacking a siege train to challenge Ciudad Rodrigo or Almeida), had driven his army into northern Portugal, moving in the direction of Sabugal. From here, Clausel's Division raided Castelo Branco, whilst Marmont's main force turned to face Colonel Nicholas Trant's and Colonel Robert Wilson's militia forces at Guarda. These forces were easily defeated by Marmont, but news that Wellington had captured Badajoz and was already moving north in pursuit, caused him to hastily retire into Spain.
2. Major General Baron Victor Alten led a brigade of cavalry consisting of the 11 Light Dragoons and 1 Hussars KGL.

ment we understand did not exactly meet [with] the approbation of Lord Wellington, who thought he need not have resorted to that measure till he saw whether the French had followed him. The Portuguese General Le Cor, who was also in Castelo Branco with some newly raised infantry, fell back on the mountains on the direct road to Abrantes, however Marmont, having heard of the fate of Badajoz (the fall of which his movement had by no means retarded) began to retire towards the frontiers, first having plundered all the property he could lay his hands on in Portugal. We halted three days at Portalegre, and one day that chanced to dine with Colonel Cuyler of the 11th Regiment.[1] I was introduced in the afternoon to his landlord, a person of some consideration and his family, one of them a beautiful girl of seventeen was just about to enter a convent very much against her inclination. The father made no secret that it was so, he regretted the measure that he was about to adopt, he said he had no money to give with her as a marriage portion and that she was not likely to marry in her own rank in society without it. I did pity her sincerely. This is the first instance of the kind that has come to my knowledge since I have been in the country. Beauty is not so often to be met with in Portugal as to justify parents in offering such a sacrifice; all idea of the religious part of the ceremony seemed quite out of the question. The father appeared to think of her taking the veil merely as a worldly establishment, just as in England, we should consider sending a girl to a boarding school, for her education.[2]

I will not fatigue you with attempting to go over again the road we have so frequently passed before, but merely say that we left Portalegre, at half past four o'clock on the morning of the 20th, and came that day to Alpalhao, the 21st to Nisa, 22nd crossed the Tagus at Vila Velha, and were quartered (our regiment only) at a miserable village with not more than six or seven houses called Retaxo, a little out of the road, and which we had never heard of, [as] often as we had passed this road before. 23rd Castelo Branco which we found sadly pulled to pieces by the French, and but a few

1. Lieutenant Colonel George Cuyler had joined 11 Regiment on 16 November 1809; he was soon to be severely wounded at Salamanca.
2. This comment regarding the education of ladies is enlightening. It is clear that in Georgian times it was quite normal for ladies of the higher classes to receive formal education and many of them at boarding schools.

of the inhabitants remaining. 24th Escalos de Baixo, 25th Aldeia de Santa Margarida. Here we were ordered to retrace our steps so returned yesterday to this place, and here we are to return again to the southward; anything for new ground, some little diversity of object!! For the idea of another summer between the Coa and Agueda, would be too much. The weather during these marches has not been favourable; heavy thunder showers; but the experience of two former seasons enable us to decide that the spring is the wettest time of the year. Much anxiety has been shown on this march, that the troops should be put under cover every night, whenever it has been possible. The army is healthy, but many of the regiments, the 53rd amongst the number, much reduced in their effective strength. Adieu.

Letter 53   Castelo de Vide, 3 May 1812

My dear Sophy,[1]

Your two letters would not have remained so long unanswered had it not been for the continued state of motion we have been in for these last two months, a state very unfavourable to pursuits of this description. We have been as you may have heard from my mother from north to south, back again, and we are now once more on our return to the southward. We have been fortunate generally speaking in our weather, although we have had one or two wet bivouacs, which to people not educated as gipsies is no luxury; use reconciles us to many things and certainly we feel our hardships are less now than formerly. I will not however pretend to say we are by any means perfectly reconciled to them, but we take the world as it goes, and hope for better days. I trust these days are not far distant, as an order has been sent for the return of second battalions to England – this order on account of our loss at Badajoz cannot (or will not) at present be acted on, but will not be delayed after the service on which we are about to proceed is over. What that service is to be, we cannot say, but we think it will prove to be the forcing Soult to raise the siege of Cadiz, and evacuate Andalusia; if we can accomplish this, you will say something to us. After an absence of three or may I say four years from my native

1. His sister Sophia was married to William Clavell Richards of Smedmore. She died without issue in 1841.

118

land, you may easily conceive the delight the bare prospect of returning to it gives rise to. I feel as a schoolboy does at the approach of the holidays, and I am almost tempted to make notches on a stick to cut off every day, till the time arrives. I own my anxiety to return has been increased by the mode which our new general of division has of carrying on the duty. He has learnt his trade from books, which teach nothing about human nature, but when we have to deal with men and not with machines, some knowledge of the former is rendered necessary. General Clinton has been very civil to me, and has paid me many compliments some of which perhaps I do not feel I deserve, but his mode of proceeding I cannot approve and therefore I shall be glad when the time comes to take my leave. We arrived here yesterday and look for ten days halt. It is a good town situated on a narrow steep ridge with a most extensive view (as its name denotes) of the plains of the Alemtejo and Spanish Extremadura. It has been fortified, but at present is dismantled; previous to the improved method in the art of attacking places, it might have been considered strong. It ought to be, and I believe it is a healthy place, from its elevated site and good water, and it is very pleasant from the number of quintas and gardens that surround it. The environs are well wooded, the trees chiefly chestnut and walnut, and from the walls you look over this beautiful foreground to a vast extent of plain, lying like a map below you, and terminated by mountains nearly the whole year tipped with snow; the spires of the town of Nisa, and Alpalhao and others, rising like the masts of shipping from the plain, add much to the beauty and variety of the scene. You can trace the Tagus by the dark lines of rocky hills on each side of it, and which from this height; do not appear more than the ordinary banks of the river. But high as this town stands, and extensive as the prospect is that it commands, there is another about two leagues from it considerably higher. It hangs in the clouds and is perched on an isolated rock that looks only fit for eagles to build on; it is called Marvao and I mean to take an early opportunity of visiting it, if we should remain here long enough. I shall soon be a better guide in Portugal than in my own country; ere long we shall have traversed it in every direction. Although the march of troops is slow, we pass over a great deal of ground. We have marched already in this year, 1812, about seven hundred and fifty miles, but this has been certainly the most active campaign we have had, and likely to continue so. But

119

my dear sister, I mean before this eventful year draws to a close, to tell you many a story of long marches, hair breadth escapes &c., when if I don't make your hair stand on end, it won't be my fault. Till then, however, adieu.

Letter 54   Alegrete, 17 May 1812

My dear Madam,

We left our quarters at Castelo de Vide, on the 9th and came to this place, which is neither so pleasant nor so healthy, and stands more in the plain. The air at Castelo de Vide, was so fine, the situation so commanding, and the town so good, the inhabitants so civil and so hospitable, that we regretted leaving it. We had a profusion of the finest cherries which are only to be met with amongst the mountains; I was able before I left it, to visit Marvao which must be like what the hill forts in India are described to be, situated on an isolated rock very high above the valley from which it rises. There are mountains which surround it on three sides, higher than itself, but not sufficiently near to incommode in a military point of view. The French, in Junot's campaign, came before it, and threw a few shells into it, but it is quite inattackable [sic], if a garrison are determined to defend it. It is a small, poor, place and is at present garrisoned by the militia of the neighbouring district. On our arrival here, we found the place full of the small pox. In my billet there were four or five children ill with it, and indeed there is scarcely a house that had not some one dead or dying with it. Our men, who have been all vaccinated have stood it, without taking the infection,[1] but the poor little children who have been born since the arrival of the regiment in this country, and some Portuguese women who have attached themselves to our men, have all had it. The town had the appearance of having been a place of more note than it is at present, but it is so unhealthy in the autumn, that the population is now but small, and everything bears the mark of decay. It is walled but the walls have fallen in many places, and there is a gate at the north entrance of the town, covered with ivy that puts me in mind of the gate at Carisbrook castle; half of

1. It appears from this statement that the British army was routinely vaccinated on mass for smallpox when going abroad. I am not aware of this fact having been mentioned in any of the numerous Peninsular memoirs that I have read previously.

the keep has fallen, the remainder hangs in awful majesty above the town. I was in hopes to have had some rest, but I have to attend a general court martial, at Assumar, six miles from this, where the other brigade is quartered and the weather begins to be very hot. I suppose we shall not be here long. Various are the rumours as to our destination, but no certainty.

Letter 55   Montijo, Spain, 24 May 1812

My dear Madam,

We were not destined to remain long at Alegrete, to experience any bad effects of the climate, for on my return from my court martial, on Tuesday the 19th I found the brigade under arms, and I had just time to snatch something to eat and off we marched. At half past ten o'clock that night we got into our old quarter at Arronches, which we left again at five the following morning. We arrived at Campo Maior at half past eleven. The weather begins to be very hot over these plains, which will now soon be burnt up again. I had never been quartered at Campo Maior before, although I had visited it three years ago when we were encamped so long in the wood near Badajoz. It is not a bad town, and fortified in the modern manner, and made a sort of defence in 1810, obliging the French to bring up their heavy guns from Badajoz, and ensuring a capitulation to the militia that defended it. There is nothing worthy of remark either in or about it, except an oratory paved with human bones, and lined with human skulls, which is quite the Portuguese taste. This is the first I have seen, although I have heard of several. We marched again on the morn of the 20th at five o'clock, and passing through the wood in which we were encamped in 1809, bivouacked about four miles to the left, and beyond it at no great distance from the solitary chapel Nuestra Señora de Botoa that I must have mentioned before. Our bivouac was very pleasant, with a quantity of fine grass for our animals, and shade and water for ourselves. How much preferable at this time of the year, and in fine weather, than the filthy towns we often inhabit. We marched at four on the 22nd, and arrived here at eleven. Montijo is a good town, and the houses, from cleanliness so great a contrast to the Portuguese. It is not so large but held our division, with Puebla [de la Calzada], another town not a mile distant from the Guadiana, and nearly opposite Lobon; where we were for a short time in 1809. On our arrival we heard that General Hill had succeeded in his attempt on the Bridge of Almaraz;[1] having attacked and carried some redoubts in the face of open day, in a most gallant style. The French were in such haste that those who first passed the bridge did not deem themselves safe on the other side of the Tagus, but cut the moorings of the bridge, which floated back to the other side, leaving one hundred and fifty prisoners in our power, and enabling Sir Rowland to burn the boats that composed it. The 50th Regiment distinguished itself on this occasion, which altogether reflected great credit on Sir Rowland and the troops employed on the services. The 23rd (yesterday) and today we have halted expecting to retrace our steps, as we were moved to support the 2nd Division in this operation, which having succeeded we are no longer wanted. Although this is a good town, yet standing as it does on a dead flat it is excessively hot already, and has the reputation of being unhealthy in the autumn, and I make no doubt but that it is so. Conjecture is as yet busy as to what we are to do for the remainder of the summer, whether we are to resume the offensive or not. I ardently hope we may, Clinton will give us no rest if we are not in the field, and it is quite as well to be on the march, as at drill. If we are to go into a quarter of refreshment in Portugal, I hope it may be Castelo de Vide, which is the most agreeable quarter I know in this part of that country. Adieu.

Letter 56   Pedrogao [de Sao Pedro], 5 June 1812

My dear Madam,

An unexpected halt gives me an opportunity of sending you a short letter (for I have just heard a mail is about to be made up) to tell you that we are here on our way to the north of Portugal again, and it now begins to be generally believed that we are to enter Spain again at or near Ciudad Rodrigo, find out and attack Marmont. This gives us new life, as we shall see a new country and offensive operations are so much pleasanter than defensive; so much more

1. General Rowland Hill led a surprise attack on the French pontoon bridge at Almaraz on 18 May 1812. The bridge was protected by a small fort on each bank but the rapidity of the attack led to the forts being captured with relatively small loss. Without this bridge communications between Marmont and Soult were made much more difficult.

exhilarating. My last was from Montijo. In that I expressed a wish that Castelo de Vide might be assigned for a quarter; in this I was gratified, although but for two days. Our march route was as follows; the twenty fifth we were at La Roca [de la Sierra], a small village fourteen miles from Montijo. I was quartered at the house of the priest, who had a spotted fawn; he was rearing for General Hill. It is surprising the popularity Hill has obtained in this part of Spain; there is nothing the inhabitants would not do to serve him, and he is deservedly popular, for he is so even tempered, so just, so exactly what an English gentleman and an English general ought to be, that it is impossible not to like him; so that it is doubtful by whom he is most beloved, by the inhabitants of the country or by the troops he commands. We hear of no squad drills in the 2nd Division, and yet nothing can be better done than the enterprises with which they are trusted; the late affair at Almaraz, and the former surprise of the French at Arroyo [dos] Molinos[1] speak for that. I often think I should never entertain a wish to leave this army, if I belonged to any other division but the 6th. A long march of nineteen miles on the 26th brought us to Alburquerque, in the time of the moors a good town, and with most picturesque walls gates and towers, equal to Caernarvon or Conwy. The twenty-seventh we were at a small village San Vicente [da Alcantara] and the twenty-eighth, over bad roads in some measure compensated for by the extreme beauty of the scenery brought us back to our old quarter Castelo de Vide. We passed near Marvao of which I should have liked to have had a sketch, but all falling out on a march, is forbidden. Formerly, when not near the enemy, the officers used to catch a hare or two, with their greyhounds, on the flank of the column, but this is now all put a stop to. The thirty-first we marched again, and I shall do no more (as I am pressed for time) than just to name the days march, to enable you to follow us, running your finger over the map, as it is a route we have so often passed before. The thirty-first Monte Claro, bivouac; June the first bivouac near Vila Velha; the second Castelo Branco; third Lousa;

1. The Battle of Arroyo dos Molinos had occurred on 28 October 1811. Hill with 10,000 men had been detached to surprise General Girard's isolated division totalling around 4,000 men. The French force was cornered and destroyed, killing some 300, a further 1,300 becoming prisoners, the rest fleeing into the mountains. Girard was recalled to France in disgrace following this action.

fourth Pedrogao a wretched miserable place, and I have preferred encamping to occupying my wretched billet in the village. We have generally marched at two o'clock in the morning, which is certainly cooler, but then the men get but little rest at night, and if the entrances and lanes about the town or village are (as is the case most frequently) narrow, it makes it difficult to get away, and sometimes an hour or more is lost in waiting for daylight. Our halt today was unexpected; our route is to Sabugal on the Coa, where we shall now arrive on Sunday, and where we shall receive further orders. Adieu.

Letter 57   Camp near Ciudad Rodrigo, 12 June 1812

My dear Madam,

My last was from a wretched place called Pedrogao. The day following we continued our march as follows; 6th to a bivouac near Meimoa; 7th we crossed the Coa at Sabugal and bivouacked in the superb chestnut groves near it, one of these immense trees serving to shade two or three companies; the turf as smooth as velvet and a delicious stream of clear water running through it. Here we began to fall in with the other divisions of the army; the 1st [Division] crossed the Coa nearly at the same time we did, and Sabugal standing as it does with its ruined castle in a very picturesque situation, with the passage of troops, baggage and commissariat was a very striking and animated scene. The 8th we halted near Aldeia [da] Ponte and were ordered to hut regularly, which we did, very neatly; oak coppice furnishing the materials, so that when our leafy town was completed, it looked very well, although it wanted the natural beauties of the day before. Near our ground the 7th Division and a beautiful brigade of heavy German cavalry were reviewed by Lord Wellington; how all this bustle contributes to raise the spirits. I would not now (except as to the division) exchange situations with any man in the world, for though my battalion is weak perhaps in point of numbers, they are now all old soldiers and men that I can depend on in any part we may be called on to perform; besides I have Mansel as my Major, and with his zeal and activity, he is a host in himself. The 9th we halted; the 10th we moved to the eighbourhood of Puebla de Azaba, where we had the same facilities for hutting as the day before; the march short and the weather fine. We took the same advantage of them, for we constructed a line of huts, so regular and neat as to call down the admiration of all who passed them. The arms were all neatly placed in arm racks made of the straightest oak branches with the bark peeled off and no holiday militia camp in England, ever looked more trim. The country was covered with troops; every direction in which you put up your glass, you saw divisions, brigades of every arm all posting to the same destination. Three brigades of cavalry, as well equipped, in as high order, and with their horses in as good order, as any at home, passed close to our lines. This year we shall have an equality, if not superiority in cavalry, which we have never had before, and we hope soon to see them regain that confidence that they have lost from having been hitherto overmatched. Yesterday we came here to the banks of the Agueda, about three miles above Rodrigo. It is rocky, bad ground, and crowded with three divisions. We are to enter Spain, in three columns; the right in which we are, composed of the 1st, 6th and 7th Divisions, under Sir Thomas Graham; the centre column 4th, 5th and Light Divisions under Lord Wellington in person; the left column 3rd Division, three Portuguese divisions which not being formed into a division are denominated independent brigades,[1] and the greatest part of the cavalry under Picton; whilst the 2nd Division, Hamilton's Portuguese Division and some cavalry are left on the other side of the Tagus to watch Soult's movements in the south. We have also with us a small battering train, in case of a siege, but I believe they do not amount to more than four guns and some howitzers. We are to move tomorrow, and hope in four days to see the famous city of Salamanca. Nothing can exceed the spirits of the army; it has never been equalled since we landed. Lord Wellington's late successes have silenced all grumblers[2], and the utmost delight and glee is exhibited in all ranks at the idea of once more becoming the assailant. I shall continue to write as often as I have an opportunity, and hope soon to give you the earliest intelligence of our successes. Adieu.

1. Besides Hamilton's Division, there were only two Independent Portuguese Brigades under Pack and Bradford.
2. It is very easy to forget due to Wellington's later fame, that for many years he endured sharp criticism from the opposition in Parliament and indeed from many of his own officers; they were not slow to air their grievances in letters home, which then often filtered through to the press to his great irritation.

Letter 58   **Camp near Salamanca, 16 June 1812**

My dear Madam,

I have just an opportunity of writing, as a bag is to be made up for England at 1 o'clock, and although I have hardly more than time to say that I am well, I would not let it slip. We are now, (after three easy marches since we crossed the Agueda) about three miles from Salamanca. The enemy's cavalry retired from the ground we are now on, this morning, after a skirmish with our dragoons; very trifling as we heard nothing about it. The roads are delightful, and the country through which we passed quite a park. Fortunately the weather has not been very hot, but constant marching and moving as we do now, in large bodies which is tedious, knocks up our people. We are now below three hundred men, and I hear we are to be dismissed soon after this affair is over. Although the French have been busy in constructing works on this side the river I am afraid they do not mean to stand, but that we shall have another dance after them, some say to Madrid, others to Valladolid. Yesterday we completed 1,000 miles; we have marched since the 1st of January by a very moderate computation of mine. We have been constantly in bivouac, for these last six weeks; this used to be pleasant formerly, as the officers were not obliged to take up their exact place in line, but pitched their tents where shade and ground was most convenient; but General Clinton insists on regularity, and as we are frequently in two or three lines, this throws the commanding officer's tent close to the men of other regiments, and is not comfortable. I am afraid of being late, and therefore conclude. Adieu.

Letter 59   **Salamanca, 20 June 1812**

My dear Madam,

By the last mail I sent you a hurried letter, to let you know I was safe and in good health. It was dated the 16th, we marched as usual at daybreak the next morning, and about eight o'clock crossed the Tormes, just above the town without opposition. It is a clear, deep and rapid river, and runs close under the walls of this once beautiful city. The French (who had been left to defend some forts they had erected to cover the bridge) retired before the light infantry of our division, and left us the town to ourselves. It so happened that those parts of the river where the other divisions of the army were to have crossed, were not fordable, so the 6th [Division] was the first that crossed, and the only division that entered the town. To attempt to describe the enthusiasm of the people would be impossible. We were nearly drawn off our horses by the women, who threw up their caps, their cloaks in the air, laughed, cried, and were quite mad. The French had persuaded them that we were to plunder, so their fear being abated, their joy increased when they saw us marching peaceably in with drums beating, colours flying. The forts, which on a nearer inspection, proved much more respectable than was at first supposed, were immediately invested, and the city that afternoon, exhibited the curious spectacle of a plentifully supplied market, and all the shops open, thronged with a busy populace of the one side, and a siege, with some sharp service at the other. I think the university must have been, when in its splendour, nearly equal to Oxford, and those who wish to see the rich and highly elaborate gothic architecture in perfection, must come to Salamanca; where either from the durability of the stone, the dryness of the climate, or other causes, the buildings look as fresh, and the points are as sharp, and clear, as the first moment they were erected. The cathedral is the most perfect, it was a source of constant revenue to the French who had nothing to do when they wanted money, but threaten the cathedral, and it was raised for them immediately. Of the numerous colleges and convents, several are entirely destroyed; the walls only left standing. Some have been thrown down to the ground to extend the fire of the forts, others have been converted into hospitals, barracks, store and such, and some have been even destroyed for the firewood their roofs, doors and windows afforded. Yesterday our batteries opened at three hundred yards distance, and produced considerable effect, but, we are very short of ammunition; ours ceased about nine o'clock, two hours after they had opened, and have since been silent. A large convent (San Vincente) has been taken into the body of the work, and forms a sort of citadel to it, for were the work itself carried, from the loop-holes of this convent there would be such a fire kept up, I doubt whether we could remain in it; our fire yesterday brought down the gable end of one part of this building and laid it open in beautiful style, but the lower part was so covered by a sort of glacis, that but little good resulted from it; is it not provoking? The thousand men left in these nasty little works,[1] have arrested our progress for three days, and they are not yet in our possession!! Only one casualty has as yet taken place, amongst the officers of the 53rd, Lieutenant Devonish has had his thigh broken by a grape shot, and that so high up, that amputation is out of the question; if he recovers, which is doubtful, he will be lame for life. A captain of artillery was killed yesterday in the trenches[2] and I hear of another officer of the same corps, and one of the engineers being slightly wounded today. I had by this mail, a note from General Wm. Wynyard to say that we are ordered home, so that I may before Christmas (God willing) shake you by the hand at Melcombe; when that time comes, I shall rejoice, for I shall have had a good share of these campaigns; at least as far as marching goes. So for the present, Adieu.

Letter 60   Salamanca, 23 June 1812

My dear Tryon,

We have just returned from a position we took up in front of this place, where we have been looking at Marmont's army for two days, leaving half the division to take care of the forts, which for want of ammunition, we were at any rate unable to proceed against. I will attempt to give you a rapid sketch of the campaign, as far as it goes, although as the baggage is in the rear, I have no pocket book to refer to for dates, and proceed on recollection. I think it was the 13th we crossed the Agueda, in three columns, the right under the command of Graham, the centre of Lord Wellington, and the left of Picton. The 16th the advance fell in with the enemy and a trifling skirmish (which drove in their outposts) took place; and the next day we crossed the Tormes (a much more considerable river than I expected to find) and entered this town. The fords allotted to other divisions to pass (the river not being practicable) the 6th was the first to cross, and we drove, without any difficulty, the French out of the town, into the forts they had constructed to command the bridge. These forts were found on inspection, to be much more formidable than they had been repre-

1. The French had converted three convents into forts, St Vincente (the largest), Cayetano and La Merced; all buildings in their vicinity had been destroyed to enable supporting fire for each other.
2. Captain John P. Elige, Royal Artillery, was killed during the siege.

sented. They were solid works of masonry, that the French had been constructing for two years, with good ditches, palisaded with seasoned timber, taken from the roofs of the public buildings of the university; a covered way, the parapet of the principal fort raised and loop-holed, and a tolerable glacis, the houses destroyed for about four hundred yards to clear it. In these forts they have mounted twenty-four guns including some large howitzers, and a garrison of between seven and eight hundred men. In the centre of the principal work is the convent of San Vincente, which I suppose gave rise to the idea we entertained before we entered the town, that it was only a loop-holed convent, which merely required a hole to be beat in the wall, to make it surrender. Our means therefore were very inadequate to our undertaking, and we had neither fascine or gabion ready, nor are there any materials in the immediate neighbourhood for making them.

Little else was done on the 18th (the day after the investment) than keeping up a fire of musketry; two battalions of riflemen of the German Legion were employed on this service, and were very useful. Two batteries were traced out in the night, but were not sufficiently advanced at daylight, to get the guns into them. The enemy threw several shells, but without any great effect. Four field pieces were got up into the gallery of the convent of San Bernardo, and although not more than five hundred yards distant, had no effect on the walls, and the fire from the forts being so superior, and one of the guns being dismounted, the rest were withdrawn. The night of the 19th, a battery was completed within three hundred yards and animated. I saw it open at 5 o'clock a.m. and before 8 the whole of the gable of the convent was down, and the interior exposed, but on examination, it was considered impracticable, as a breach; as by the ditch the lower part was so covered that you could not get up by means of ladders or otherwise; and our ammunition being expended, the firing ceased. They got the exact range of our battery, and threw their shells with great precision. Between these and their musketry, the casualties during the day were considerable. On the night of the 20th, a sort of battery was scraped out of the ruins, to the left of the former, into which two eighteen pounders, and one howitzer were removed; at noon some ammunition arrived, and they opened and beat down another part of the convent, and buried as we understood their bread and spirit room in the ruins, and also several men who were firing from loop-holes at the time. I did not see this for I was

129

on the working party, opening a communication in rear of the battery. Whilst there I received a contusion on my right shoulder from a stone which their shells made fly about at a great rate; it fortunately struck the pad of my epaulet, or it would have broken the arm; it flattened two or three of the bullion, as if they had been under a hammer. Although it knocked me down, I was not obliged to quit my working party, till relieved at the regular hour. It was very painful, for some days, and I was obliged to wear my arm in a sling, but as you may perceive by my writing, I am now perfectly recovered. The construction of this new battery was so bad, and being within grape range, the artillery who served the guns suffered severely, and we have already lost more men of that corps than we did at the siege of Rodrigo. Well! This new battery having beat down another large piece of the convent wall, ceased as before for want of ammunition, and the engineers gave it as their opinion that the breach was not practicable. In the mean time Marshal Marmont having assembled an army sufficient as he thought to oblige Lord Wellington to retire, advanced in front of the position of San Cristobal, which our army occupied. There was some sharp skirmishing that evening, and drove in our outposts.

On the morning of the twenty first, our brigade and one Portuguese regiment from our division left town at three o'clock, and found the army in position, about three miles from Salamanca, and at daybreak observed the French in the vale below. I might have been mistaken as to their numbers, but they did not appear to have more than 25,000 men, and everybody allowed we had 45,000. We looked on all that day, and in different detachments we saw about 3,000 more join them.[1] Yesterday the twenty-second, passed nearly in the same manner, except that there was a pretty sharp skirmish on the right of both cavalry and infantry, who were attempting to get round that flank; this was about 9 o'clock in the morning. After dark they began their retreat towards Valladolid, and our brigade returned to the town. Now as Lord Wellington wants the bridge, we are to have the forts, coûte que coûte [2] to night. The batteries

1. It is true that on the morning of 21 June Wellington's 43,000 men faced Marmont with only 30,000, as his rearguard of a further 10,000 men was yet to arrive. The French numbers in the plain were clear to see and it is strange that Wellington did not launch a concerted attack unless he suspected that the rearguard would arrive very soon.
2. Coûte que coûte translates as 'whatever it takes' or 'at all costs'.

are to open at noon, better provided they say with ammunition. I shall keep this letter open to let you know the result of our assault, which is ordered at midnight. If Picton were here, I make no doubt the place would soon be ours, but our chief goes poking about on the church steeple, and I am sure will do anything else than head his division; time will show; if he fails, I will never trust a martinet again. Adieu, for the present, I am just going to see if our batteries are ready to open, and if their effect will be equal to our expectations.

At half past one the batteries opened, with only half the number of guns they have brought up, and they fire very slow; this looks like want of ammunition. The light companies are ordered to be kept off duty and I suppose will be employed in the storm.

27th. I have had no opportunity of either adding to or sending off this letter, our brigade has been so frequently taken from the siege and added to the covering army, and our baggage has been so frequently sent away, that I have been unable to do anything in the way of writing. Our storm was attempted the day I last added to this letter, and failed; partly from mismanagement, and partly I think from not employing a sufficient number of people. The light companies of the division alone were called on, and were to assault the two small detached works, called Cayetano and [La] Merced. The false attack on the large work (San Vincente) did not take place till the other attacks had failed. The ladders for the escalade, had not been examined since they arrived on cars from Rodrigo; they were made of green wood, not properly fastened, and they came to pieces in the men's hands as they were carrying them. General Bowes,[1] poor man, who was killed, and who had no business there in person, chose to neglect the advice of the engineer, and would take the troops straight across the glacis, when by a detour he might have got within fifty yards of the place, or less under cover. Our loss was serious, and Hamilton[2] of the light infantry 53rd Regiment and ten men of the company are hors de combat. The morning after we were again called on to join the army; Marmont had crossed the Tormes near Alba, and had turned our right. The whole day we

1. Major General Bernard Foord Bowes had been severely wounded at Badajoz where he was shot through the thigh and bayoneted. Having recovered, he was wounded on 23 June but went back to duty and was killed on 24 June.
2. Lieutenant James Hamilton was slightly wounded and recovered.

passed in manoeuvring, without a shot being fired, and it ended in the French recrossing the river.

Yesterday I was on duty the whole day in the trenches. About three o'clock the batteries, four 18 pounders, and four howitzers, opened; and the enemy's fire became very slack, and our casualties consequently few; about seven o'clock, we set the convent on fire with hot shot. The storming party, under Colonel Davies of the 36th,[1] was in the trenches, and I was to have made the false attack on San Vincente; but the breach in Cayetano was not deemed practicable, and the attack was postponed. Lord Wellington was in the trenches himself, in the course of the day. The batteries fired hot shot at intervals during the night, but the enemy did not fire to interrupt our working parties who carried the approach between the two smaller forts and the large one, and cut off all communication between them.

What can Marmont be about? Whilst he is delaying in this neighbourhood, the Spaniards have overrun the whole of the country in his rear, so that like Massena last year in Portugal, he has only the ground he stands on. His people, officers as well as men, desert fast. At present the firing has ceased. I suppose the firing will open at the same time as last night and that the assault will take place; Adieu, again for the present.

Three o'clock in continuation. The batteries opened soon after I concluded, and at eleven o'clock the convent having been effectually set on fire, and the flames that had smouldered all night, burst out with great fury, the forts were assaulted, and carried without loss. The breach in Cayetano being practicable, the fort was summoned, and having refused to surrender, the troops carried it in about four minutes, with the loss of five men. The great fort hung out flags of truce, immediately after, which were ordered down, and the 9th Cacadores entered without the loss of a man.

The place on our entrance appeared much stronger than we had an idea of, and every means of defence was resorted to, as at Badajoz. Amongst others twenty musket barrels fixed in a frame to discharge by a train at once. The garrison consists of six hundred effective men, besides killed and wounded. The commandant says they have had thirty of the former, sixty of the latter. We hear from

1. Lieutenant Colonel Lewis Davies 36 Foot.

the south that Hill and Soult are looking at each other, and perhaps have ere this come to blows. If he should be beat, it will be a great thing for us.

June 28th, in continuation. Marmont moved off last night in the direction of the Douro, and tomorrow we are to follow. I have just been to the cathedral, to assist at a Te Deum; the music was very fine, but the performers hardly sufficiently numerous to fill the church. Tonight there are to be illuminations, fireworks, a play, also a ball and supper.

Seven hundred and six prisoners were taken in all, in the forts; and John Mansel has marched with them, today to Rodrigo. The officers were, most of them, members of the Legion of Honour, and all had been promised promotion, if they held these forts till relieved. As there will be a mail made up on this occasion I close this long letter. So once more, Adieu.

P.S. Devonish[1] died of his wounds on the 25th and we were allowed by the Spaniards to bury him in the church near the square.

Letter 61   Camp near Foncastin, 4 July 1812

My dear Mother,

I hope this will find you more comfortably settled and enjoying the shade and pure air of Melcombe; and the business of the militia settled, both to yours and my father's satisfaction. I wrote to you on the 20th of last month, and continued my account of the siege of the forts at Salamanca, in a letter to Tryon of a much later date; although they both went by the same conveyance. My arm was very painful, for a few days, but now, thank God, it is quite well again. If the stone had hit me on the head, it would have prevented my moving with the army which I should have been sorry for. I grieve to tell you I am likely to lose my good friend and commander General Hulse who expects to be removed to the Brigade of Guards; a distinction he well merits, and is anxious to obtain. Indeed our chief of division is so violent, everybody is anxious to exchange out of his division. Hulse's removal will give me the

---

1. The gazette states that Lieutenant J.A. Devonish died of his wounds on 24 June 1812, however Bingham being there is probably correct in stating that he died on 25 June. From the description given he is presumably buried at the Iglesia de San Martin which stands just off the Playa Major.

temporary command of the brigade, an honour I do not under the present circumstances aspire to. I would rather command a regiment in any other division in the army, nor do I see any advantages that would accrue to me; my reign would be so short. No, I trust shortly to return to England, to be permitted to have one or two years of your society. My military fits are now very short, and my desire to see home and wish for rest and quietness almost constant. Much longer we cannot remain, we have two hundred and sixty-eight rank and file present and fit for duty, and we get no recovered men from the rear. We move as fast as they do, and we must have a long halt, to enable them to overtake us.

To be sure a Dorsetshire man has no reason to complain of any country being open and without wood, but this is more so than any country I ever saw, between this and Salamanca forty and odd miles, there is but one wood, and not a straggling tree near a town or an enclosure of any kind. Grapes and corn grow as it were in a common field without a division.

The inhabitants make use of straw for fuel. There is however no want of villages; from a height near this place, I counted thirty, all springing up like mushrooms, naked on the plain. These towns and villages are not so good as those in Spanish Extremadura, and are in general built of brick burnt in the sun which gives them the appearance of mud building, and in fact they are little better; the water is very bad here, which is the case in general throughout this part of Spain.

Whatever the inhabitants possess they freely give, and their behaviour towards us has been much altered within these last two or three years. Reverses teach people wisdom, and they have suffered severely. I pray [to] God it may never be our turn as a nation to experience similar ones. My servant, two days ago went a short distance from the road, to endeavour to buy some eggs; he entered a village in which he was eyed with looks of suspicion. They asked him if he was a Frenchman, or an Englishman; he told them the latter, they were still incredulous [and] they examined the money he offered them, which being chiefly Portuguese, and an old lady discovering he wore tight pantaloons (whereas the French were always dressed in loose trowsers [sic]) they gave way to their feelings; they screamed, rang the bells, forced him to drink wine, and having loaded him with eggs, pigeons and milk; all the village afforded, for which they would not allow him to pay, they suffered him to depart. Had he been a Frenchman they would have murdered him; what a delightful thing it would be if our army could always inspire such sentiments. I shall write Nora a long letter from Valladolid, if we get there, and we are entertained with balls and plays, as we were at Salamanca. Adieu.

Letter 62   Alaejos, 13 July 1812

My dear Mother,

I will not let this packet pass without dropping you a line, although I have in truth nothing to say. We have been a good deal harassed with night marching and are now leading a curious life, we march into this town early every morning, and march out again into the fields, just at sunset, where we remain for the night. The French cross the Douro occasionally but in no very great numbers, and retire almost immediately; it is reported they are in want of provisions, and will shortly be obliged to retire on that account, leaving us a free passage of the river; which otherwise will cost us some men to effect; the banks on the right commanding entirely those on the left. I wish something was decided! Our present situation is not very comfortable, on account of the uncertainty.

This town is a very good one, and I am billeted on the house of an old deaf lieutenant colonel in the Spanish service, whose wife is one of the greatest termagants I ever met with.

There is not a tree in the whole country, and if old houses were not bought and pulled down, we should be badly off for fuel.

There is a handsome church and a beautiful steeple built of brick; as there is no stone in this part of the country. I was not aware it was possible to erect so handsome a structure of such materials. The brick towers we have in England are very ugly in general. If we want to improve in this particular, we must come to Alaejos.

A great part of the harvest is already in; it is considered a good crop, they are however sadly at a loss for mills; there are no such things as water mills in a country which scarcely at this season, affords water to drink. And there is only one windmill in the neighbourhood, which I should think would scarcely grind enough to supply the population. The four pound loaf, which a few days ago sold for seven shillings, is now reduced to five. War is a sad evil, and I pray to God we may never know what it is at home. They have a curious way of separating the corn from the straw here; the

135

whole of the harvest is brought to the threshing floors near the town, where it is spread abroad. Two mules are fastened to three strong boards, a little curved upwards at the end next the animals, the bottom of the boards are thick set with flints; on these boards a boy stands, who drives it about, till the grain is quite rubbed out, the receptacle for the grain, when so threshed, are large cellars underground, outside the town, which have been made for centuries, and are said to have been the work of the Moors. And such is the dryness of the climate, and soil, that the corn is preserved for years without suffering from damp. One great luxury in this part of the country is ice, which we get in all the towns, and though you must not fancy the rich ice creams you get in England, cold water and cold wine are delightful, in these parched countries. Adieu.

Letter 63   Salamanca, 24 July 1812

My dear Sir,

I trust this letter may reach you before the official details of the glorious victory of the 22nd, as by a mistake of the surgeons, I understand, I am returned severely wounded, which is not the case, as this letter will convince you. Towards the end of the day, as the 6th Division ascended the hill to attack the last position of the enemy, I received a musket ball in my neck, which entered in a slanting direction, and was cut out a little way under the skin, by an assistant surgeon of the 11th Regiment.[1] When the surgeon of the 53rd,[2] was called on for his return of the wounded, as he had heard that I had had a ball cut out of my neck, he chose to take it for granted, that the wound was a severe one, and returned me accordingly. I am now nearly fit for duty, if I could get my coat on, and shall be with my regiment I hope, by the first of August. I know but little yet of that memorable day; those who play a part only know what is going on immediately about them.

We had not been engaged till we were brought up to support a Portuguese regiment of the 4th Division, which soon gave way,[3]

1. Assistant Surgeon Alexander Stewart 11 Regiment.
2. Surgeon Sandel was chief surgeon to the 53rd.
3. It is sometimes assumed that once Wellington took the offensive against the

and our left was uncovered just as the French gained a temporary advantage on our right. In this situation, unsupported, we were attacked by the enemy's heavy dragoons;[1] we retired in good order, in line, and twice stopped their advance by halting and firing.[2] At last, a circular rocky hill, about two hundred yards in the rear, offered an advantage; I determined to profit by it, the dragoons being too near, and the ranks too much thinned to attempt a square, we made a dash for the hill. The dragoons came thundering on in the rear, and reached the hill just as our people faced about. The fire checked them, and it was soon obvious they would make no impression. At this moment I saw a part of the regiment which had not reached the rock, running down the hill in great confusion, without however being pursued by the dragoons. Giving the charge of the hill to Mansel, I dashed through the dragoons who made way for me, and succeeded in rallying the men round the regimental colour that I had with me.[3] The several attacks of the dragoons on the mass failed, although at one time they seized the end of the King's Colour, and there was a struggle who should have it; when a

---

strung out Army of Marmont, that victory was assured. However following the crushing defeat of Maucune's Division by Leith's 5th Division and Le Marchant's heavy cavalry, the French launched a serious counter-attack. Marshal Marmont and his second-in-command, General Bonnet, were both wounded and command devolved on General Clausel. When Cole's 4th Division advanced against Bonnet's Division and Pack's Portuguese Brigade stormed the Greater Arapile, the defeat of these attacks gave the French a momentary advantage. Clausel launched a well coordinated infantry and cavalry offensive which drove the 4th Division back. Wellington was however, well aware of the danger and the 6th Division (Clinton) stemmed the French tide and eventually forced it back with heavy casualties on both sides. The 6th Division suffered nearly half of all British casualties at Salamanca and clearly decided the crisis of the battle in Wellington's favour.

1. These were from Boyer's Heavy Dragoon Division, which consisted of 2 squadrons each from the 6, 11, 15 and 25 Dragoons.

2. Oman states that the 53rd repelled the cavalry attacks in squares; Bingham makes it clear that they resisted the cavalry in line. As a primary witness I choose to believe his account.

3. Regiments always carried two colours. The King's Colour always a union flag with the regimental crest and number in roman numerals and battle honours; and the Regimental Colour in the facing colour of the regiment (buff for the 53rd) with the regimental crest and number.

sergeant of grenadiers[1] wrested it from the dragoons who held it, or rather tore the silk from the pole, which I rather think remained with the enemy; at the same time our people gained ground on the right, and the dragoons retired in confusion. They would not have been with us so long, had not our men been almost left without ammunition. We got our battalion into order, told it off again into four divisions, and joined our brigade; soon after which we advanced to attack the last position of the enemy. We crossed a valley in line (nearly dark) exposed to an ill directed fire of artillery. Just as we were about to ascend the hill, I received the wound I mentioned before. I cannot tell what happened afterwards as I went to the rear to get the ball extracted. Ten officers of the regiment besides myself, are here wounded,[2] and I hope all doing well. I think the number of men hors de combat will be about one hundred and twenty, many of whom are slightly wounded. We went into the field only two hundred and fifty-four.[3] The other regiments in the brigade have suffered more than we have done.[4] Adieu.

1. There were two sergeants present with the grenadier company at Salamanca, Sergeant Abraham Peele and Sergeant James Millar. Unfortunately it is not clear which he describes here.
2. There were indeed ten other officer casualties from the 2/53rd at Salamanca, apart from Bingham. They were Captain Andrew Blackall (severely, died 28.08.12); Captain Oliver George Fehrszen (severely); Captain John Fernandez (severely); Captain Duncan Macdougall (severely); Captain Thomas Poppleton (slightly); Captain John Robertson (severely); Lieutenant and adjutant John Carss (slightly); Lieutenant John Hunter (severely); Lieutenant Joseph Nicholson (severely); and Ensign Peter Bunworth (slightly). One could also add Volunteer Mars Morphett (severely), but he was not officially an officer until becoming an Ensign in the 36 Regiment on 22 July 1812; he transferred back to the 53rd as an Ensign on 1 October 1812.
3. Bingham's figures of 120 killed and wounded from a total of 254 (assuming both figures refer to the other ranks) would show a casualty rate of forty-seven per cent. Oman states that the 2/53rd went into battle with 341 rank and file, and suffered 142 casualties, giving a casualty rate of forty-two per cent. Both, however, show a severe loss.
4. Oman shows the figures for the other two battalions in the brigade as follows: 1/11th incurred losses of 340 rank and file from an original 516 (sixty-six per cent) and the 1/61st lost 366 rank and file from an original 546 (sixty-seven per cent). Bingham is quite correct therefore in stating that the other two battalions had come off worse than the 53rd.

To my mother,

[The first part of the letter is identical to that to his father, Letter 63, and is omitted.]

Although our loss has been severe, our success has been brilliant. I understand upwards of seven thousand prisoners have already passed through this town; nineteen pieces of cannon,[1] have fallen into our hands. Marshal Marmont is wounded, he was seen in that state by Captain Fehrszen, who was left in the hands of the French, but who has [since] returned to us. His history is rather a curious one, he was wounded in the foot; the ball still remains in it, when the cavalry charged, they picked him up. Notwithstanding the pain he suffered from his wound, they made him take hold of a horse's tail, and so dragged him till he was in the rear of their line. They then put him on a wounded horse, and sent him to the rear; this horse fell dead under him. He was mounted on another; on this he rode till faint from loss of blood, he fell. He was then placed in a blanket, and borne by some English prisoners, till they arrived near the bridge of Alba de Tormes; the confusion here was great, and the passage blocked up by baggage and fugitives. Marshal Marmont's carriage, in which he had been placed after he had been wounded,[2] was stopped by the press, and hearing that a chef de bataillon was in the blanket, he ordered him to be brought to him. He asked him a few questions: - what reinforcements Lord Wellington had received the night before the action? Whether our men were not drunk and such, and then dismissed him, his guards cutting a way through the mob on the bridge. Fehrszen after this was taken to a house in the town, and attended by a surgeon, who put him to great pain, ineffectually trying to extricate the ball. The confusion in the town was great during the night, and in the morning favoured by the people of the house, the guards withdrew one by one, without appearing to heed him. The landlord's daughter was continually ascending to the top of the house, to give him, from time to time, the intelligence so interesting to him. The infantry were all leaving the town; the cavalry were preparing to mount; they were beyond the houses. The English cavalry were in

1. The number of cannon captured was actually twenty.
2. Marshal Marmont was wounded in the arm, and did not serve again until 1813.

sight; they were galloping down the street; and in a few minutes, she brought to him an officer of the 14th [Light Dragoons], to whom he was known, and who gave him a horse to convey him to this place, where from the exertions he has made, it is much feared he must suffer amputation. I forgot to mention that a small party of the enemy's cavalry fell into our hands, who had been sent back for the express purpose of carrying him off.

Marshal Beresford is severely wounded,[1] and Sir Stapleton Cotton,[2] Generals Cole[3] and Leith;[4] Tryon's friend General Le Marchant was killed,[5] and is the only General we have lost. The loss we have sustained in this battle will accelerate our return to England, and if the conduct of the 53rd merits being mentioned, which I really think it does, I shall be doubly happy as I know it will give you, and all my friends so much satisfaction; I would not have missed the battle for twenty such trifling wounds as I experienced. You must not expect details, all I can tell you, is only as far as we ourselves are concerned; those who play the game know less than the lookers on. Adieu.

Letter 65   Salamanca, 7 August 1812

My dear Mother,

My wound is (thank God) nearly healed and I intend starting for the army, on Monday next.

General Hulse has been removed at his own request to the 5th Division, and all the staff that have interest to get away, have left the 6th Division, where the chief I understand makes the duty more unpleasant than ever. Besides his conduct on the day of the action,

1. Marshal Beresford was severely wounded in the chest.
2. Sir Stapleton Cotton was shot by a Portuguese sentry during the night following the battle as he returned from a patrol.
3. Major General Galbraith Lowry Cole was wounded severely in the arm.
4. Lieutenant General James Leith was severely wounded.
5. Le Marchant's Heavy Cavalry Brigade took advantage of the confusion in Maucune's Division and struck with such force as to rout virtually the whole division and the leading elements of Brennier's Division. Having destroyed no less than eight battalions, the cavalry was scattered and worn down. Whilst attempting to charge again with a small group of his men, Le Marchant was shot and killed. His loss was a severe blow to the cavalry arm, being one of the few really professional cavalrymen in Wellington's army.

was such as does not add to his popularity,[1] I succeed to the command of Hulse's Brigade, which however does not muster four hundred men.[2] Eight hundred men and fifty-six officers was the loss of the three regiments at the Battle of Salamanca.[3]

The officers of the brigade have come to the determination of offering Hulse a sword on leaving us; when it was first mentioned to me, I with great satisfaction acceded to the proposal, as there is no man in the army, or indeed anywhere else beyond our little circle, for whom I have greater respect. I did not however expect they would have made it so expensive; Mansel has just put his name down for twenty guineas; half that sum is as much or more than I can afford.

I have been living principally with General Cole since I have been here; he has behaved in the most handsome manner towards me; first making a general offer of his table, and then finding I did not avail myself of his invitation, asking me whenever he happened to have anyone to dine with him whom he thought I should like to meet. He is very badly, but not dangerously wounded; one of his ribs broken, and the blade bone shattered; it will be four months before he will be able to rejoin the army.[4] He talks of removing to Oporto, as soon as he is able to get about.

---

1. This criticism of Clinton must refer to the closing stages of the battle at dusk. Ordered to advance and harass the French retreat, Clinton came across their rear-guard, which consisted of Ferey's Division, who had not yet been involved in the fighting. The French were deployed in line, with a square on either flank and were clearly determined to stay the British pursuit. Clinton's troops were much thinned, clearly exhausted and low on ammunition; despite this he chose to take his battered division forward without waiting for the support of the fresh divisions then coming up. The French infantry produced a hail of fire that all witnesses agree was the heaviest they had ever seen. The fire-fight continued for the best part of an hour until the French eventually broke and fled, but by this time the 6th Division had been decimated. The losses in the division were horrendous (Oman's figures of rank and file for the 6th Division, show a casualty rate of forty-one per cent whereas the average loss for the British army at Salamanca was nine per cent) and it is perhaps not surprising that Clinton was censured by his troops for ordering them into such a murderous fire without support; suspicious that the lives of their comrades were forfeited just so Clinton could claim the lion's share of the glory.
2. Oman states that the brigade mustered 555 rank and file after the battle.
3. Oman states the losses of the brigade at Salamanca as fifty officers and 798 men killed or wounded.
4. Cole was indeed unable to take up his command again until 15 October 1812.

The first, second, and third of August, were dedicated to fêtes, on the proclamation of the new constitution;[1] it was read both in the Plaza Maior and in the cathedral. I don't think two hundred people attended at either place and it was received without interest. The picture of Ferdinand the seventh, was exhibited under a velvet canopy, and was not much respected. 'He is something of a beast, like his father', was the expression made use of respecting him, to an officer of my acquaintance. If the kingdom of Spain were put to the vote, the whole of the people of Salamanca would give theirs to Lord Wellington. If the French or any other foreign government would be moderate in their demands and temperate in their contributions they would be much more popular, with the generality of the nation, than any free constitution of their own, the advantages of which they have no idea of, and it never enters into their calculation. They appear as if they would be glad to get rid of the trouble of governing themselves at any rate.

Amongst other amusements on this occasion, bull-fighting was one. The capital bull fighters would not enter the lists against the young bull which was produced. The animal was tied by the horns, and tortured for two days in the most barbarous manner. How can women enjoy the spectacle! And yet great numbers of all ranks and descriptions assembled to see goads thrust into the sides of the poor beast, which after all they could scarcely make savage enough to avenge his ills on his tormentors. The great joke seemed to be, a man held up a cloak before the bull, who ran at it, and then the man slipped dexterously on one side. The fireworks on the second night were very brilliant, and worth seeing. The ball I did not go to, as my wound was still open; I did not think it prudent to expose myself to the jostling of a crowd, and I considered if officers could figure away at a ball, they had better have been with the army.

I am very anxious to see the Gazette account of the business of

---

1. The Cortes proclaimed a new Constitution for Spain in 1812, ensuring civil liberties for all, but not religious. It established equality before the law; freedom of employment; universal liability to taxation and military service; the King's power restricted and the Cortes had to meet annually, controlling all taxation and retaining a dominant role in all legislation. No changes to the Constitution were allowed for eight years and Ferdinand was expected to sign the Constitution immediately on his return to Spain.

the 22nd July. If the 53rd are mentioned in terms of approbation, it will I hope make amends to you for my not having been with you sooner. And I do not forget that my father said it was the happiest day in his life, when he read the account of the Battle of Talavera. I think they must give another medal for this decisive action, and one of these days I may make my appearance, loaded with these marks of distinction[1]. After all we look forward to retirement, as the end of all these exertions and I often sigh for the round hat, and the cottage, the long morning walk with my father, and the social evening in the Melcombe drawing room.

The 82nd have been here, since I last wrote.[2] Of course the regiment has changed since I left them eight years since. I met however some old acquaintance, that made the two days they remained here pass pleasantly enough.

Marshal Beresford is also here, wounded. He publishes daily bulletins of his state; these are entered in a book, in which enquirers put down their names. They are not numerous; I was admitted one day, to the honour of an audience. Every body laughs at his affectation of state and grandeur.

The ball is not yet extracted from Fehrszen's foot, and he suffers great pain; I am however in hopes he will not lose his leg. Adieu.

Letter 66   Cuellar, 21 August 1812

My dear Mother,

Yesterday I received three letters. Yours of the 23rd and such. The date of my letter will convince you of my recovery; the wound is not completely healed, but I feel not the least inconvenience from it. I came from Salamanca here in five days, and halted one at Medina del Campo, travelling very early in the morning to avoid the great heat. Nothing can be at this time of year more uninteresting than this part of the country; nearly a perfect flat, and so burnt, and parched up that there is scarcely an appearance of vegetation. There are only two pine woods between this and Salamanca, and these of

1. Lieutenant Colonel Bingham of 53 Regiment was particularly mentioned in Wellington's dispatch on the Battle of Salamanca dated 24 July 1812.
2. The 82 Regiment had just arrived from Gibraltar and was initially placed in the 4th Division but was transferred in November to the 7th Division.

no very great extent. And the distance is nearly eighty miles; there are plenty of villages which though in some instances, preferable to those in Portugal, are very dreary. Not a garden near any of them, and I believe the vegetables with which this market is tolerably well supplied must come from the clouds.

I have succeeded to the command of General Hulse's Brigade and I understand there is no chance of my being superseded. We only muster six hundred men out of two thousand, there are in the country; but our strength will increase as the slightly wounded recover. At present I have a battalion formed of the convalescents of the army nine hundred strong attached to my command.

General Clinton has been very quiet since the battle, so that our time passes pleasantly enough. The 82nd are here, amongst the regiments lately landed who are detained at this station, which gives me a further opportunity of seeing my old friends, but by our being halted I have lost the chance of seeing Madrid, and the palaces of San Ildefonso, Escorial, and Aranjuez; however we have escaped some very hot marches and I should have found it difficult to have overtaken the division had it been in movement.

I yesterday got hold of Lord Wellington's official account of the action of the 22nd in the Lisbon Gazette; I was glad to find my name mentioned, as I know the satisfaction it will give my father and yourself. The conduct of many others both in our brigade and division, deserved to be named more than mine did; the insertion of my name therefore, must in this instance be attributed to Lord Wellington's previous good opinion. I hope I may never forfeit it, as you will agree that being noticed by such a man must be considered as highly flattering.

My having the command of the brigade will I am certain reconcile you to my remaining longer than I expected in the country but yet I expect every week an order for the return of the 53rd to Lisbon, to embark. We are reduced to four hundred and forty-four rank and file, in the country, whereof only one hundred and sixty-seven are present at head quarters; a number too inconsiderable to make it probable we shall be long detained.

The fever as usual at this time of the year makes great ravages especially amongst those not accustomed to the climate.[1] The

1. Hence Wellington's efforts to retain old campaigners like the 53rd despite their lack of numbers.

Honourable Captain Percy, a son of Lord Beverley's[1] died here last night. Adieu.

Letter 67   Arevalo, 28 August 1812

My dear Mother,

I hope this will find you enjoying the autumn at home and such. I am happy to tell you that my wound is nearly completely healed and that I never enjoyed better health than I do at this present moment although fever and ague is very prevalent amongst all ranks. We found poor General Hulse very ill here, he was not out of bed yesterday; today he is up, but very weak.

We marched last Sunday from Cuellar to Olmedo, a town which has seen better days. If the country was not so parched up as it is, just the neighbourhood of Olmedo might be pretty, at least for this country, and our next days march to a bivouac on the banks of the Piron, where we found a fir grove, was more so. One of the advantages of commanding a brigade is getting a house to live the heat of the day through in, but it is only one day that I have enjoyed or availed myself of that privilege, but if we continue our march, it may save me a fever.

I am anxious to have an opportunity of seeing the palaces and Madrid. Those of the army, who have been there, speak in raptures of them. It must have been very interesting immediately after the English entered; the joy of the population was so great, and the illuminations and balls, beyond anything. Hulse says the palace was the most complete thing he ever saw, and most beautifully furnished. Lord Wellington lived there in great style; he is now gone to Toledo.

The bridge at Almaraz being repaired, the great road from Lisbon to Madrid is now open by Talavera, Truxillo, Merida, Badajoz and Elvas.

Arevalo, in which we are now stationed is certainly the best town I have seen in this part of the country, next to Salamanca; never having been made a station by the French, it has not been much pulled to pieces; there are the remains of an old castle of brick, much like that of Medina del Campo, but not so perfect. Two small

1. Captain the Honourable Francis John Percy 23 Regiment, DAQMG, seventh son of the 1st Earl of Beverley, died on 20 August 1812.

streams that after rains, swell to mighty torrents, unite just below the castle. There are two bridges over one stream and one over the other. One of the bridges is handsome. The banks of the stream, which are steep, are a little wooded, and the sight of a tree or bush in this apparently barren and parched up country is a treat not to be described. Adieu.

Letter 68   Arevalo, 2 September 1812

My dear Mother,

I do not know when I may again have an opportunity of writing so that I sit down with very little to say, having written a few days since. Troops have been pouring in here for the last three days, and tomorrow another division, and the headquarters of the army will be here; there are three divisions in the town, already, so that if we do not move tomorrow, we certainly shall the following day, and perhaps shall not halt till we arrive at Burgos, for I do not think the French will make any stand short of that place; what may take place afterwards I cannot foresee. The command of the brigade as it will eventually (I hope) turn out so much to my advantage, reconciles me to remaining in the country and when the business is going on so favourably, and with a prospect of a glorious termination, it would perhaps be a pity to leave the army, and although I know you will feel every moment of my absence, when you consider how beneficial it may turn out to me, and the satisfaction you will experience, if you hear my name well spoken of, you will also be reconciled to my stay a few months longer than we at one time expected.

The days continue very hot, although the nights are cold, and we have a great many ague cases. I am sorry to say my servant is laid up with the fits as severe, or more so than ever and I am afraid he will not be able to move with us, and what to do without him, I cannot tell. Besides, as I am in the command of the brigade, I have the Brigade Major (Cotton by name[1]) attached to me, which renders the want more severely felt than it otherwise would be.

We have been very gay here; balls almost every night. The ladies have learnt English country dances, and perform very well. There is one very pretty girl here, and only one. The Spanish ladies look

---

1. Captain Thomas D'Avenant Cotton 7 Foot, a first cousin of Sir Stapleton Cotton, he was later Brigade Major to Byng of the 2nd Division.

more to advantage in a morning, and in their native dress. Of an evening they are dressed in the French fashion, and in white which does not become their complexion.

General Hulse continues ill, and must be so weakened by his attack as to oblige him to go to the rear, when we move forward. He will feel this severely, as he has just been appointed to the command of the 5th Division, but there are so many general officers ill, and wounded, that scarcely one is left to each division.

I am very anxious for your next letters, as they will have been written after the official accounts of the Battle of Salamanca has reached England, and I long to know if my letter reached you before the Gazette.

I shall call on Lord Wellington, if we remain tomorrow; on the night of the 22nd, he heard I had been killed and expressed himself to an aide de camp of General Clinton's who went to him for orders, in terms of great regret, for my loss. The wound is all but healed; the surface is not larger than a silver penny. Adieu.

Letter 69   **Camp near San Isidro [de Duenas],**
                                         11 September 1812

My dear Mother,

I was made quite happy, yesterday, by receiving your letter of the 20th and to find that my plan had been successful; that my letter conveyed to you the first news of the action, and my wound. It is now all but healed; it rather broke out again a week ago, but it is now not much larger than a pins head.

My last was written to you from Arevalo, since which we have been constantly marching. On the 3rd we left the town, but merely went into bivouac, a mile from it. My servant John, had a severe fit of the ague, the day before we left the town, and on the 4th, on which day we marched into the neighbourhood of Olmedo, was so ill as to be left on the road side; he was however brought in, in the afternoon so ill, that being left, as we moved on the following morning in the little village of Calabazas, I almost despair of seeing him again. This has been indeed a sickly season, and poor General Hulse who had been ill only a few days, and who during the three years he has been in the country has hitherto enjoyed uninterrupted good health, died at Arevalo, last Sunday morning. He will be universally lamented; I believe I told you we had ordered a sword, value two hundred guineas, to present to him on his quitting the command of the brigade. General Wheatley [1] died the week before; as he belonged to the 1st Regiment of Guards, it will make a vacancy for Robert Bingham,[2] and will give him a company; he has been a long time kept waiting for it.

To continue my narrative, on the 5th we crossed the Eresma, and on the 6th the Duero,[3] and came (very unexpectedly I believe) on the enemy, who were strongly posted in front of Valladolid, near the village of Asternas. An attack was planned and was postponed on account of some guns having arrived too late. We bivouacked that night on the right bank of the Duero; the enemy retired in the night; we moved forward about seven o'clock in the morn; the enemy blew up the bridge about ten, and we entered the city. Valladolid, which was formerly a royal residence, is a large town, the plaza or square is not at all equal to that at Salamanca, or are the public buildings in general, but the streets are broader, and the environs much more cheerful, well wooded, and pleasant. There is a public walk on the banks of the Pisuerga, which although I saw it to great disadvantage, the French cavalry having picketed their horses on it the night before, appeared to me the prettiest thing I had seen in Spain. There is a very neat theatre, coffee houses, public and private baths, and all the luxuries of great cities. We halted on the 8th, which gave me an opportunity of seeing much of what was worthy of attention. The royal palace is a good building, but nothing extraordinary. The Convent of San Pablo is a beautiful specimen of gothic architecture much destroyed by the French. The cathedral is a large building in the Grecian style,[4] with nothing

1. Major General William Wheatley, 1st Foot Guards, died of typhus at the Palace of Escurial 1 September 1812.
2. Lieutenant and Captain Robert Turbeville Bingham, 1 Foot Guards was George's cousin, being the first son of his father's brother, William, Archdeacon of London. He had been a lieutenant since 1798, although made a brevet major in 1805 and was only confirmed in the rank of captain and lieutenant colonel on 23 September 1812. He retired from the service 8 April 1813. I must thank Barbara Chambers who has produced a book listing the service records of the officers of the 1 Guards for this information.
3. I have amended the manuscript which states 'Douro' the Portuguese name for this river; it is however known in Spain as the 'Duero'.
4. The model in Valladolid museum explains why the cathedral is so plain and unimpressive. Only half of the original design was ever completed and the overall effect is simply plainness and severity.

particularly worthy of observation except a beautiful highly worked iron railing that separates the choir from the altar; it has two good organs.

In the evening we went to the play, it was called the 'Triumph of Innocence'; the story turned on the return of Christopher Columbus, (or Colon, as he is termed by the Spaniards) from the new world, a prisoner; and his liberation by Ferdinand and Isabella. It appeared (for I was not master sufficiently of the Spanish language to understand more than the outline of the story) rather a dull piece, and was purely historical, unenlivened by any under plot, as I think it's called. Lord Wellington was there, and was received with great acclamation, and enthusiasm. Whenever any passages could be applied to him, as when Columbus was created a Duke, there was incessant 'Viva's', and a cheer of 'Nuestra Duque de Ciudad Rodrigo'; but Valladolid is not considered a very patriotic town. There was after the play a bolero, beautifully danced. The farce I did not stay for. The night after we came away, Lord Wellington gave a ball, which I understood was numerously and brilliantly attended.

We marched on the 9th and crossed the Pisuerga, at the bridge of Cabezon, and rather unexpectedly found the enemy at Duenas, four leagues from Valladolid, to which place they had returned finding we did not immediately follow them, and having been reinforced by a division under Caffarelli,[1] they occupied very strong ground, and yesterday we closed up to them; but the Spanish army having appeared at Rio Seco, on their right flank, they moved off last night. Today we passed through Duenas, and at present occupy with our division the Convent of San Isidro, which the French have as usual, pulled much to pieces. We are encamped in the park, which might have been beautiful, but is now a wilderness. The River Pisuerga runs near it. We are two leagues from Palencia, into which town we expect to march tomorrow, and from thence to Burgos, is fourteen leagues; (the leagues in this country are about three miles and a half) and the rain that is falling today will lay the dust, cool the air, and make marching pleasant. The road, which is the great road from Madrid to Paris, is excellent. Quite as good as any turnpike in England. Near the town the sides of the road have

1. General Marie Francois Auguste Caffarelli du Falga took command of the Army of the North in 1812.

been planted for miles together with trees, but the French who spare nothing that suits their temporary convenience, have in several instances cut them down. The country here is much diversified, and more wooded than on the arid plains near Salamanca. From Burgos we expect to see the lofty Pyrenees.

I continue in the command of my little brigade, which is so much pleasanter than a regiment that I hope to retain it; the Brigade Major, is a son of the late Dean of Chester, by name Cotton, and a first cousin of Sir Stapleton's; a pleasant well informed man and I am glad that he is so, for we of necessity have much tête-à-tête. Adieu.

Letter 70   Camp before Burgos, 21 September 1812

My dear Mother,

We arrived here three days since, and are likely to stay some days longer, engaged in the siege of the castle of Burgos, which has for the present brought us up.

Our march from Valladolid to this was in very bad weather, rain every day, and we were always in bivouacs. With any other officer but General Clinton, as commanding a brigade, I might have been under cover, but that indulgence has been refused to me, and I was not anxious to press it, which I should have done had my rank entitled me to have been regularly on the staff. I do not find he ever encamps himself, although he made a great flourish about it.

The country in this part of Spain, is I think the pleasantest we have been in, the more so perhaps, because it puts me in mind of Dorsetshire; high chalk hills, well cultivated valleys, with trees along the sides of the brooks; frequent villages, which are doubly pleasant after the plains we have left, where neither hill nor tree was to be seen.

The Spanish army under the command of Castanos, 11,000 strong, joined us on the sixteenth; such a set of scarecrows I never set eyes on!! Complete jail birds! The officers being, in appearance, little better than the men; no discipline amongst them. One of their divisions has been attached to ours, and it is the best; but they are so filthy, that in camps they are bad neighbours. Their cavalry and artillery are considerably better looking than their infantry.

You will be contented to hear that the 6th Division has nothing as yet to do with the siege which has been carried on by the 1st

150

Division, and Pack's Portuguese Brigade. The night before last, they carried by assault, a horn-work, within three hundred yards of the place, which will greatly facilitate its reduction. The loss has been considerable owing, it is said, to the cacadores of Pack's Brigade having commenced firing at four hundred yards distant from the place. Had it not been for Major Cocks of the 78th Regiment,[1] the attack would have failed. He entered at the gorge of [the] work at the head of the light company of his own regiment, by which the party without, who were about to relinquish, were encouraged to persevere in their attacks. The casualties in the approaches have been few, considering the distance.

I have not yet been into the town, from which we are two miles distant; in crossing the bridge you have to run the gauntlet of a fire of musketry, at three hundred yards distant. And as I may have an opportunity of examining it at my leisure, some days hence, it is not worthwhile paying for my curiosity or running the risk of it. The cathedral is supposed to be the finest gothic structure in Europe. I cannot however think it can exceed that at Salamanca.

The public walks about the city are very pleasant; trees planted thick in rows are so refreshing in this ardent climate. The rains have ceased, and the atmosphere is again clear. The nights are very cold; the days very hot.

Previous to the French retiring to the castle they set fire to the town to burn the houses nearest their defences, as the wind blew strong from the westward, a number of houses were burnt. Indeed the fire is not yet out, and this is the third day. I really think if the wind had continued to blow as strong as on the first day (the 19th) the whole city would have been burnt. There is not so much wood in the composition of the houses as in those of Valladolid and Salamanca, but had the whole town become a prey to the flames, it would have excited no compassion in the breasts of the French, who have no sentiment but inordinate ambition. From Burgos to Santander is not more than eighty miles, and the road now quite open. In a good ship, in four days I could be in England; this is a dream too pleasing to be realized. Adieu.

---

1. Major the Honourable Edward Charles Cocks, 78 Regiment, received a slight wound (not recorded) during the successful storming of the St Michael's horn work.

Letter 71   **Camp before Burgos, 27 September 1812**

My dear Mother,

Here we are still, and likely to remain much longer than we at first had an idea of. The castle is so strong and our means have hitherto been so inadequate. On Tuesday night an attempt was made to escalade the lower part of the works, which failed. The officer, who commanded, Major Lawrie,[1] a very fine young man, was killed, and several officers were wounded. An officer of our brigade, Lieutenant Stewart of the 61st,[2] who had volunteered his services as acting engineer, and who had only arrived from Salamanca (where he had been left in the hospital wounded) had half his face carried away by a round shot; of all his features, one eye only is left. On Wednesday the 23rd, there was a truce to bury the dead, and bring off the wounded, who had been lying there twelve hours exposed to the cold of the night and the heat of the day. That same evening we broke ground on our side [of] the castle (the west) within twenty or thirty yards of the works, covering our advance by the ruins and houses, and taking advantage of what in Dorsetshire would be called a lancet of ground, under the wall, and sheltered from the fire of it; here we began a mine which is to go directly under the exterior wall. The guns we understand are to be in batteries, the north side, and will open when the mine is ready to spring. We hear some more guns are to arrive,[3] and as soon as our fire is equal to theirs we shall soon I hope knock the castle about their ears. This is the eighth day of the siege, and our loss they say amounts to seven hundred killed and wounded; some make it more. We formed both covering and working parties yesterday, that is the brigade and our loss was seven killed, two wounded. The distance is now so small and everybody so well covered that if a man gets hit at all, it is through the head. We are in fact so near, that when the Portuguese are on duty, they abuse the French, who return it all day long. My being in the command of the brigade, and doing the duty of colonel in the division, prevents my taking part in the duty of the trenches, and people do not go there for their amusement.

1. Major Andrew Lawrie of the 79 Regiment was killed on 22 September 1812.
2. Lieutenant Gilbert Stewart of the 61 Regiment. It is surprising given Bingham's statement, that he was only described in the returns as 'slightly wounded'.
3. The Navy was sending guns from Santander, but they did not arrive before the siege was abandoned.

I have broken up my encampment, and have got into a small mill which is pleasantly situated and commands from one of its windows, our works and the castle; it is certainly more comfortable than a tent at this time of the year. The night being very cold, the days exceedingly hot; but I now care so little about these things that I should have remained in my tent had not my servant returned from Salamanca recovered indeed of his fever and ague, but so weak as not to be able to stand any hardship. My horses too were suffering from standing out, and as I can see the camp from another window, of my aforesaid mill, I feel no scruple of conscience in getting under cover. I have not yet gone into the town although by going round you may proceed there without risk. I want nothing there but to see the cathedral which from its towers must be a beautiful building. Mansel has experienced and indeed still labours under a severe attack of fever and ague; it will be some time before he gets round again; these attacks weaken people so much.

I expect to see Robert Bingham with the 1st Regiment of Guards, one battalion of which has landed at Corunna and are on their march to join the army. His stay will be short for as he will get poor General Wheatley's company he will soon return on promotion. Adieu.

Letter 72   Camp before Burgos, 3 October 1812

My dear Mother,

I did not expect to have addressed you from this place again but I am sorry to tell you we are as far off as ever from obtaining possession of the castle; our means are so miserably inadequate, and we have not talent enough amongst our engineers to compensate for the want of means. I see no end of the siege, which had already cost us very dear, and it is likely to be more expensive yet, in the articles of men and time, both precious in war.

I am sorry I have written in so sanguine a manner, about returning home, as I find by your letters of the 3rd of September I have raised expectations not immediately likely to be gratified. The 1st Battalion of the 53rd, as you will have seen by the papers, has suffered severely in India,[1] and this may be a means of accelerating our return, to fill up the vacancies occasioned by their loss; but

1. The 1/53rd were involved in operations around Allahabad in India in 1812.

Lord Wellington is very averse to sparing a man; and the two words 'Return home', puts him into a fury. We ought to consider that patience is a virtue we may well exercise; since it has pleased God to give me good health, and sound bones, and I know you would rather hear of my remaining in Spain, than see me obliged to return on account of wounds, or ill health. My profession alone renders me independent, I have embarked in a cause from which I could not withdraw, even if I wished it, without returning in that sort of way, that you would feel nothing but sorrow, after the first meeting was over; and it is a sensation I hope never to excite.

Yesterday it began to rain, and last night which was wet, I felt the comfort of my mill; although it swarms with fleas to that degree, that at first it was quite terrible. Today they talk of getting our men under cover in the Hospital del Rey (a collection of large buildings that before the invasion was made use of as such). It is so near my mill, that I shall not change my quarters; the hospital is quite within range of the fort and I doubt whether the enemy will let our people live in it, after they know that they are established there; which cannot be concealed notwithstanding it is well shrouded with trees.

I have not yet been into the town to see the cathedral, of which I hear so much, and the Calle d'Espolon a beautiful walk in the centre of the town. I have also two convents to see with the tombs of several of the Kings of Leon; these will furnish subject for my next letter. Adieu.

Letter 73   **Camp before Burgos, 6 October 1812**

My dear Mother,

I wrote to you only two days ago, but as Mansel is going home by Santander, I cannot allow him to depart, without a line to let you know that I was on duty Sunday in the trenches and although we had hot work of it, escaped unhurt, and I hope gained some credit for my exertions. I was quite knocked up when I came off duty, not having sat down except just to eat my dinner, for twenty-four hours. At five o'clock in the afternoon the mine was sprung, and the breach made by the former mine, rendered practicable, and both these points were carried in a very gallant manner by the 24th Regiment, supported by the covering party in the trenches, under my command; the supporting and covering ourselves on the wall, after we had gained it, was a point of great difficulty. It was however affected notwithstanding a sortie, made in the night to interrupt the work, and the incessant fire of the musketry, and of shells which the enemy kept up; frequently five or six in the air at the same time, besides others that they rolled down the glacis, at the foot of which our work began. These on a dark night together with the fire balls consequently thrown to discover our workmen, was a truly sublime sight. I prayed heartily for a stout heart, that I might do nothing that any of you might be ashamed of, and it pleased God to grant me presence of mind to enable me coolly to direct what was necessary. I do not know exactly the amount of our loss. Of our brigade we had two officers and thirty-one rank and file killed and wounded. Our total loss that night must have been a great deal more than that.[1] Much more might have been done had some pains been taken about the previous arrangements. I did not know that the storm was to take place till the commanding officer of the 24th[2] reported to me that he had marched his regiment into the trenches for that purpose nor had I any orders till just about half an hour before the mine was sprung, when Lord Fitzroy Somerset[3] rode down from Lord Wellington, to say I was to support the 24th; the directing engineer, Major Jones,[4] was wounded in moving out to make the signal that all was ready, and his loss was most severely felt. Yesterday afternoon the enemy made a sortie and completely destroyed almost all the work we had done the night before. The field officer who relieved me was severely (I believe dangerously) wounded, and since that our work has gone on so slowly, that if we make no more progress than we have done for the last eight and forty hours, we shall be a long time before we are masters of the second line of defence, and then the third line and castle still remain. I was called on to make a report and I was glad to be able to mention the name of

1. According to Jones, the total loss that night was thirty-seven men killed and seven officers and 189 men wounded.
2. Captain Hedderwick of the 2/24th was in temporary command of that regiment.
3. Captain Lord Fitzroy James Henry Somerset, 43 Regiment, ADC to Wellington, who later became infamous as Lord Raglan in the Crimea.
4. Brigade Major, Captain John Thomas Jones Royal Engineers, was severely wounded on 4 October 1812. He later wrote his *Journal of sieges in Spain 1811–14* which was published in 1856.

young Fraser,[1] who is as gallant and fine a boy as ever lived, and in whose behalf you may recollect my having mentioned, I interested myself to get a lieutenancy; and a Captain Campbell of the 42nd[2]; his father was an old acquaintance of yours ages ago, at Portsmouth, who was then waiting to join a regiment in Canada, before I went into the army, and in whose regiment you were anxious I should get a commission. If the unfortunate result of last night's sortie, does not put the Marquess out of sorts, I think I stand a fair chance of seeing my name in the Gazette again, and as it will be unaccompanied by the drawback as of a wound at Salamanca, I am sure it will give you satisfaction, and make you some amends for my not appearing in person.

Pray don't let this letter go beyond your own circle; in writing to you, my dear mother, I am apt to talk more in the first person than I should do to other people, and I am afraid the Lemons and other to whom you showed my letter after Salamanca would think me a great egotist. Nothing could have behaved more to my satisfaction than the remains of the 53rd; they are become as soldiers valuable as old gold, and were the other night my principal stand by; there were only three wounded.

What a lesson this siege has proved to everybody, and perhaps more so to Lord Wellington whose uninterrupted success required some check of this kind, to make him more cautious; and shows the folly of undertaking jobs with inadequate means; it's like trying to cut down a large tree with a blunt saw, when a sharp one might be had for going a mile for it.

Letter 74   Camp before Burgos, 10 October 1812

My dear Mother,

I wrote Tuesday to Mansel whose presence in England being absolutely necessary; he being executor to his late mother's will, he with great difficulty got leave to proceed. In this letter I detailed all that happened to me when I was on duty Sunday last at 'the deadly imminent breach'; since which I have not been on duty, and I have enjoyed myself by seeing sights as much as the continued wet

1. Lieutenant John Fraser 53 Foot led a ladder carrying party in the storming of the second line on 4 October and, having planted the ladders, was the first up.
2. Captain John Campbell, 42 Foot.

weather allowed. I have found a way to go into the town hardly at all exposed to the enemy's fire, and I have been three times to visit the beautiful cathedral which although quite different to that at Salamanca, yet I think nearly equals it, in beauty. It is not so richly ornamented on the outside, but it is perhaps more so within, and there are fine alto relievos at the back of the great altar, that are worth much attention and a wheel window with painted glass of very brilliant colours, finer than anything I have ever seen out of England. The space between the choir and the high altar is filled with an immense pair of bronze gates; I think the finest I ever saw. They cannot be less than fifty feet high. The chapels are numerous and some of them handsome, and would be more in unison with the building were it not for the too tawdry ornaments with which they are decorated, and the difference in the order of architecture; most of them are Grecian, as is also the choir, which is of marble but takes off from the general appearance of the building.

In one of the chapels is some very fine tapestry, representing the Roman emperors, but how they came in company with Nuestra Señor de Burgos, I cannot divine. To this image many miracles are attributed.

There are no good pictures; there is one of San Nicolas four or five times larger than life, carrying our saviour over the sea, which seems to have nothing of merit, but its size.

The martyrdom of a female saint, by having her breasts cut off, is a subject so horrid, that very good painting would hardly compensate for the subject.

About two miles from the town is the convent of Cartuja de Miraflores, standing in a beautiful situation richly endowed and must certainly have been one of the most delightful retreats any monastic order could have enjoyed; round a large cloister closed with windows of painted glass and opening to a garden with a fine jet d'eau in the centre, there are apartments for forty monks of the Carthusian order; each cell was a separate house, it had one room below, with a fireplace, which opened into a small garden with a covered walk. A small staircase conducted you to a very good sized room with a recess for a bed, and an oratory. All these were pulled to pieces by the French who have made stables of the cloisters, and lower apartments, and their present desolation forms a strong contrast with the comfort that must have once reigned within these walls. The convent was very rich and has conveniences for farming that lead you to suppose the monks could not have been the drones they are represented to have been. The principal church of the convent is of gothic architecture, and is a striking object from the surrounding country; it is most highly ornamented, and even the French have respected the most beautiful specimen (except Batalha) of that style I ever saw. The tomb of white marble of the founder, John the second and his queen, is before the high altar. I think it is decidedly a finer ornament than that of Henry VII in Westminster Abbey, and probably of a similar date; although I have no history of Spain to refer to. All the pictures worth removing have been carried away, and many wantonly destroyed. But one chapel contains several that I suppose were thought not worth carrying away; amongst them, one of the celebrated Bruno, who is mentioned in Charlton's[1] memoirs as having given rise to the strict monastic order which we call that of 'La Trappe'.

The story is briefly this; Bruno passed for a man of extraordinary piety in the convent, and was elected Abbot (having refused the mitre several times) to dedicate his days to the service of God, in this Convent of Cartuja where he died, in a most exemplary manner, and was brought out to be buried, but while he was laid out on the bier, and the brethren chanting the service de functis over him; to their great astonishment he raised himself up, and cried out with a loud voice, 'Vocatus sum'; the service proceeded, and shortly afterwards when they had got him half way to the grave, he again sat up and pronounced 'Judicatus sum', the monks had hardly recovered from their surprise, at this second astonishing appeal, sufficiently for the service to proceed, when with a horrible and ghastly look, which is well represented in the picture, he again raising himself, called out 'Damnatus sum'. Upon which the monks, in a very inhospitable manner turned out the corpse on a dung-hill. The founder of the order of La Trappe, who was one of those present at this extraordinary scene, turned in his mind what could have brought down so severe a punishment on a man of such known piety; when it struck him that eating meat and drinking wine was the cause. The only way they could avoid the fate of poor Bruno, and his most summary punishment, was abstaining from

1. This almost certainly refers to *Letters to a friend, intended to relieve the difficulties of an anxious inquirer . . . on the subjects of conversion and salvation* written by Thomas Charlton.

this indulgence. Before I quit the church of the convent I must call your attention to the Abbot's seat; representing a spire of gothic work, that would suit the Abbey church at Milton. It is of wood and the workmanship as fine as the ivory fans you get from China.

At a small village called Huelgas, near the city is a nunnery which was occupied by forty nuns. It has been the burying place of many of the royal family, whom it would seem in general, preferred being deposited with the sisters in the vale, than with their neighbouring brothers on the hill above.[1] The buildings of this convent have been more destroyed than the others, having been fitted up as a permanent cavalry barrack. Of its size you may form some idea, when I tell you that the cloister and lower apartments are calculated for seven hundred horses. The church seems to have been preserved till lately; the tomb of the founder, in the choir has been opened, and a body in royal robes, in tolerable preservation appeared in it; these by having been exposed to the air, and much touched have gone to pieces.

Since I wrote on Tuesday the enemy have made another successful sortie, in which a very fine young man and promising officer, Major Cocks of the 78th, formerly in the 16th [Light] Dragoons, lost his life.[2] It is quite lamentable to think how many people we have lost in this villainous siege; and we are not now a bit nearer the end of it, than we were a week ago. If we had had a proper battering train, six days, and three hundred men, would have given us the place. They talk of forty officers and 1,200 men having fallen already; two out of our three guns are disabled so that our case appears to me to be hopeless. My people are on duty today, but at present all things look quiet. Adieu, my dear mother; how rejoiced I shall be to meet you all, and talk over these days of anxiety, and night of watching, in peace and quietness.

Letter 75   Camp near Burgos, 17 October 1812

My dear Mother,

I hardly know how to make out a letter for this packet; this last week has been so barren of interest. It has rained every day. We have made little, or no progress, in the reduction of the castle,

---

1. This is now the Monasterio de las Huelgas, run by the Cistercian order.
2. Cocks was killed whilst rallying his troops during a sortie.

which I am sure everybody in the army (I won't except the Marquess) ardently wishes was underground, or anywhere else, unless we were provided with more suitable means to reduce it. Our batteries have opened three times, and have been very soon silenced by the superior fire of the enemy. They have opened again this morning, and there may be an attack this evening if the weather should be more favourable, but it is now raining as hard as it can pour, and this makes every part of the work so difficult of access, and renders our muskets nearly useless, so that I think it will be postponed. I much wish it could take place this afternoon, as we have no men in the trenches, the 1st Division being on duty; tomorrow, we take the duties, and I cannot afford to lose any more men. As for myself I shall not be on duty again these three weeks, and it must be settled one way or other, before that time. Clausel[1] threatens to relieve the place, and for these last two days Lord Wellington has been looking out in front at positions to resist the attempt.

[The remainder of this letter was removed by Bingham as private.]

Letter 76   **Camp in front of Tordesillas**
                                          [30 October 1812 ?]

My dear Mother,
   I have, I am afraid missed one post having been on the constant march since I last wrote, and hardly time to eat and sleep, writing quite out of the question. Our narrative is, shortly, this:- General Souham[2] having taken command of the French army, and great reinforcements having arrived from France particularly cavalry, it was necessary to give up the ill-fated siege of the castle of Burgos, and retire; which determination was carried into effect on the night of the 21st; our battering guns, three in number, that were in fact not worth bringing away, were destroyed and part of the covering army passing through the city of Burgos, over the bridges, which were previously prepared with dung to prevent the noise of the guns and horses being heard in the castle, which commanded them within musket shot.

1. General de Division Comte Bertrand Clausel commanded the Armée du Nord.
2. General Comte Joseph Souham commanded the Army of Portugal.

Favoured by the darkness of the night, the whole of the baggage, artillery, cavalry, and a part of the infantry made the passage without being discovered, having only a random shot from a sentry now and then. The remainder (our division forming a part) left the town on our left, and being much detained by dreadful roads we arrived at Celada del Camino, by noon, of the 22nd.

I should have told you that we had been moved up to the covering army on the night of the 20th through the town so that the 21st, the first night of the retreat was the second we had been on the march. We moved again at seven o'clock on the morning of the 23rd and arrived after dark at our ground, near Torquemada, making as we computed it, a distance of nearly sixty miles in the two days. Fortunately fine weather! And after we had got into the great Madrid line, the road was broad and good. The retreat was unmolested on the 22nd. On the 23rd the enemy's cavalry followed very closely. The brigade of heavy German cavalry, having failed in a charge, the enemy's cavalry broke in on ours and there was a complete race and melee for three or four miles.[1] Lord Wellington and his staff were in the crowd, and it was who could get off the fastest. The enemy's cavalry were brought up by a square of light infantry, who stood very steadily, and behind them our cavalry rallied and formed. After all, the loss was not great. Colonel Pelly of the 16th [Light] Dragoons was taken.[2] The French who came up in no state to make any impression on our squares of infantry, suffered from their fire. On the morning of the 24th, our brigade was moved at daylight, into the town of Torquemada; a masked battery of eighteen guns was established opposite the bridge (the great road here crosses the Pisuerga, which though not a very wide, is always a deep river) and we were placed in the houses which we loop-holed to protect the battery. The remainder of the army, who moved off at the time we went into the town, was in a sad state. On the outside of Torquemada on the side where the enemy bivouacked there was a small hill, which had been hollowed

1. This refers to the action of Venta de Pozo, where Anson's (11, 12 & 16 Light Dragoons) and Bock's (1 & 2 KGL Dragoons) Brigades were overthrown by the French cavalry until brought up by the squares of Halkett's Brigade (1st & 2nd Light Battalions KGL) of the 7th Division.
2. Lieutenant Colonel Raymond Pelly, commanding the rearguard of the cavalry was wounded in two places and made prisoner.

into wine vaults, and where the inhabitants kept their wine; as the troops took up their ground after dark this was not known, and no safe guards were posted; these vaults were soon discovered, and as soon as discovered entered. The consequence was the whole army was drunk. The brigade I commanded was fortunately farthest from the scene of disorder, and it was not till towards morning that our people made the discovery. I heard a noise, and got up and found some men of the 61st drinking wine out of a camp kettle, which I immediately overset. I immediately awakened all the officers, and as we had the officers of three regiments, to somewhat about 1,000 men, we contrived to keep the people sober; and so were able to undertake the post of rear guards. About 11, the [French] advanced guard of cavalry made their appearance, and were allowed to pass nearly over the bridge, when the masked battery opened on them. This rendered them cautious throughout the day, and we retired twelve miles to the position Duenas without molestation or interruption, and fortunate that it was so! The army from drunkenness being in a complete state of disorganization. On the 25th we remained in position; the enemy made a smart attack, on the left where the Fifth Division were posted, and heavy columns were directed towards Palencia. At first they appeared to carry everything before them, but in the afternoon they were driven out of Villamuriel [de Cerrato], which they had possessed, and across the river, with the loss of about 100 prisoners.[1] At another point on our right they were successful, their cavalry charged at the bridge of Tariego [de Cerrato], which was preparing for explosion and dispersed a party of the 1st Division. Our cavalry retired and left the point in their hands, as well as a party of about sixty infantry; the immediate guard at the bridge who were made prisoners.[2] On this day the 1st Guards joined, and Robert Bingham, the same good fellow he ever was, breakfasted with me, and would have stayed to dinner, but we were ordered away to another part of the line. On the twenty-sixth, we fell back again twelve miles, to

1. This describes the combat of the Carrion, General Oswald commanding the 5th Division is criticized by Napier for failing to hold the village of Villamuriel with sufficient force. The loss of this position seriously compromised the army and Wellington launched a major counter-attack to reclaim it, which was successful.
2. The mine on the bridge at Tariego failed to explode properly, allowing the French to rush across and capture a small party, but they failed to utilize this success.

the strong position of Cabezon, which the enemy dare not attempt. Robert Bingham was just sitting down to dinner with me at the fashionable hour of noon, when we were moved in a hurry to Santovenia [de Pisuerga], to cover a ford and support the cavalry. Here we remained the whole of the twenty-seventh. On the twenty-eighth (the enemy having extended themselves along the right bank both of the Pisuerga and Duero, and pushed on as far as opposite this place) we retired also, having blown up the bridges of Cabezon, Valladolid, and the Puente Duero [-Esparragal], after the army had passed. We halted for the night on the banks of the Duero, and yesterday morning we came to this place, a report having been sent that the enemy had repaired the bridge and crossed. And our baggage having been sent away, we prepared to give battle. On our arrival we found the report not correct, a small picquet only having crossed. Our baggage did not join us till nine o'clock at night, and our situation in the middle of a dreary plain, raining hard, with nothing to eat, and nothing to make a fire with except thistles, was not very pleasant. The enemy have moved again in the direction of Toro. He will have to fight with the river in his rear, and we could always be at Valladolid before him, and then his line of operations being cut off he would be obliged to escape in some manner, very difficult if not impossible. In the meantime Soult may and will advance and occupy Madrid; but will not be able to penetrate the passes of the Guadarama. So that if we could gain a decisive advantage over Souham, he might find his retreat difficult to accomplish.

These campaigns, very interesting to lookers on, are very fatiguing to those engaged in them; and constantly being in the field at this time of the year, the shortness of the days, the difficulty of getting forage from the length of our marches, and shortness of the notice of our motions, are not very pleasant circumstances, so that notwithstanding my brigade, I rather envy Robert who is on the eve of returning to England again, having seen enough of this style of campaign, to make him enjoy what we call luxuries, viz. a bed to sleep in, a house to cover him, and regular hot meals, once or twice a day. We have lost nine men on the night of the 22nd. I don't exactly know where, but I believe that as we were passing a camp where brandy was destroyed for want of means to carry it off, they rendered themselves incapable of marching. I am afraid the loss of the army in that manner, amounts to something considerable. Our men are so greedy of drink, and so utterly careless of consequences, that a night march, a retreat, or a forced march of any kind, costs us as many men, as a smart skirmish. Whether we succeed in this campaign, I hope it may dispose the world to peace; I do not at all foresee how we are to get on. We are now only paid half of last May's subsistence, and the officers have had neither pay or bât and forage money since that time, although of the latter three hundred and sixty five days are now due; and I see no likelihood of any arrears being made up, for there is no money at Lisbon or anywhere else that I can hear of. Adieu.

Letter 77 — Camp in the position of San Cristobal near Salamanca, 10 November 1812

My dear Mother,

I have just heard that a mail for England is to be closed at 4 o'clock this afternoon, and although the time is short I cannot let it pass without dropping you a line as we have a halt today, and indeed a prospect (but a miserable one in camp at this season of the year you will allow) of continuing here for some time. I am sure I forgot from whence I dated my last letter, I think from the camp in front of Tordesillas. We broke up from that camp on the 6th, at four in the morning, and marched twenty-two miles to Castrejon [de Trabancos]. At the same hour on the seventh, we marched again to Pitiegua, twenty-four miles; wet day, and miserable ground to encamp on. The eighth we came to the gate of Salamanca, where tents were served out, and the men covered by them. I got into a clean, comfortable, peasant's house, outside the town; the first I had been in for a fortnight, and where I was most kindly and hospitably received by the inhabitants, and I hoped to have remained, if but for a few days, for rest and refreshment. Yesterday morning however, we were started at daylight, and here we are in the same position we took up in the summer to cover the siege of the forts. The French have not followed us in any force; their videttes are in force on the distant hills. Hill's force are at no great distance; somewhere near Alba de Tormes. They have been followed from Madrid by Soult, and a force commanded by the King in person; so that the whole of the two armies are concentrated near this place.

Robert Bingham left the camp at Tordesillas, two days before we did. He travelled alone, and only arrived at Salamanca the day we did. I heard he had been ill, and I searched Salamanca, three hours yesterday, without finding him. I therefore conclude he has continued his journey. He has not been long enough in the country to understand how to make himself comfortable, and on this sort of service, a good deal depends on this. I am convinced here, some people live in luxury, while others starve; and starvation always predisposes people to illness. We are sadly off for forage. The neighbouring villages are full of the other divisions of the army; of course they will not allow us to forage on them. We have three or four leagues to send for straw. Yesterday, we got none, and wood is so scarce, I was obliged to burn my tent mallet yesterday, to boil my kettle. All wood that is to be procured comes from the houses, for not a tree the height of one's knee, grows within sight of us.

All these misfortunes, incidental to a campaign, I should bear with patience, but I cannot bear with equanimity, General Clinton, who is one of the greatest fools I ever met with. He expects men are made like the little wooden figures you move and manoeuvre on a table with so much facility. He makes no allowance for weather, fatigue, or any other cause. I wish every day I was clear of him and the trade of war, altogether, if carried on by such masters. The fate of our little brigade which now musters nine hundred and seventy-five rank and file, is not yet decided. The 3rd Battalion 1st Guards, who came from Cadiz, joined the 1st Division today. This makes two brigades of Guards and it is reported that the Highland Brigade is to join our division, and that the little brigade is then to be dissolved. It is also reported that Lord Wellington will make no more provisional battalions,[1] in which case we must go home, which I would much rather do than continue where I am. I have no time to say more; Cotton the Brigade Major is going into town and will take this with him. Adieu.

1. 'Provisional battalions' were a device to retain battle hardened troops with Wellington, when their parent regiments had been reduced to such low levels of manpower, that they could no longer operate independently. Two such regiments would be amalgamated into a provisional battalion, and the excess of officers and NCOs returned to the regiment's headquarters to recruit. At this time there was only the 1 Provisional Regiment in existence, being formed from three companies of the 29th; four companies of the 2/31st; and three companies of the 2/66th; all of whom had suffered horrendous losses at Albuera.

Letter 78 Martillan, near [the] Agueda, 22 November 1812

My dear Mother,

After the most severe retreat of five days, from Salamanca to Ciudad Rodrigo, here we are once more, under cover. Marshal Soult crossed the Tormes above the town of Alba on the night of the 13th and morning of the 14th. On the 15th, our whole army was assembled in the old position of the Arapiles, and we looked forward to a second Battle of Salamanca. Soult and Souham also formed a junction, and their force amounting to between 80 and 100,000 men,[1] in the afternoon we began to retire; the weather being very unfavourable, raining as hard as it could pour, the soil being clay, and the roads at the best of time not very good, the marches were very distressing. Add to this on a retreat it is seldom prudent to have the baggage with you, so that after being drenched with rain all day, we had but the wet ground to sleep on at night. Neither ourselves nor our horses had much to eat, and both men and officers three days without bread. Our loss has been very severe, many men exhausted by fatigue and want, died on the road; others were left with their legs in a state of mortification from cold and wet. One day only did the French press us, but obtained no great advantage except picking up the stragglers. Sir Edward Paget [2] was taken, the French cavalry having penetrated between two columns; he fell amongst them being near-sighted, without recognising them.

I have enjoyed (thank God) good health and have not even a cold, although except one night at Salamanca, I have not been in a house since I was at Santovenia, the other side of Valladolid. In other respects I have suffered less than others, as my servant has always contrived to have a painted baggage cover for me to sleep on, and plenty of blankets to keep me warm; and always something to eat and drink, so that I hardly felt the loss of a tent. The last two nights we had our baggage up, and as all our comforts are by comparison, enjoyed myself, having a candle, a box to sit on, and a small table to eat off. Many corps have suffered considerably, and lost many men. Only fourteen of our brigade are missing, two only of the

1. Oman calculates that the combined forces of Soult and Souham numbered some 90,000.
2. Lieutenant General, the Honourable Sir Edward Paget 80 Foot was second-in-command of the Army.

53rd. I am sorry to tell you my brigade is dissolved, and I have again returned to the command of the 53rd, two hundred rank and file.[1] But I console myself that it will not be long before we shall meet, and talk over these affairs. This village which is within a mile of Sexmiro (where we were with Moysey this time twelvemonth) is so confined that we cannot stay long. Three troops of the 16th dragoons are with us, and we are so crowded that we have a fourth of our men under canvas. It is supposed that after Soult has dispersed his army which he must have done ere this, we shall retire into quarters of refreshment in Portugal, to be nearer our supplies. We want something of the kind; our men are in rags, and look more like beggars than soldiers. We have had no rest these eleven months, in which time we have marched two thousand miles; the army has been engaged in four sieges, and fought one general action besides repeated affairs and skirmishes. Do not we deserve some rest and a spell at home after nearly four years of this work? Adieu.

Letter 79   Santa Comba 4 December 1812

My dear Mother,

Since I last wrote I have received two letters from you &c., I am very well satisfied with our winter quarters in this beautiful country at the foot of the Estrela, two miles from Seia; and although my house does not possess the comforts of glass windows, yet after having lived so long in the field, it is quite a palace, and as the weather is open I do not feel the want of such luxuries as windows, fireplace &c. Our march from Martillan was as follows (so you may trace our route on the map) 25th Vale da Mula; here we passed the frontier; 26th Peva, a miserable village, having crossed the Coa at the bridge of Almeida; 27th Freixedas; 28th Barracao; 29th two miles to Aldeia Rioa, where there were not more than six houses. On this day we stepped into Celorico, and put our men into their new clothing. On the 30th we came to Melo, where I was quartered at one of the neatest houses I have seen for some time, and I was

1. An order dated 11 November 1812 amalgamated the remains of the two brigades of the 6th Division as a new 2 Brigade; and transferred the brigade of Stirling into the 6th Division from the 1st Division which became the 1 Brigade. Bingham no longer commanded the 2 Brigade as Colonel Samuel Venables Hinde, 32 Regiment, became senior officer by the amalgamation.

complimented by the patrona, a widow, with a present of fruit and sweetmeats, which put me in mind of old times. I never received from any person, except the mere peasants in Spain a present at my quarters of the most trifling value, and the best friend I met with in that country was an old gardener, who would insist, after I was wounded at Salamanca, upon carrying me upstairs, and who came every day afterwards whilst I stayed there to enquire after me with an offering of flowers and vegetables, and whom as I last passed Salamanca I had the pleasure of shaking by the hand.

The 1st December we came to Sao Martinho, where I was quartered at the house of Dona Francisca, the sister of my worthy hostess of the night before; who gave me grapes and the finest apples I have seen since I left England, and I left her house this morning promising to call on her. We are only two miles from it across the Val de Maceira. I shall not attempt to give you any description of this part of the country, which I have so often described before, but shall only say that the weather on the march was clear and frosty; our marches short; and we moved by regiments. We met with little inconvenience, and it has been perhaps the best way of terminating our active campaign. Adieu.

Letter 80   Santa Comba, 12 December 1812

My dear Mother,

Since I last wrote Lord Wellington has decided on a measure which I am sorry to say puts my return to England out of the question. So we must look forward to peace or some other equally fortunate event to restore me to my home, which at all times and under all circumstances I cannot help looking forward to as the end of my labours. The measure alluded to is this; he has ordered all the effective men in this country of the 2nd and 53rd Regiments to be drafted into four companies of each corps; the remaining six companies of each, comprising only officers and non-commissioned officers to return to England; these eight effective companies to be formed into a battalion, and removed into the 4th Division.[1] To be again under the command of Cole is some qualification for the disappointment I feel

1. Bingham was to command this amalgamated regiment of the 2 and 2/53rd, to be known as the 2 Provisional Regiment by order 6 December 1812. On the same day the remains of the 2/24th and 2/58th were amalgamated into the 3 Provisional

at having my return delayed; from which delay I see no advantage likely to arise to myself. Lieutenant colonels rise by gradation, and those people of that rank who are enjoying themselves at home, get rank equally with those who are fagging here. As for the rewards, they go no further than Lord Wellington. The end of our labour will be making him a duke; but as to any reward, that is quite out of the question. The army is not a little out of humour with his Lordship at present, who (in a circular letter he has addressed to the generals commanding divisions) has laid the blame of the losses in the last retreat to the want of energy and ability of the officers commanding brigades, regiments and companies. He affirms, the army suffered no privations except such as they were exposed to from the severity of the weather; but the wearied, famished wretches who perished by numbers on the roads, and were left unburied, and half devoured by dogs and wolves, as an encouragement I suppose to others, is a refutation of this accusation. The army were (for the greatest part) twice, three days without bread, and the whole were six months in arrear of pay; having no money to buy salt or vegetables after marching all day. The time the men ought to have rested was employed in cooking, in fact the men were worn out with constant marching, having travelled over two thousand miles of country in the last eleven months; each man loaded with sixty rounds of ammunition, a greatcoat and a blanket. Are these no privations? It is however always the practise of the great to kick from under them the stool by which they have been exalted. The headquarters of the 4th Division is at San Joao de Pesqueira, six days march from this, on the Douro. To that neighbourhood we go in a few days; in the course of next week perhaps. I only hope the weather will be a little more settled than it has been or rather is at present. It has rained without intermission these last two days, and the valleys are all under water.

I am so comfortably settled here that I have no wish to move for the winter. The country about the village is beautiful, and the walks round pleasant and interesting, and supplies abundant. I have had woodcocks at my table, which as there has yet been no severe weather to drive them from the mountains is rare. Adieu, direct to me in future 4th Division. I leave the 6th without regret.

Regiment. The 2 Provisional Regiment was placed in Major General Sir William Anson's Brigade of the 4th Division, which also comprised 3/27th, 1/40th 1/48th and 1 company of 5/60th.

Chapter Four

Operations in 1813

Despite the inglorious retreat that ended the 1812 campaign, Wellington was in a strong position. His army was steadily increasing in numbers and improving in quality, whereas the French armies were being bled dry to replace the horrendous losses incurred in Russia. Wellington misled the French by remaining with a corps near Ciudad Rodrigo facing their entrenched lines, while the bulk of the army, led by General Graham, performed a wide turning movement through the mountainous regions of the north. These movements outflanked the French and they were forced to abandon their defences and retire rapidly.

The French forces to the great relief of Wellington's army abandoned Burgos, but stood at Vitoria confident of success and were heavily defeated by Wellington. The French rapidly retired across the Pyrenees to lick their wounds, leaving a few garrisons at key points. Wellington split his forces between maintaining command of the Pyrenean passes while actively besieging San Sebastian and blockading Pamplona. Soult was given the job of sorting out the French forces and he launched a daring strike aimed at relieving these two fortresses. He nearly succeeded but was eventually beaten at Sorauren and forced to flee back into France. San Sebastian was eventually stormed at a high cost to the British infantry and Pamplona was starved into submission. The year ended with Wellington's forces driving deep into southern France itself with actions at the Bidassoa, Nivelle, Nive and St Pierre. The 2 Provisional Regiment had a prominent part to play in all of these operations.

My dear Madam,

I received on my arrival here your letter of the 10th ultimo, and am glad to hear you received all mine and that you are going on so well &c, &c.

We have not at all changed for the better in point of situation, we are here amongst rocks and precipices which have not even the picturesque to recommend them; the first two days, the fog was so thick that we could not see the end of the street, to day is somewhat better but the cold is great, from the high situation of the town, several degrees beyond Santa Comba, and the houses are not [at] all calculated to keep out the cold; my room is like a large old barn, with chinks in the floor, that I can plainly see everything that passes in the stable below, a heavy carved oak ceiling, over which the rats gallop with great rapidity, dirty white-washed walls, no glass in the windows, worse ten times worse than any castle rackrent you can imagine.

We had fortunately very fine weather for our march the whole of which I walked from choice, Vila Cortes [da Serra] the first day, a village completely ruined by being on the public road; the priest at whose house I was billeted, lamented his hard fate, he said his house was an inn without the emolument, scarce a day passes without a detachment passing through and each detachment he says rob him; if a day should elapse without a detachment passing, and a single officer comes, he is sure to make for the padre's house. The day before we were there, the servant of an officer of the 48th Regiment stole the key of the stable, almost the only moveable appertaining to the house. The door of the room in which I slept, had been used for fuel. I could do no more than pity him. The next day I was billeted on the small cottage of the prior of Celorico, whose fate was nearly as bad. He had two good houses, one at Celorico, the other at Lamego, both occupied by officers, and he had retired to this cottage to be out of the way. He had living in the house a young lady that passed for his niece but appeared to merit a more intimate title. There was a fine little boy that was denominated an orphan, but who looked too like both the prior and the niece to be mistaken. I was very agreeably (and as far as their means went) hospitably entertained, and passed a very pleasant day with them, although the place was so small that there was only one sitting room with two closets as bed chambers. Trancoso, our next march looked a good deal better than when we were last there; it had been cleaned. I paid a visit to the grate of the convent; Doña Bernardo looked older, though still handsome.

The Juiz de Fora gave our youngsters a dance in the evening, and all the ladies in the town were put in requisition. I did not hear anything of it, till the next morning. I was quartered at the principle house in the town, which was large, gloomy and cold. I did not see anything of the people of the house who kept their own apartments; they were very merry however, a deformed negro servant was playing for them, as I understood from my servant, on a guitar, and dancing all the afternoon in wooden shoes, not a very pleasant thing for me a stranger and who, fatigued with the day's march, wanted to go to sleep. Adieu.

Letter 82   Ranhados, 30 January 1813

My dear Mother,

I have missed one packet but will not let another pass without dropping you a line &c.

Since I last wrote I have spent three very pleasant days with General Cole at St. Joao de Pesquiera &c &c.

I met at General Coles', Colonel Ellis[1] of the 23rd, who told me he had seen not more than three leagues from this place at a grand chasse last year, eleven wild boars. I am quite agog to go wild boar hunting, to see the immense savage beast as he is described. Adieu.

Letter 83   Ranhados, 12 February 1813

My dear Richard,[2]

I am quite ashamed when I recollect the date of my last letter &c, &c.

1. Lieutenant Colonel Henry Walton Ellis commanded 1/23rd. He lost two fingers at Albuera, was wounded at Badajoz and severely wounded at Salamanca.
2. Written to Major General Richard Bingham, his elder brother, whom it is recorded, was on the staff at Malta at this time, but the letter appears to have been sent to Sicily.

It is now too long since it occurred, to enter into the afflicting details of the siege of Burgos, where the division, the 6th, which I then belonged to, was employed.

I retained the command of the brigade not only during the siege, but during the subsequent retreat, when it was my good fortune to have kept the regiments well together and our loss from stragglers was very trifling. Lord Wellington gave us several opportunities, had the enemy come on, of doing something; when the brigade was detached from the division we were placed in the village of Torquemada to support the artillery, and prepared to form square, covered the retreat of the cavalry as far as the position of Duenas that same day, but nothing came near us. On our arrival at Salamanca my brigade was broken up, but I commanded the same three regiments as far as Ciudad Rodrigo, and covered the baggage of one of the columns as far as San Munoz the day Sir Edward Paget was taken. On our arrival at our cantonments, the Queen's and 53rd were formed into a provisional battalion consisting of four companies of each regiment and we were removed to the Fourth Division (General Cole's).

I command at present General William Anson's Brigade consisting of the [2nd] Provisional Battalion, 3rd Battalion 27th, 1 Battalion 40th, 1st Battalion 48th Regiments, whilst he is on a court martial at Lamego. At a brigade field day Tuesday last, at which I commanded, we had 1,859 men under arms, which in these days is considered a strong brigade.

We expect to take the field again in March or April, not before; I am anxious to see what will be done in the ensuing campaign. I trust we shall have no attacks of regular strong fortifications without proper means; attacking forts with musketry does not answer.

The brigade of blues and lifeguards have left Lisbon, and the hussars have landed to supply their place;[1] we cannot take the field till the green corn will allow us to subsist them, and as in Spain the army that has the superiority always wins the game, we cannot

---

1. The statement is unclear; two squadrons each of the 1 and 2 Life Guards and the Royal Horseguards were marching to join the army where they were to form a new brigade. Another brigade under Major Colquhoun Grant composed of the 10, 15 and 18 Hussars had also just landed on route to the army. The 4 Dragoon Guards, 9 Hussars and 2 KGL Hussars were ordered home.

move without them. I trust this year the cavalry will retrieve their character; the army was loud in their dispraise last year. Adieu &c.

Letter 84 Ranhados, 22 February 1813

My dear Mother,

There seems no immediate chance of a move, the army in general are far from healthy and as yet no forage on the ground to enable the cavalry to live. Well, when the orders come it will be time enough as rest is everything; I have no objection to remain in these quarters till April or May, when we shall be very strong; I mean my battalion, 700 bayonets.

I have dined out in this country this week with a young Portuguese gentleman or fidalgo as they are called, who lives with his mother in a Quinta about two miles from this; the mama, who is young enough to be the wife of the fidalgo, did the honours of the house. Ten were invited; only six sat down to a dinner that would have served sixty; exceedingly well dressed after the Portuguese manner, a capital dessert and coffee immediately after dinner. We sat down about five o'clock and were at home at Ranhados at eight; no time lost. The wine made on his own estate excellent. The lady of the house was pleasant, and lively, and did the honours of the table very well. Nothing would serve the gentlemen, but they must ride home with us. It was a dreadful road to be sure, I do not know how we should have found it without their assistance, but they are tiresomely polite and to please a Portuguese, you should have studied the fourteen books of Chinese ceremony, there are so many bows to be made at the top of the steps, and again at the bottom of the steps, that there is no end of it, even after these gentlemen had turned out to show us the road, there was no getting them to ride first, but they must keep their post in the rear, and direct you which way to go. Nothing I suppose could have induced the fidalgo to ride on my right hand. The conversation during dinner was not very brilliant; we talked about coursing and shooting, and shooting and coursing till we were tired. If we had not been relieved by a poodle dog that could walk on its hind legs, and tumble, we should have been badly off indeed; it was made worse by our being bad Portuguese scholars. To my shame be it spoken, I have been three years in the country and cannot converse fluently, but it's seldom we get any person beyond

174

a peasant to speak to; now there is the patron of this house as he is called a fidalgo, and who is a Major in the Ordenanca;[1] there is no associating with him. He locks himself up with such companions in such a room, and he drinks brandy and eats garlic. They say we are proud, but there is no standing this.

Letter 85   Ranhados, 23 February 1813

My dear Mansel,

Your two letters entrusted to General Brisbane[2] reached me this afternoon. I hope to be in time to save the packet. I have not written lately expecting to have heard of your arrival in Lisbon, as you said your stay in England was to be so short. I do not regret your not having come, as it would have put you to great trouble and expense, without answering the end proposed. I had been partly promised the light infantry of the brigade, if not of the division for you, which would have been a temptation, but the fact is my dear fellow, the army is so sickly that there is little chance I think of our opening the campaign much sooner than the time we crossed the Agueda, last year; the accounts from the rear if only half of them are true, are frightful; from the absence of General Anson on a court martial, I have commanded the brigade nearly a month, and fifty men have died in that time, two hundred and fifty-nine are today sick present, and eight hundred and fifty-four absent. This fatal sickness diminishes our force in this country to nearly nothing, and we are considered one of the most healthy and effective brigades in the army. The 2nd Provisional have only twenty-six [officers] present on the list, and five hundred and twenty-seven effective rank and file; our numbers in the rear are however considerable.

Army news I have none to give you. It is reported Sir William Erskine[3] has thrown himself out of a window and has broken his

1. The Ordenanca was effectively a levee en masse, with little organization and usually armed with pikes.
2. Major General Thomas Brisbane was originally appointed to the Staff on 7 January, but took command of a brigade in Picton's 3rd Division *vice Kempt,* on 25 March.
3. Major General Sir William Erskine Bt., had commanded the Light Division for a period in 1810 and Hill's cavalry on the advance to Madrid. He was, however, declared insane and cashiered but committed suicide.

neck, in a fit of frenzy fever. It is also said George Murray[1] is coming out again as Quarter Master General; everybody hopes it may be the case. I have not heard to what part of the army your friend Brisbane is to go; Pakenham[2] commands the 6th Division during Clinton's absence. Adieu.

Letter 86   Ranhados, 27 February 1813

My dear Mansel,

Tomorrow we move I believe towards the Coa, the order says a short march and this is all we know. I wish we could have remained here, we had for ourselves at least plenty of forage, and our people remarkably healthy, and as the fine weather had set in we should have increased in strength surprisingly; we have today five hundred and thirty fit for duty, twenty-eight sick, of whom fourteen are to be left behind, and we have twenty-nine recruits for the Queen's to be up in eight days, so that we hope to begin the campaign with six hundred men if they will let us alone till the beginning of April (for this movement is certainly not the opening of the campaign) we should start with seven hundred which would ensure our being tolerably strong in the day of action.

I do not enter this campaign with much heart, the army is so sickly and four months in arrear of pay, and ill supplied even then with provisions and all these things you know are so essential that there is little hope of affecting anything without them.

[The remainder of the letter has been removed by Bingham]

Letter 87   Almofala, 6 March 1813

My dear Mother,

We were last week on the march which prevented my writing; had I written I could not have sent it.

---

1. Major General Sir George Murray had served as Wellington's QMG until 1811 when he had returned home. He did return in 1813 and served in the same capacity until the termination of the war.
2. Major General Sir Edward Michael Pakenham was brother-in-law to Wellington; he is perhaps more famous for his death at the Battle of New Orleans in 1814.

We came to this place from Ranhados in four days very easy stages, it not being more than forty-one miles. We had very pleasant weather, and altogether I like this place better than the last; we are out of the mountains and our rides and walks more practicable. I have been able to secure a fortnight's forage which will be sufficient I hope till the grass is up which it soon will be, for the weather is quite pleasant, and I had left off fires before I marched from Ranhados. I do not see any immediate prospect of a move; we are by no means prepared yet so that I think we may calculate on a fortnight to three weeks or even a month's rest before our troubles begin. There is nothing but fox hunting and plays going on at and in the neighbourhood of headquarters where Lord Wellington is I understand in his usual spirits.

I gave up the command of the brigade the day before we marched to General Anson; as I was not to continue in the command I was not displeased at this circumstance, the temporary command yielding neither pleasure nor profit. Some of the regiments are in bad order and as I never can be a sleeping partner where my duty is concerned, I only got ill will by putting people right who would in general rather be wrong and did no good for as soon as my reign was over the old bad habits will return.

There has been a trifling affair in the south between the 50th Regiment and a party of the French who thought to surprise them.[1]

This place is three leagues from Almeida and two from the famous pass of Barba del Puerco which I intend to explore today.

Except the 4th, none of the other divisions of the army have moved. General Cole is at Pesquiera[2] seven and General Anson at Mata de Lobos three miles from this.

Tomorrow we are to march to the latter place, to hear divine service for the first time since we have been with the division; the establishment of chaplains is much too small, one to a division. Now there are seven regiments in the division which is more duty

1. Foy had conceived the idea of surprising Hill's outlying detachment, consisting of the 50 Regiment at Bejar. However Colonel Harrison, commanding the 50th, was cautious by nature and had repaired the town's crumbling walls. Unknown to the French, the 6 Cacadores had been sent to strengthen the position. The surprise attack failed at the gates of the town and the French were forced to flee precipitately before being trapped.
2. I cannot find a village of this name in the vicinity, I suspect it should read 'Penha de Aguia'.

than one person can perform. There should be one to each brigade as it is the appearance once now and then of the chaplain serves to remind us we are protestants and no more; in general although the order on their appointment stated they were selected by the most eminent prelates I do not think they do much credit to their choice; the man who is with this division of the army and has been with it three years is the best I have seen; his name is Jenkins. Adieu.

Letter 88   Almofala, 12 March 1813

My dear Mansel,

Your letter of the 8th found us on the banks of the Agueda, instead of the Tagus, making every preparation for the ensuing campaign instead of embarkation. I was certain Lord Wellington would not let us go; he said to General Cole that he had got into a scrape about the formation of the provisional battalions, but said not a syllable about complying with any orders from the Horse Guards he might have received on the subject. He concluded by saying he would rather have a few men that had been some time in the country than double the number sent out fresh from England.

Tomorrow I go to Ciudad Rodrigo to dine with his Excellency who has removed his head quarters to that place for the installation of Sir Lowry Cole as Knight of the Bath. There are fifty officers asked to dine and one hundred and fifty to a ball and supper in the evening. It is seven good leagues from this and the weather likely to be wet, so I have not a very pleasant prospect before me.

We had very fine weather for our march and crossed the Coa at the foot of the mountains near Pinhel and passed close to Castelo Rodrigo from which we are distant two leagues. Our battalion is on the right of the division which extends to the left as far as where the Coa and Agueda run into the Douro.

We are not likely to take the field before the first week in April by which time the green corn will be very high and I hope the army very strong. We are healthy, but several regiments in the division are far from being so.

An alteration has taken place in the establishment of company mules. The captain's winter or short bât and forage allowance is increased £10. The mule that formerly carried the camp kettles is to be more efficient and to have three bell tents as a load instead, and tin kettles are to be served out instead of the iron, and to be

178

carried by the men as you may recollect the Portuguese troops did. I doubt whether the plan will answer; the first action away will go the kettles.

[The remainder of the letter was removed by Bingham]

Letter 89 Almofala, 21 March 1813

My dear Mother,

[The start of the letter removed as private by Bingham]

No talk of moving at present. General Murray, Tryon's friend, our Quarter Master General came from Plymouth to Freixedas in eight days, a very quick passage; everybody is delighted to see him again at the head of that department and 'Caleb Quoton' as Colonel Gordon[1] is called removed. Theory, alone, in this country will not do; the person who directs from behind his desk at the Horse Guards is not likely to answer for active service in the field.

Auchmuty, who was General Campbell's Brigade Major, has joined General Cole who has now a better selection of Staff officers, with more talent than any other general of division in the army, and does great credit to the person who selected them. They all live in great harmony and good humour and it is a great relief to me occasionally to enjoy their society.

I gave my sister an account last week of Lord Wellington's fête at Ciudad Rodrigo. I understand another is in preparation to be given by his staff (family they are called) to the Earl on his being made a Knight of the Garter; as the aides-de-camp are in general men of rank and fortune no expense will be spared and I think I shall be tempted once more to emerge from my solitude. These parties are no expense to the person attending them. You get a billet in the town, take your bed with you, and get forage for your horses from the commissary. Adieu.

1. Colonel James Willoughby Gordon was a political appointment by the Duke of York. Wellington was not happy with the loss of Murray to a post in Ireland and soon discovered that Gordon was inept. He campaigned hard to have him removed and eventually succeeded in having Murray recalled in his place.

Letter 90   **Almofala, 29 March 1813**

My dear Mansel,

We have arrived at the strength of five hundred and seventy rank and file, exclusive of sick present but have no idea when we move. Money is as usual much wanting; the army is not paid beyond 24th November and supplies of every kind getting scarce, cattle especially. It is said the First Division is on the march to Oporto to feed on salt provisions, having been on half rations for some time will show what we can do this campaign, but I think it will be our last effort. A very formidable party is forming in Spain against Lord Wellington, and you know that the Spaniards (who to do them the credit hate us as much as possible) are very much dissatisfied with our inaction, so that unless the Russians gain ground I am not very sanguine as to our success. We may and I believe we shall put the French beyond the Ebro, but that will be doing nothing unless the Spaniards can organize a force sufficient to prevent their crossing it again, or with our assistance driving them further back; but those who trust to the Spaniards trust to a broken reed.

We are all praying for rain, that we may get some grass for our cattle; forage is very scarce but we have had a constant supply of corn since we have joined the Fourth Division.

Letter 91   **Almofala, 6 April 1813**

My dear Mansel,
[Extract from larger letter]

Nothing has taken place since I last wrote and both the army and the battalion remain in status quo. It is indeed reported Hill's corps have moved forward as far as Oropesa but we have not made nor do we expect to make any movement on this side the water.

Letter 92   **Almofala, 12 April 1813**

My dear Mansel,

This leaves us in the same situation as when I wrote a few days since. We have had some rain which has done great service in the way of grass and green corn, articles that you have no care about, yet it is not believed that we are likely to move before next month although it is said head quarters are to be at Fuenteguinaldo for the purpose of hutting the First Brigade of Guards who arrived at Oporto about the beginning of the month and will require some time to get round again. It is not improbable they may move up on the right bank of the Douro to turn that river, which if they do not some other troops will. Our tents have arrived and we expect to be complete in our camp equipment in a few days. The Hussar Brigade is moving up and we expect to have seven hundred British sabres in the field; I hope they will be better wielded, that is, to more purpose than they have ever hitherto been.

The provisional battalion is upwards of six hundred rank and file, exclusive of sick present; another month ought to give us one hundred more, perhaps it may fifty, so that we have a fair chance of bringing five hundred into action especially as many of them have served four, most of them two campaigns, and ought to be worth double that number of men just arrived from England.

Letter 93   Almofala, 16 April 1813

My dear Mansel,

Next week it is reported we are to move and many are the speculations as to our line of march; some say we shall cross the Douro here and go up by Torre [de Moncorvo] and Zamora but I do not think this will be the case. The cars for our division are collected here, which would hardly have been the case if we were to have proceeded by the other side of the river. As usual Lord Wellington is so close that all is conjecture. Hill's corps it is believed will be augmented to twenty-five thousand men including a corps of Spaniards under the Duke Del Infantado,[1] it is also said a corps is to be embarked at Alicante to proceed to Tortosa to threaten the rear of Suchet's army and to render the line of the Ebro indefensible.[2] We talk I assure you very grandly not of the Tormes and Douro, but of the Pyrenees and Ebro.[3]

1. This is incorrect; it should read the Duque Del Parque.
2. An Anglo-Sicilian force of approximately 14,000 British and 7,000 Spanish commanded by Sir John Murray, was holding Alicante. The Spanish General Elio and his 'Second Army' lay close by, totalling 30,000 men.
3. It is noticeable how confident the army was of success in the forthcoming campaign, despite their sufferings in the last.

181

Letter 94 Almofala, 2 May 1813

My dear Mansel,

We are all in anxious preparation for a grand inspection which is to take place by Lord Wellington on Tuesday; on the 29th ultimo the strength of rank and file [of the 4th Division] was six thousand six hundred and sixty four, of which four thousand and eighty-five were British. Since that several drafts have arrived from hospital, and we are likely to be considerably stronger on that day; the provisional battalion we had seven joined yesterday, three today, and shall have exclusive of the working party building huts, five hundred and sixty under arms.

Letter 95 Almofala, 10 May 1813

My dear Mother,

The weather this week has been in general wet notwithstanding which we were inspected Saturday by Lord Wellington, who was satisfied. The ground however was very bad and we did not manoeuvre altogether so well as we ought to have done, but the fault certainly did not lie with the troops who had never been together before. There were nearly seven thousand men under arms and for lookers on the spectacle must have been beautiful. The army was never in better order, never better equipped so that, please God, we ought to do something next campaign. We understand we are to march the 15th and I believe all the divisions in the rear will be in motion in a few days. Lord Wellington looked very well and was very civil to me at a luncheon, or rather dinner, he took at General Cole's after the review was over. Sir Lowry detained me and I returned yesterday morning. I met there Lord March[1] and a Mr Russell, nephew of the Duke of Bedford.[2] The former would be thought a fine young man in any situation; he is very lively and somewhat forward, but this is not his fault; but of education and station in life. Sir Lowry appeared for the first time with two stars; Lord Wellington with only that of the garter. The Prince of Orange[3]

1. Captain Charles Earl of March, 52 Regiment (as of 8 April 1813), ADC to Lord Wellington.
2. Lieutenant the Honourable Francis Russell, 7 Foot, ADC to Sir Lowry Cole.
3. Colonel His Royal Highness William Prince of Orange served as an extra ADC to Wellington 1811–13.

was not with him; indeed he was but slenderly attended, only four aides-de-camp with him.

A great part of the army have crossed the Douro in Portugal and are to proceed on the right bank of that river. I wish we had been fortunate enough to have been of this party as it would have been new ground to us.

The absence of the Paymaster is a serious grievance to us; we have not received any pay since December, and on the 24th of last month £150 was due to me. It is most severely felt by the junior officers, who are absolutely starving on their pound of meat and pound and [a] half of bread which goes but little way with young gentlemen who have been used to gorge themselves at a regimental mess.

Letter 96   Almofala, 10 May 1813

My dear Mansel,

The rains which have fallen during the last fortnight have retarded our movements, and leave us in the same state as when I last wrote. We however understand that on the 15th the whole army is to be in motion, which I shall not be sorry for as I am quite tired of an indolent life.

Saturday we were reviewed by Lord Wellington. It rained the whole of our march to the ground, six miles from this, and when we began to move the whole field was a swamp. We however got over the thing better than I expected and as my battalion was the first to march past I remained and saw the whole division. The Welsh Fusiliers were certainly, though few in number, in the best order. The 7th [Regiment] were neither as to men or officers what they were. The 20th is a fine looking veteran regiment, and will make play I am sure if they ever get near enough to Johnny. I send you a card of the division, which pray don't let the newspapers get hold of, but burn as soon as you have looked it over. Exclusive of the number under arms we have large working parties building hospitals and making roads down to the Douro, which river a great part of the army will pass; two brigades of heavy cavalry and one of light crossed as low down as Oporto and proceeded to Braga, and will enter Spain by the Tras-os-Montes. The 3rd and 5th Divisions, Pack's and Bradford's Brigades are also said to be about to move on that side of the river and it is said many other troops are to follow. Roads have been made down to the Douro close to our left, but whether we are to cross or no we cannot divine. Today Lord Wellington sees the Life Guards and Blues, on Friday the Light Division, and on Saturday it is said we all start.

The 2nd Provisional Battalion today is six hundred and thirty-two, exclusive of sick present; we ought to carry six hundred of them as far as Salamanca.

[The remainder of the letter was removed by Bingham as being purely on regimental business.]

Letter 97   Almofala, 16 May 1813

My dear Mansel,

I am quite aware that after we march much time will elapse before I shall be able to send letters. I therefore take the last opportunity before we move, although I have written so lately and not having had a mail this week I have so little to say. It is uncertain whether we march tomorrow or the day after. The 7th Division are today on this side of the Coa; the 6th cross that river today. It is yet uncertain whether we cross the Douro or not, or rather the arrangement is not known, for since Murray has returned to the Quarter Master General's office things go on in their old train; there is no such confusion as when Colonel Gordon was at the head of affairs. Mr Commissary Fernandez who has entered on his functions in that department is gone to Torre de Moncorvo to prepare a million rations, and he says we are to move by that route. Blackie[1] arrived yesterday from Lisbon. He passed the Hussar Brigade on the way up; they have arrived with the army in as good order as when they landed at Lisbon, perhaps ere they reach Burgos their note may be changed.

Wonderful liberality! We are to be paid up to the 24th of January before we start, but we are warned it will be a long time before we are to expect another issue.

We shall start from this with six hundred and forty rank and file, but many of them won't get beyond the first three days march, but it will I think ensure at this period of the year our having five hundred late in the campaign.

The affair near Alicante as far as we can learn seems to have been

---

1. I believe the spelling to be a mistake and that he refers to Lieutenant Colonel Sir Edward Blakeney, 7 Foot.

altogether a good one and proves that if the Spaniards won't fight, the British will for them;[1] the many easy victories the French troops have gained over the Spaniards have done them no good.

The celebrated Mina[2] if you can believe his own accounts has been very successful in Navarre.

The 4th Provisional Battalion composed of the 30 and 44 Regiments[3] is ordered home and have been taken leave of in the orders of today. I should think no great loss to the army.

The route has just arrived and is as follows:-

18th Escalhao; 19th cross the Douro at Bonca d'Alva;[4] 20th halt; 21st halt; 22nd Fornos and Logoaca; 23rd Vila de Ala; 24th Sendim; 25th Miranda [do Douro].

The division join and move together after the 22nd. Adieu.

Letter 98   **Camp near Vila de Ala, 22 May 1813**

My dear Mansel,

Your two letters of the 20th and 25th ultimo met me the day we left Almofala. On starting we only left nine men in general hospital, which is now established at Escalhao, a place to which no person (not even the most determined hospital ranger) will ever wish to go, I should think. It is to be under the superintendence of Lieutenant Colonel Royall.[5] We march therefore six hundred and fifty-two rank and file, of whom we have today only three sick. On the 19th we crossed the Douro, our brigade in boats at Barca de Alva, the other two brigades lower down at a flying bridge at Pocinho. The 7th and 6th Divisions had crossed before and we are followed by the Hussar Brigade and the pontoons, the 18 Portuguese Brigade and 9 Portuguese Brigade[6] accompanied the 6th and 7th Divisions; another column move by Vila Real and Braganca consisting of the 1st, 3rd

1. Murray's force won a victory over Marshal Suchet at Castalla on 13 April 1813, before embarking his army to land at Tarragona. The comments against the Spanish forces seems to be unfair on this occasion as Whittingham's Spanish at Castalla stood bravely and drove the French attacks off.
2. General Francisco Espozy Minas, a celebrated guerrilla leader.
3. Composed of the 2/30th and 2/44th.
4. I cannot find this village on modern maps.
5. Lieutenant Colonel William Carr Royall, 61 Regiment.
6. The Portuguese line regiments had two battalions each; this is what Bingham refers to as brigades.

and 5th Divisions, Pack's and Bradford's Portuguese Brigades of infantry, three English, one Portuguese, one Spanish Brigade of cavalry which are I understand to all appearance excellent. Sixty pieces of artillery are said to be attached to this column, chiefly nine pounders. It is said we are to form a junction somewhere about Alcanices on the frontier of Spain. Lord Wellington was yesterday at Rodrigo having with him only the Light Division and two brigades of cavalry; he is to join at Tamames, Hill's corps of 25,000 men and move on Salamanca; the Tormes most likely will be given up, and we think the Douro. The Esla, a river that runs from Benavente to the Douro is expected to be defended, but it is doubted whether we shall not have gained that river before the French have collected force sufficient to afford a considerable resistance. A superb battering train is all ready at Corunna including ten eighteen inch mortars with which we must pound the castle of Burgos about their ears. Every exertion has been made to complete the army and we are equipped in a very superior style, not a single article wanting, and every department brushed up, particularly the artillery. Three out of four commanding officers have been sent off as too old within as many weeks.

All things go on quietly and well in the division. The duty must be done and well done, but there are no long lectures on nonsense, but standing orders have been carefully collected and are expected to be strictly adhered to. I never saw a division march so well; to be sure we have had as yet only short marches, and move early, but the weather is already hot when the sun is up. In short, things go on so pleasantly and differently from what they did last year that except to see my friends, I have no wish to return to England and the goose step.

Notwithstanding the French never have been in this province there is nothing to be procured except forage. The villages are very poor and quite as dirty as any other part of Portugal. I prefer much being in camp; we generally have shade for our tents.

I saw the 11th and 61st the day before yesterday. The former had five hundred and seventy, the latter about one hundred less; they are both in high order. Pakenham commands the division, Clinton not having as yet arrived; he is not much wished for.[3] Adieu.

1. This comment is slightly obscure as Clinton still commanded the 6th Division (Pakenham in his absence), Bingham's Provisional Regiment was in the 4th Division and therefore unaffected by this situation, but his dislike of Clinton still remained.

Letter 99   Camp near Vila de Ala, 23 May 1813

My dear Mother,

We left Almofala last Tuesday not sorry after so long a spell of winter quarters once more to take the field; so natural to all is the desire of change, the remembrance of the fatigues of last year was totally obliterated, and everyone started with a cheerful heart. Our first day's march was a very short one to Escalhao, where we got into bad quarters. This town is chosen as a station for a hospital and except it is with a view of making it disagreeable to those who are not really ill but retire from the army under pretence of being so, I cannot conceive what should have determined the choice. It is situated amongst rocks, near the confluence of the Agueda and the Douro, without wood, with scarce water enough for the inhabitants in the summer, and with the expectation of being the most aguish place in the country; but it is a large village and by looking on the map appears an eligible position for embarking on the Douro, when twenty-four or thirty-six hours would land you at Oporto so that the hospital could (in case of accidents) easily be removed.

On the 19th we marched at four o'clock, day break, having sent our baggage off at one o'clock, seven miles down hill nearly the whole way brought us to Barca de Alva. The Douro here has been sunk far below the level of the surrounding country and although both on this side of the river as well as the other you fancy yourself on a level country, you find on approaching the river that you have a mountain to descend to get to the water; with four large boats that held one hundred and fifty men each, and our baggage having nearly all passed before we got there, we were soon safely landed in the province of Tras-os-Montes by nine o'clock, but then all our troubles were to begin. We had the hill to ascend, a narrow goat path the only road; it was an exceedingly hot day, and more severely felt as being the first. We were two hours reaching the top of the hill but the men were very much exhausted, and it was three o'clock in the afternoon before we arrived at Macores, which place many of the men were so knocked up that they did not reach before dark. It would have been better not to have made so long a march, which might have been managed; we had our tents with us and there was no absolute necessity to put us into a town. It was quite a rarity to be in a village in which neither French nor English troops

187

had ever been before. The appearance of comfort, the fences entire, the vine props perfect, the gardens in order, the trees, elm, in high luxuriance, after the naked country about Almofala, made us amends for our fatiguing march. My billet except that it was full of bugs, was comfortable, and there was a garden to it in better order than I had seen for some time, and plenty of strawberries. Few however were ripe, such as were given to me with cheerfulness by the abbot, who was living there with his sister, and who had been but a short time before, presented to the living, which was not valuable, and he lamented being buried alive amongst these mountains without society. He appeared ignorant, and the lady was vain and ugly. We halted the 20th which quite set us up again; as it proved quite as hot as the preceding day I was not sorry to have the shade of the town for our people. On the 21st to avoid a bad road we went round by Carvicais to Mos passing another small village called Felgar, or some name like it, for it is in none of the maps. It is one of the most romantic in situation of any I have seen in Portugal. Mos was a wretched place and I was much better pleased to have my tent pitched on clean grass under the shade of elm trees, in which two nightingales notwithstanding the noise of drums and bugles, the smoke and bustle of camp, kept their station the whole night. At Mos is an old castle with nothing very particular about it. On the 22nd we started about six o'clock, the weather being very cool and pleasant; passed again through Carvicais, which is on the great road from Torre de Moncorvo to Miranda [do Douro]. The roads are excellent and although the country is hilly it is not mountainous; very steep however when you descend to rivers, that are all sunk below the level of the surrounding country. A short march brought us to Fornos where we had another pleasant camp amongst the elms. General Cole, and one of his aides-de-camp Auchmuty, breakfasted with me. I dined in the town with General Anson; it is a wretched place, and I did not envy the General being under cover; our camp now being so much preferable, especially as I carry with me a nice camp table about the size of a backgammon board and a stool which tends in some measure to make this letter so long a one.

The villages in this province are very miserable, and quite as filthy as those in the other parts of Portugal, nor are there any fidalgo's houses as you meet with elsewhere, but the war never having extended here, the diversified face of the country and the trees, render it much pleasanter than any other part we have lately been stationed in. The farms are in general well cultivated and the people seem robust and healthy. Such are the blessings of peace contrasted with the miseries of war; for it makes this province, which in other times would seem a desert, a most abundant country, and the fine plains we have left a desert; let no one wish for war who has not had some experience of the misfortunes attending on it. Tomorrow we go to Sendim and the day following to Miranda, which we understand is a good town. Next week I suppose we shall meet the French on the Esla, the only river that will on this side present a momentary barrier to our progress; I say momentary, for with our pontoon bridge we shall cross where we like, not expecting much resistance as the enemy can hardly by the time we arrive there, have collected sufficient force effectually to oppose our progress. Every branch of the army is this year better managed than I have ever seen it before, and if it pleases providence, I hope for more brilliant and what is better more substantial results than we have hitherto attained. Adieu.

Letter 100 Camp near Ampudia, 6 June 1813

My dear Mansel,

Many thanks for your regular correspondence &c.

In four days more we shall be at Burgos and shall be able to form some judgement of what the French mean to do. At present we see nothing of them; reports vary as to their strength when they shall have assembled, some making them thirty-five, some seventy-five thousand, but they must show more than even the latter number to check us; our army continues effective beyond former example, I have only one subject for the general hospital.

We ought to be much obliged to the enemy that they did not oppose us on the Esla; the river was nowhere (near where we passed) fordable, and some men of the 7th Division were drowned. So little were they advised of our movements that a small picket of cavalry were taken at Almendra, and by an intercepted letter from General Villatte, who commanded at Salamanca, it appears they thought the whole army was advancing on them; part of their rear-guard stayed too long near that city and were taken.

On the 2nd there was a very brilliant affair of cavalry in which the Hussar Brigade commanded by Grant were the only people engaged. They behaved exceedingly well, and took upwards of two hundred prisoners; it was in fact as far as we can learn the best affair the cavalry have performed in the country. The French opposed to the hussars three regiments and three guns; our artillery was not up.[1]

Since the 2nd we have not seen a Frenchman; we have marched about twelve or fourteen miles a day and the weather has been by no means hot.

The army moves in three columns, with Hill's corps in reserve. It is said they are to have Burgos, which we will willingly give them. The left column, composed of the 1st and 5th Divisions, is under Graham. The centre, 3rd, 4th and Light Divisions is under Picton. Lord Wellington generally moves with this column. The right have the 6th and 7th, under Lord Dalhousie.[2] The hussars are with our column and three reserve brigades of artillery besides those attached to divisions.

Tomorrow we expect to cross the Carrion at or near Palencia. As yet there has been no want of anything; the supplies exact and regular so that this has hitherto been a tour of pleasure and not like our former campaigns.

Clinton has arrived in this country and is expected up with the army. The difference of commanders has changed my views and wishes and although last year I was very anxious to get home I am by no means so this year, and am very well content to remain where I am. I should like, if I am above ground, when the campaign is over, a few months leave of absence, as it is now so long (six years) since I have seen any of my friends and relations, but Lord Wellington told Brisbane a few days ago that we were to return after the campaign was at an end, and expressed his regret at being obliged to part with us. Adieu.

1.This refers to the Combat of Morales, 2 June 1813. Grant's Hussar Brigade pushed up the road to Tordesillas and fell in with the French cavalry rearguard at Morales. The Hussars charged immediately the two regiments of French Dragoons (16 and 21), broke them and chased them for two miles until they found the protection of the French infantry rearguard; when Grant called off the pursuit. Oman states the French loss as two officers and 208 men captured from the 16 Dragoons.
2. Lieutenant General the Right Honourable George, Earl of Dalhousie, Colonel of the 26 Foot, commanded the 7th Division.

Letter 101   Camp near [Villa]sandino, 12 June 1813

To Mr Gundry

My dear Sir,

I promised before we broke up from winter quarters, that I would from time to time give you a sketch of our proceedings in this part of the world, and a day's halt gives me ample time to put my threat into execution. From the 10th to the 16th of May the divisions of the army in the rear, closed up to the Coa, and every preparation having been made for the advance on Salamanca, on the three following days six divisions unexpectedly turned to the left, crossed the Douro, and advanced in three columns on the Esla, at all times a formidable barrier, but become so now in truth by an unexpected fall of rain, that rendered it impassable for infantry. It was however crossed on the 31st May and 1st of June, without opposition, on pontoons; so much had the attention of the enemy been distracted by the movements of General Hill in the south, and by Lord Wellington remaining in the neighbourhood of Ciudad Rodrigo, that we were certainly never expected to enter Spain on this side and the Douro and Tormes having been both avoided by this able and well executed manoeuvre, the enemy fell back on Burgos, and we have arrived thus far without having seen anything of the infantry; the Hussar Brigade had an affair at Morales, with an equal force of cavalry, supported by artillery in which great coolness and judgement was shown by Colonel Grant and great courage on the part of the officers and men; upwards of two hundred prisoners were taken. An affair also took place on the enemy's leaving Salamanca, in which place their rearguard were shaken, and it is thought had Lord Wellington chosen to have risked a few cavalry, the whole fifteen hundred men might have been taken,[1] but it is evidently our commander's plan this year

1. On 26 May 1813, the advance of Fane's division on Salamanca caused the French rearguard commanded by General Villatte to hastily retreat. Fane, pushing on with his cavalry, the French dragoons covering the rearguard of infantry was quickly scattered but charging the infantry squares proved ineffectual. The cavalry skirted around the French infantry, picking up the numerous stragglers that fell out of the column on this stiflingly hot day and Gardiner's Horse Artillery that came up, played on the squares whenever opportunity arose. They continued this for some five miles until Wellington arrived and called off the troops.

to keep his army in the best possible state, for on one grand struggle depends the fate of this country. He therefore declines secondary advantages and allows nothing to divert him from his plan; hitherto he has succeeded admirably, for the army was never in better health not even in quarters, and I don't believe the whole army have left two hundred men behind since we quitted the frontiers of Portugal.

It would appear by our present movement as if we were likely to leave the castle of Burgos behind us, in the first instance blockaded, until the proper means arrive to undertake a siege; these are embarked and are at Corunna, and will proceed to Santander, as soon as that road shall have been covered by our advance, which two or three day's march will do. Our supplies will also come by that line, which will be of the greatest utility, as the land carriage will be saved in a great measure; the sea coast not being the third of the distance to our magazines on the frontiers of Portugal, and the canal of Castille, will be of great service; it is in excellent repair, and will begin at Palencia to Reinosa, which if we cross the Ebro is likely to be our great depot.

The country we have passed over since we have left the frontiers of Portugal has been rich beyond measure in grain, but very uninteresting in a picturesque point of view, not a tree or enclosure to break the prospect of an immense sea of corn with villages and churches frequently seven or eight to be seen at a time, appearing scattered amongst the straw, which is the only fuel they have to make use of.

The villages throughout Leon are poor, the houses dirty and wretchedly constructed; they are bricks hardened in the sun, which is, in brick making, but a poor substitute for fire. They have few gardens, and scarcely cultivate vegetables, so that with a soil and climate the most productive in the world, they are the most wretched. Here the peasants are dirty and ugly in their persons, and features; in the south they are clean, and handsome, and I think the further we advance the more miserable they appear. The churches which are built of stone, are spacious, and handsome and as usual over ornamented. The cathedral at Palencia is certainly a fine building but not to be compared to either that at Burgos or Salamanca. There is a very fine organ under which, as if supporting it, as large as life and painted in colours, are two Saracens, which at a certain part of the service, are made to open and shut their mouths, loll out their tongues, move their hands as if (so it was explained to us) they were joining, against their inclinations in part of the church service. This childish invention, not better in point of execution than the Dutch nut crackers the very reverend old canons were very anxious to point out to us, and very ready to laugh at the conceit, which is played off as often as service is performed in the choir.

I have not yet seen any of the Spanish corps that have joined the army; individual soldiers I have met are much improved in appearance; as far as clothing and appointments make soldiers, they are very much better than they were, under the old Spanish government, but the officers are of the same bad description. A certain education is necessary to make an officer and I fear there are no traces of that through the country; there seems an equality of cultivated intellect, between the possessor of the soil, and the labourer that tills it.

Every village has the remains of a castle, and some of these would have an excellent effect if placed in picturesque situations. That at Pina de Campos was particularly light and airy. Living as we do constantly in camp, we have little or no intercourse with the inhabitants of the countries through which we pass; we are well received as far as ringing of bells &c, goes, but they are unwilling to part with the necessary supplies for the army; without the money down, and this considering the villainy that is practised near great armies by contractors, commissaries, and that description of persons, is not to be wondered at, and notwithstanding our boast of principle and probity, we deal as largely in that way as any nation under the sun. Adieu.

Letter 102   **Camp near Espejo, 18 June 1813**

My dear Mother,

We have been continually on the move since I last wrote, and the affairs of this campaign are becoming every day more interesting; we have few sick, and until yesterday have never outrun our supplies. We have left the tedious monotonous scenery of the Castiles, are in the mountains and enjoy every day new and diversified prospects, with pure exhilarating air, peculiar to these regions. My last letter was from Villasandino where we had a day's halt. On Sunday we marched by Villadiego, and encamped near [Las] Hormazas; the roads bad from the rain that had fallen the preceding day. On Monday 14th we started at 4 a.m., the road bad and tiresome, but the scenery along the valley through which we wound was magnificent. We were welcomed on our halting ground by the pleasing intelligence that the French had blown up the castle at Burgos and had retired. To us (who recollect the many weary days we spent before it last year) the news was most exhilarating, and we sat down to our frugal meal, and retired to rest, with double satisfaction. The 15th saw us in motion again at an early hour; another tedious march through a rocky sterile country, till about six in the evening we opened on a valley with the Ebro running through it; there was everything growing in the utmost luxuriance, the land parted into fields, the hedges planted with fruit trees; we were refreshed after a march of eleven hours, during which time we had not gone more than fourteen miles, by cherries, so large and fine, that it is few years in England they attain that perfection trained against a wall. We encamped near Puente-Arenas, in a grove close to the river, which we crossed the next day without opposition; indeed we had not even seen any of the enemy's parties for some time. It is reported they are concentrating near Vitoria. When we arrived on our ground near Bustillo,[1] I heard, to cheer me, that my name is included in the late brevet as Colonel,[2] which if it is of no other advantage, will save me the unpleasant duty of commanding the picquets.

On the 17th we made a short march to Oteo, not more than ten miles. We passed the 2nd Division near the bridge of Medina [de Pomar], and about four in the afternoon arrived at our most beautiful encamping ground, shaded by large forest trees, and rendered interesting by the finest mountain scenery. Today we were under arms at six, and found the enemy strongly posted near Osma;[3] our light infantry dislodged them, and we encamped near Espejo, at the head of the pass, which was by nature so strong that I wonder the enemy relinquished it so easily. Whilst my dinner is preparing, I just find time to write to say I am right glad to hear you are so much better and to assure you how glad I shall be &c, Adieu.

1. I cannot identify this village for certain.
2. His promotion to colonel was dated 4 June 1813.
3. I cannot identify this village for certain.

Letter 103   Camp near Pamplona, 25 June 1813

My dear Sir,

A short march today affords me an opportunity of giving you an account of the battle fought near Vitoria last Monday, a very important one in its results, for it will put the French back into their own country and give to the Spaniards and ourselves the natural barriers of the Pyrenees to defend after we are in possession of the place I am now looking at from my tent, and San Sebastian, which although very strong cannot hold out long, whilst being on the sea coast will enable us to bring up such superior means of attack to any we have ever before employed.

For some time during our advance we heard that the enemy were concentrating their forces near Vitoria. Many were the reports as to their force, and as many conjectures as to whether they meant to make a stand there. I think the general impression throughout the army was that they would not. It was known that there was no position at Vitoria itself, but that many occurred in the mountains behind it, in fact it was all one defile from the city, or rather the plain on which the city stood to the frontiers of France, but I believe the fact was that Lord Wellington pressed them too hard and that they could not file off their baggage which was beyond calculation, so they thought they must make a fight for it.

Our army had advanced in several columns and each column the night before the action was stationed at the head of a separate valley that opened on the plain. There was very little possibility of communication between the columns, a mountain as it were parted each, and had the enemy commenced the offensive by attacking with their whole force any one of the columns, I don't know how the affair might have terminated.

The battle did not begin very early in the morning; for hours we were gazing on the plain below on the French troops, who were formed in two lines across the plain below us. About ten o'clock Sir Rowland Hill who was on the right, and on the great road from Burgos to Vitoria, began the engagement by an attack on the enemy's left. This movement we saw very plain, and he soon gained the height on the extreme left of the French which seemed to give them great uneasiness as they were continually sending reinforcements in that direction. It was soon however apparent that this was not the real attack; enough was done to keep the enemy employed;

a village was taken by the 34th and retaken by the French,[1] and this occurred several times. In the mean time the heavy and incessant firing away to our left kept us no longer in doubt where the real strife was. It was not till due impression was made in that quarter, that we moved forward, at nearly two o'clock, when we followed three brigades of artillery across a bridge in our front, which the enemy complaisantly left to us.[2] The batteries moved forward to a height beyond the river, and we formed in rear of them. A cannonade from the eighteen guns immediately opened and was as instantly returned. We had hardly formed in rear of the hill when up went one of our tumbrils of ammunition. The shot that went over the artillery struck our columns. One shell burst in the centre of our fourth company and killed and wounded eight men, and all of them from your militia regiment. The cannonade soon ceased. We formed in two lines, covered by our light infantry, following the French and marching in line as well, as well as I ever saw men move on a field day. The Second Division were close on our right, and a brigade of heavy cavalry in our rear. No stand of any consequence was made by the enemy in our part of the line, till towards evening.

They had been completely beaten by Graham on the right, who had cut them off from the great road to France by Tolosa, and they were now seen in great confusion getting towards the Pamplona road; the ground here was intersected with steep ravines that did not appear till you were close to them. Frequently towards sunset, we saw the enemy apparently in the greatest confusion, regiments intermixed, and all huddled together. You expected to be up with them in a moment; the ravine passed they were all gone; you saw no more of them till they had passed another of these obstacles. There was one period of the day that was to me particularly interesting. I wished I had been a painter to have availed myself of it; it was near sunset, and we were on high ground interspersed with forest trees.

We overlooked the whole plain and the bright evening light was streaming on the towers of Vitoria, the battle still raged in our

1. The 2/34th was part of O'Callaghan's Brigade which fought hard to take the village of Subijana de Alava.
2. The upper bridge at Nanclares was used by the 4th Division to cross the River Zadorra.

front, and on our left towards the city, but it was all confusion and smoke. At this moment Lord Wellington rode up with all his staff; as he passed the battalion which was halted, he desired us to move on: I asked 'In column or line?', never shall I forget the animation of his countenance 'Any how, but get on' was the reply. Night brought us up under a hedge, and here Fehrszen and I talked over the occurrences of the day.

Every moment brought us fresh intelligence of the loss the army had sustained, of the wealth and plunder we [they?] had abandoned, everybody had something. My servant had the sense to empty one pig-skin of the bad wine of the country, and to fill it with excellent burgundy he had picked up in some French officer's baggage. We with difficulty kept our people together. Could the French have seen what was passing at our bivouacs and returned, they would have found us in a sad state to receive them.

The Quartermaster[1] of the 53rd had a curious adventure; he fell in with one of the treasure wagons of the enemy, deserted, and without horses, in a narrow lane. He sat down on it, waiting till he could get some assistance to carry it (or its contents) away. Before he had been there long, a party of Spanish guerrillas came up, who minded not the right of possession as he had no force to back it. They however allowed him to take as much as he could carry away, so he stowed some things he had in a valise, behind his horse, and contrived to stow away fifteen hundred dollars in it, and came to me:- I advised him to keep his own counsel, so he saved the whole. Had the wagon contained gold what a prize it would have been.

The following day was wet and dreary, and we kept plodding on in rear of some other divisions, till sunset, without a skirmish in front to enliven us. Madame Gazan[2] and another lady of rank passed through our columns, to join their husbands. They had been left behind in the town, during the scramble, and dined with Lord Wellington after the battle, and were well satisfied to be allowed to return to their own country. The 23rd and 24th still found us on the Pamplona road, in rear of the column. The weather wet and the roads dreadfully cut up, and our bivouacs cold and wet, and having been occupied by the French dirty and disagreeable. There was a skirmish

1. The Army List 1813 states that the Quartermaster's name was Hanson.
2. The wife of General Honoré Theodore Maxime Gazan, who commanded the Army of the Centre.

the last day to cheer our spirits, and the last gun the enemy had with them was captured.[1] A short march this morning brought us in view of Pamplona, a regular fortification, placed in the centre of a fertile plain, and only to be taken by the regular modes of approach. As yet, we are all uncertainty as to whether we are to follow to the Pyrenees (whoever thought at the beginning of the campaign that we should so soon, if ever, reach them) or remain here for the siege; the former I should prefer. I am sure both my mother and you will be thankful that I am spared and have a chance of seeing you again after all these affairs are at an end. &c, &c, &c. Adieu.

Letter 104   Gallipienzo, Navarra, 29 June 1813

To Mr Gundry

My Dear Sir,

I think you will have received in England, with great satisfaction, the details of the battle of Vitoria, which must long ere this have reached you. We had a very small share in the action, except the light infantry; not having fired a shot, nor should we have lost a man but for an unlucky shell that burst in one of the companies.

Both before and since the action we have been marching from ten to twelve hours per day, with but one halt before today for sixteen days, with the worst weather I ever remember so late in the year on the peninsula. We are considerably reduced by mere fatigue, and I have nearly two hundred men less with me in the battalion, than I had on the day of the action; many of whom I am afraid are wandering about the country committing the most wanton depredations; for these last eight days we have had only one pound and a half of bread and had it not been for some wagon loads of flour we took from the enemy we should have been starving.

The loss to the French in money has been very great, but the benefit derived from it by our army small; some worthless individuals that remained in the rear made immense booty, whilst those who preferred doing their duty in the ranks, got nothing. Much fell

---

1. Actually two guns were saved by the French from the rout at Vitoria. Bingham is right to state that one of these was captured, but he is mistaken in saying that this was the last one; the other got away.

to the share of the peasants of the country; perhaps they are the people to whom in justice it ought to belong. Several French generals have been ruined, and have their fortunes again to make from some other miserable and oppressed people.

Clausel,[1] who was not in the action, with 13,000 men is somewhere on the Ebro, and we have moved on Jaca to intercept his return to France. I am not sanguine enough to hope we may secure him, but our victory would be complete if we could add his force to out former captures.

Nothing can exceed the beauty and fertility of the country north of the Ebro, and the people appear a most industrious race. The valley of the Ebro where we crossed it is beyond anything rich and picturesque; it reminded me of the banks of the Arno between Pisa and Florence.

I did not enter Vitoria, which appears a good town, as is Pamplona. Tafalla, through which we passed yesterday, though small, is very pleasant with large gardens around it abounding in fruit. At Olite, a few miles from it, is a garden of the Marquis of Frias, said to be a league in circumference, in which amongst other rarities are currants, and the fruits of more northern latitudes.

The people in this province seem very well satisfied to get rid of the French as well as their own guerrillas; Mina who commands one corps is very well spoken of and is as much beloved as Longa[2] appears detested.

Amongst other things taken at Vitoria, the King's correspondence fell into our hands with the keys to all his ciphers so that spies of every description are detected, and several curious circumstances have come to light.

I met with a letter, addressed to Baron Daricau, a general of division in the French army, from a friend in Paris, dated last autumn. In this letter it is stated that he met with a gentleman who has resided nineteen years in England, and who was intimately acquainted with several members of the English administration, and who affirmed that the policy of England was never to terminate the

1. General de Division Bertrand Clausel commanded the Army of the North. His force had not arrived when the French lost at Vitoria; Wellington sought to destroy him, but he rapidly retreated into France.
2. Colonel Francisco Longa, an ex blacksmith turned guerrilla leader; now commanding a division in the Spanish Army.

war in the peninsula; the English well knowing from proximity and mutual wants, as soon as Spain and France were at peace, a good understanding must ensue, and says the Baron's friend, this has been proved to a mathematical certainty by Lord Wellington's last movements. The letter concludes by an eulogium on the urbanity and politeness of the French, and animadversions on the arrogance and want of manner of the English. Altogether it was a curious production, and I much wished to have sent it to you. Adieu.

G.R.B.

Letter 105   Camp near Pamplona, 10 July 1813

My dear Mother,

It seems a long time since I last wrote, but on our return from the pursuit of Clausel we were posted here and have been much occupied in the blockade of the place, in the construction of redoubts, &c, &c, changing occasionally our ground. The weather has been very different from anything we have experienced in our former campaigns. Hitherto at this time of the year you were certain of fine dry though hot weather. Here, whether from the vicinity of the mountains or some other cause the weather is as uncertain and the rain as frequent as in Devonshire. It is however more healthy, we have few if any returns of the ague complaints that the warm and dry weather always brought on.

Our little trip to the south was much pleasanter than the monotonous life we pass here, the country we marched through was pleasant, and diversified and several of the towns, Tafalla and Olite for example though not large were very neat and well situated, and we found a better looking and more industrious race of peasantry than we have been accustomed to see.

We work day and night to complete the redoubts, that are to surround the town at a long cannon shot from the city. They throw shells occasionally but without effect as there has hardly been one casualty. I was much amused the other day whilst standing in one of the redoubts, at a private soldier of the 40th Regiment, who laying his spade coolly down, exclaimed 'My fortune is in that there town'. But in this I think he is for once mistaken, for as we hear the siege of San Sebastian is determined on, this place will fall by blockade, if we can keep the French from returning, and his hope will be disappointed.

Almost every day from three in the afternoon till five, there is a skirmish. Seldom on our side of the town, but generally where the 3rd Division are stationed. The French come out to try and cut and carry away the corn round the place and our picquets strive to prevent it. We see the ramparts crowded with all the beauty and fashion of the place to see the sport; as the corn is close to the foot of the glacis, they generally succeed in getting part of their harvest home. As they do not apprehend a siege, they are not sparing of their ammunition and they frequently fire their eighteen and twenty-four pounders at individuals. I was riding leisurely along the road the other afternoon thinking I was quite out of range on my way to see Fehrszen, who was on picquet, when one of these shot of heavy calibre struck the road so near my horse that he sprung up the bank and fell backwards with me. I quickly removed both myself and him from that neighbourhood.

I dined last Thursday with General Fane, who has a house not far from this. I met several officers of the cavalry brigade under his command and passed a pleasant day. Adieu.

G.R.B.

Letter 106 Camp near Biskarreta[-Gerediain], 19 July 1813

My dear Mansel,

When I recollect how amply you used to detail all the movements of the army last year to me while I was confined at Salamanca, I look back on the last fortnight that has passed and take shame to myself that so long a period has been suffered to elapse without having employed myself in writing. But we have been so harassed and kept so much on the alert, and the weather too for this time of the year and for this country has been so wet that I have found no convenient opportunity to address you, so that all things considered I hope you will hold me excused and accept my promises for the future.

First then, I must thank you for your letter of the 10th and am glad to hear you have succeeded so admirably in recruiting. No one that I can hear of gets men but you. Doctor Sandell wishes you may be sent to the West Indies, for he says if you go on as you have done, he will never have a chance of getting to England. On looking back to my diary I see my last was written when I was looking on as a spectator of the blockade of Pamplona. I say a spectator, for nothing could have come more apropos than the brevet, for it was just in time to take me off the sortie as Field officer of the day, and left the three Field officers of the brigade all the pleasure to themselves. On the day I wrote, the enemy nearly reached the camp with their shells and struck a work we have named 'Sir Fletche's fancy' several times without doing much damage, except knocking down one of the officers of engineers with a stone. On the 11th the whole garrison turned out to forage and were opposed by the picquets and cacadores of the 6th Division, who drove them in, although I think they took some forage with them. Our people got up some field pieces, and threw some shells very well. The 12th and 13th passed quietly; our redoubts which we numbered from one to ten are getting on fast, six embrasures opened in each, the guns not come up. They are well situated and about eleven or twelve hundred yards from the work and when completed will prevent anything moving beyond the covered way. On the 14th before day break we relieved the 6th Division which had moved towards San Sebastian and our brigade took the picquets south of the town, the 3rd and 4th Divisions being alone employed on this service. On the 15th, at five in the morning the enemy drove in the picquets of the 3rd Division from an old work east of the town, and began to forage. There was a very smart affair for about two hours; our people drove them from the old work but they succeeded in getting in some wheat. The loss amounted to thirty men killed and wounded, and was nearly equal on both sides. The nine pounders were placed in some of the redoubts and fired with some little effect but heavier metal is wanting. On the 16th that part of the Spanish army that was to relieve us appeared looking in tolerable order, and wanting nothing but officers to make them very respectable. They formed in front of our camp, and immediately primed and loaded. They went that night on picquet with our people. The French found them out, and treated them with a double allowance of shot and shell. On the 17th at seven in the morning we marched and left them to themselves. We took the road to Roncesvalles, the pass by which the French army unencumbered by baggage or artillery took their way to France. Byng's Brigade[1] of the 2nd Division occupy the pass, and we are about five miles in the rear, as a support.

1. Major General John Byng's Brigade consisted of 1/3rd, 1/57th, 1 Provisional Regiment (2/31st, 2/66th) and 1 company 5/60th.

The enemy have about seven thousand men at St Jean Pied de Port, the first town within the frontier. There is a report that Clausel who retired from Spain by the pass of Jaca after losing his baggage and destroying his artillery has joined their army. It is said they have committed the same depredations in France as they were accustomed to practise in Spain, and that the peasants are up in arms as much to prevent their own people from plundering as to resist our invasion. As soon as San Sebastian has fallen (and it cannot hold out long, fifty pieces of artillery having opened on it yesterday) we shall enter France and change the scene to that country. What is become of Suchet we do not know; we hear he has left Valencia, and is on his way home. If the Alicante army had any dash about them they have now an opportunity. I hope Sir William Clinton, who has arrived will be something better than Sir George Murray,[1] who by all accounts made a second Ferrol business of Tarragona.[2] Adieu, believe me &c.

G.R.B.

Letter 107   Camp near Biskarreta, 23 July 1813

My dear Sophy,

The weather has been so wet and stormy since we have been here, that I have hardly had any opportunity of exploring this beautiful neighbourhood, in which we have now been five days. The hills,

---

1. This statement is slightly muddled. Lieutenant General William Henry Clinton had originally landed a force of 12,000 from Sicily at Alicante in September 1812 but was superseded in the December. In March 1813 Sir John Murray (not George Murray as stated in the letter) took command of this force and Clinton took the 1st Division of this army. Lord William Bentinck superseded Murray on 17 June 1813, but on his departure the following September, Clinton once more assumed command of the army. This army, under Clinton, does eventually appear to have been of use to Wellington, as it kept the army of Suchet in check and unable to support Soult.
2. Sir John Murray's army had invested Tarragona, but with the merest hint of a relief force approaching and without ascertaining the size of this force (which was not actually large enough to seriously threaten him), Murray ordered the army to rapidly re-embark; to the point of abandoning his siege guns to the French. Bingham's reference to 'a second Ferrol', refers to a similar failure by Lieutenant General Sir James Pulteney who, having gained the commanding heights, probably should have captured the port of Ferrol with ease in 1800; but was frightened off by fears of imaginary reinforcements, and re-embarked.

the forests of large trees in which the beech and ash of our northern climate flourish in great luxuriance, have been almost denied to me, by the continuance of heavy rain with which we have been deluged, swelling every mountain brook to a torrent. I have not been under canvas myself for I found in the immediate neighbourhood of the camp, an old fashioned chateau, which I had no hesitation in occupying. It had been uninhabited except by rats and owls, I suppose for nearly half a century; a large square building with heavy towers at each angle, with high and very steep sloping roofs with which all the houses in the mountains are built, to throw off the snow. Damp and dingy as it is the corner of one of the upper chambers which I occupy, is dry under foot, and keeps out the rain better than a tent and I wander from one part of the house to the other for exercise. The day before yesterday I did get as far as the pass beyond Roncesvalles, passing through the beautiful valley of that name, which is shut out from the world eight months in the year by the snow. The roads to it are dreadful, worse a great deal than those we have been accustomed to in Portugal. The town or village stands in the centre of the plain, and must have been pretty before it was pulled to pieces by the adverse armies. A few miles further brought us to the outposts of the army, occupied by General Byng's brigade, and from this we looked over the fertile plains of France, and the opposing army below, which appeared as if concentrated near St Jean Pied de Port, the first town in France. They surely cannot intend any attack on our posts in the mountains, where we seem to hover over them as a kite does over a partridge.

The following day (yesterday) was fine; afraid to go beyond the sound of the bugle, I rambled on foot in the woods round the camp, and followed as far as I dared a most lovely glen, the stream of which increased by the rains broke into continued cascades. The verdure too looked so fresh, and profusion of wild strawberries are scattered in every direction beneath the trees. Paths there are hardly any, and those made by the sheep passing through to the higher part of the hills, where the turf is always verdant and affords pasture all the summer to the large flocks of the Mesta who return to the plains of Castile for the winter. How happy should I be without restraint and in better weather to explore these highly picturesque and beautiful regions where the foot of man (certainly not a traveller) has hardly ever passed; through passes known only to the shepherd and smuggler and these latter perhaps increase the difficulties of single strangers, as deeds of murder and robbery are frequently attributed to them, if they are not much misrepresented.

The siege of San Sebastian and blockade of Pamplona are still going on, and must fall soon, if Soult does not relieve them. Our position in the mountains is much against him, but we too labour under some disadvantages which I will not enumerate as perhaps you would not understand them if I did, so wishing your health, &c, Adieu.

G.R.B.

Letter 108   Camp near Etxalar, 3 August 1813

My dear Mansel,

My last left us in a very quiet camp at the foot of the Pyrenees, where we continued for several days, the weather being during the time dreadfully wet, and unpleasant, and the roads in the mountains hardly passable. On Saturday with Fehrszen, I rode to the outposts, viz., Byng's Brigade, stationed beyond Roncesvalles looking down on France. The day was beautiful and we could see vast plains before us, intersected with rivers as far as Bayonne. St Jean Pied de Port was below us, and the French bivouacs in the neighbourhood were in a state of repose; constant drilling of conscripts and nothing beyond it apparently. We returned late to our camp pleased with all we had seen, for independent of the interest excited by looking over that fair land, we never expected to arrive at, and the cheering prospect of the enemy's army driven to take refuge on their own soil, the country we passed over was highly picturesque, and the verdure and freshness of these mountain regions after having been of late years accustomed to the arid plains of Spain, inexpressibly pleasant and refreshing. The following morning at daylight we were unexpectedly put in motion, and proceeded to Espinal, where we cooked, then turned to our right out of the Roncesvalles road, and proceeded through the woods towards Orbaitzeta, and the iron-works. About half way to the former place we were overtaken by an aide-de-camp who informed us that the left brigade and Byng's were attacked in force. We hastened to their assistance, but we had many miles to traverse and it was late in the day before we arrived. The firing had by this time ceased; we found the remainder of the division on the crest of the mountain, and on a little green hill that projected as it were to the front, and which had been wrested by superior numbers from the 20th Regiment by the enemy, were their columns, with an endless train of troops winding up the narrow paths to join them. The 20th Regiment had behaved with its accustomed gallantry and spirit, had made a charge on the first of the enemy established on the hill, but were repulsed, the dead and wounded having been left in the enemy's hands.[1] Byng's Brigade on our right seemed to have kept their ground, but the hill before us appeared to intervene in a very awkward manner between ourselves and them. The evening was spent in conjecture as to how we were to give or receive the attack, the following morning. But our speculations were soon put an end to after dark, by an order to fall back. It seems the French had forced the pass of Maya, so that our left was exposed. Leaving therefore people to keep up our fires, we commenced our march; the darkness of the night was increased by the thickness of the wood we had to traverse with nothing but a shepherd's path to follow, intersected frequently by trees felled across it, we were obliged to pass the word from man to man, to keep us from deviating from the track, and it was broad daylight before we arrived at our old ground at Biskarreta. Here we halted to cook, and it was 2 o'clock on the 26th before the advance of the enemy made their appearance. We retired quietly before them till we were in the rear of Lintzoain and we then took up (with Byng's Brigade) a strong position across the road to check the enemy's advance. They attacked the part of the line occupied by our brigade but not with any vigour. Their cavalry got at one time amongst our skirmishers, but the ground was against them. Just at this time in advancing up a hill to the support of the skirmishers, poor Fraser was severely wounded.[2] A musket ball entering at the side of the nose and passing through the roof of the tongue was spit out of the throat. I was afraid we should lose him altogether, but I have heard once since, he has been in the rear doing well. He behaved as did all the men of the company most nobly, being as cool and collected

1. This refers to the Combat of Roncesvalles on 25 July, where the 20 Regiment and the rest of Ross's Brigade of the 4th Division fought tenaciously to hold the Linduz against Foy's forces which was advancing along the Airola ridge whilst Anson's Brigade supported Byng's Brigade of the 2nd Division which sought to stop the advance of a second column on their right at the height of Altobiscar.
2. Lieutenant John Fraser, 53 Regiment.

when the cavalry were amongst them, as I ever saw them in my life. We came off very well with only eleven wounded, and at sunset the firing ceased, we having maintained our post and having stopped the enemy's advance. They had several pieces of artillery up; ours were in the rear. We fell back again on the 27th just before daybreak, crossed the river without molestation and by ten o'clock occupied a position in sight of Pamplona. Byng's Brigade remained with us, and Picton's Division that had moved up to our support was on our right. Our baggage that had passed Pamplona the day before, had been cannonaded, and much confusion ensued, and diversion was afforded to those who happened to be present, at the very speedy manner in which women, sutlers and batmen hurried out of the line of fire. The enemy followed us in the course of the day, and made some feeble attempts to drive the Spaniards from a hill in our front, which ultimately became our position, and to which we moved up in the course of the afternoon. In the course of the day Lord Wellington made his appearance, which acted like magic on us all. You know falling back before an enemy is not very exhilarating; we had in the plenitude of our wisdom, criticised the position; it had in our eyes, every fault a position could have. A few short words from him reassured us, and we were convinced from that moment, a better could not have been selected between the Pyrenees and Ebro. In the night we were amused with a storm of thunder, lightning and rain, equal to that you remember last year before the Battle of Salamanca, and thus in this shivering expectation without cover, with hardly brushwood enough to make a fire, we passed the time till daylight of the 28th showed us the French very strong indeed on the opposite hill, almost within musket shot, a deep ravine dividing us. Lord Wellington was with the centre of our division on the summit of the hill; the 40th and two Spanish regiments were on our right, the remainder of our brigade with the commander in chief, the Portuguese brigade in rear of us, the left brigade to the left, with Byng's lower down the hill. There were two roads leading to Pamplona, the one on the right, the other on the left of the position; beyond the right road Picton's Division was stationed rather in our rear, the cavalry behind him again; on the plain the 6th Division was seen to the left, advancing towards the road on that side of the position, and it was to prevent the junction that Soult (who had assumed the command of the army, nearly the whole of which he had up) commenced the action. He had calculated not only on relieving the blockade, but of penetrating far into Spain, for we could see guns and wagons on the roads very far in the rear of his position. The marshal had stationed himself on the hill in our front, on a mule, passing orders by his aides-de-camp and staff along his line. He was so near as to be perfectly discernable. Our people were not at all daunted by the force opposed to them, and seemed to think Lord Wellington equal to two divisions of the army. It was the anniversary of the day of Talavera, and our men decorated their caps with box, the only stunted shrub that grew on the hill. It was about 11 o'clock then that the action commenced. As I said before, the approach of the 6th Division was the signal for attack on the part of the Duke of Dalmatia, which took place simultaneously all along the front of our division, as well as an attempt to interpose between our position and the division arriving to our assistance. The attack was very brisk and the French appeared to wish to show their new commander they were determined to wipe out the stain of the defeat at Vitoria. Under cover of a distant fire of musketry from the opposite bank, which however was sufficiently galling, they dashed into the ravine, and attempted to ascend on our side. Our people waited till they were near the summit and then charging drove them down again. About the close of the first attack, I was detached with my battalion to the support of the 40th Regiment and Spaniards, so that on descending from the highest part of the hill, I found myself in command of four battalions.[1] Repeated attacks were made on ours, and other parts of the position; they were all repulsed, the enemy suffering severely from our fire in retiring down the hill again which they did with the utmost rapidity. The latter part of the day till sunset, was passed in a useless skirmish. On my first arrival in rear of the 40th, I found a person whom I considered a French officer, and I desired my orderly Sergeant Dove[2] to take to the rear; it turned out to be the commandant of the Regiment of Princessa,[3] who had come up to solicit a supply of ammunition; when I looked again I saw the red and

1. Oman describes this heroic defence, but fails to mention the involvement of the 2 Provisional Regiment.
2. Sergeant David Dove, 53 Regiment.
3. This is almost certainly an error. The Spanish regiments with the 40th were that of Principe and Pravia from O'Donnell's Andalucian Reserve; it is therefore most likely that the officer was from the Principe Regiment.

white cockade. During the action, there stood by me a sergeant of the Regiment of Pravia who spoke very good English and who was very useful to me in carrying orders to my new friends the Spaniards. On my interrogating him after the business was over, how he came to understand our language so well, he told me that he had been taken by the English at Manilla, had entered into the East India Company's service, and having served his term of enlistment had returned here, and was now combating for the liberties of his country. We had reason to congratulate ourselves on the conclusion of the day; only two divisions and Byng's Brigade had been engaged, and yet Soult's plan of relieving Pamplona was completely frustrated. Two other divisions were expected to join either during the night, or the following day, which would enable us to resume the offensive.

The 29th passed quietly enough, not a shot having been fired or a movement made. The 7th Division joined on the left at the spot where I was stationed. About the middle of the day, an officer from the enemy's advanced picquet came forward and asked permission to look amongst the slain, who were laying pretty thick on our face of the hill, for that of a favourite aide-de-camp of the general officer who commanded the attack the day before, and who had been killed nearly on the crest of the hill, and almost close to our line. Permission was immediately given; then they requested permission to remove as they said for burial, the other bodies, and this was also granted. It was soon discovered to be only a ruse; under pretence of removing the dead they were carrying off the muskets that had been thrown down in the haste of their retreat. The truce was immediately broken off. The next morning when we advanced, these arms and several others were found near the advanced guard, regularly piled, and in no inconsiderable numbers.

On the 30th the action began on the left. Soult had employed himself the preceding day in sending back to France all the artillery and material of the army which became useless as soon as he had ascertained he could not penetrate by the Roncesvalles road. This having been accomplished, he strengthened his right, and attacked Hill's Division, that were just in sight, rather beyond the spot where the 6th Division had been attacked the day before. As soon as his right was seriously engaged, we were ordered to advance and attack his left. We ascended with some difficulty the hill in our front and succeeded in driving the enemy back, with a trifling loss, and we continued following them along the ridge that separates the two roads. The attack on the 2nd Division was relinquished, and a general retreat of the enemy commenced in the direction of the pass of Maya. It was towards the afternoon of this day an opportunity was afforded to our friend Fehrszen of distinguishing himself, of which he promptly and nobly availed himself. The part of the French army we were pursuing were retiring in one long column by the high road; the 4th and 6th Divisions on the hills on each side of the road; our progress impeded as well by the enemy disputing the ground in our front, as by the nature of the ground itself, which was stunted brushwood, Fehrszen being near the road with his light company observed an interval between the two last regiments and the rest of the column, he did not hesitate to place his company on the road in the interval. The commanding officer of the leading regiment actually seized hold of him, and required him to surrender. 'It is you that are to surrender', he replied. 'You see you are surrounded'. His requisition was complied with, and the two regiments laid down their arms; about 1,400 prisoners were the fruits of his daring intrepidity.[1] Night arrested our pursuit. On the 31st we resumed the pursuit and passed through Lantz keeping the Maya road. Had our general of brigade been a little more enterprising the rear guard, again here might have been taken.

Byng captured a convoy of provisions coming to the enemy from France, and added to the number of our prisoners.

The 1st of August we moved again to our left, and passed through the beautiful valley of Bastan. In the afternoon our left brigade came up with the enemy and pressed them very hard and they left many of their wounded in our hands. We had the satisfaction at night to get our baggage, which we had not seen for eight days before. Yesterday I had a most refreshing bathe in the Bidassoa before we moved off. It was a very tedious day; the left brigade were engaged, and we were in support behind a mountain which totally prevented our seeing anything that was going on, and moving at the rate of a quarter of a mile in two hours. Towards

1. It is usual for this exploit to be described as having captured two battalions; but Oman states that the prisoners were made from at least three French regiments; namely the 34 Leger losing thirteen officers and 531 men; the 55 Line losing 282 men and the 58 Line losing 348 men prisoners. Fehrszen was made a brevet major for this exploit.

the afternoon the 7th Division became engaged, and dislodged the enemy from ground that appeared almost inaccessible. General Barnes[1] and his brigade distinguished themselves very much on this occasion. We did not arrive at the top of the mountain till after dark and the road was so narrow and the hill so steep that our baggage did not arrive at all. Today we have a halt, most welcome I assure you, having undergone much fatigue since the 25th ultimo, and one part or other of the division having been engaged every day (except the 29th) since. The enemy have retired within their own frontier having been foiled in their plan for relieving Pamplona with great loss. We hear four thousand prisoners have been taken. What they have done on our extreme left near San Sebastian we have as yet no opportunity of knowing.

Our fellows, both Queen's and 53rd, have behaved admirably. Our loss is [1?] killed and 41 wounded[2] sufficiently to be sent to the rear. I must now bring this long letter to a conclusion hoping it may afford you some amusement. To the official despatches I refer you for a general idea of the whole of the operations, which, as they were carried on over an extent of country forty miles in extent, with hardly any lateral communication, we can know but little about, but as far as we ourselves were concerned you will find this a faithful narration, and so for the present, Adieu.

Letter 109 Camp on the Pyrenees, above Etxalar, 8 August 1813

My dear Sophy,

Many thanks for your kind letter, written just after your return to Smedmore which found me in a most romantic but uncomfortable situation, an old chateau near Roncesvalles. We have had a short, arduous and brilliant campaign since that, of eight days continual fighting, in which I escaped with my battalion fortunately not losing more than two officers and fifty men killed and wounded together. One of the officers, a young man for whom I am much interested received on the 26th a shot, which entered by the nose,

1. Major General Edward Barnes, commanded a brigade in the 7th Division.
2. Oman underestimates the casualties for the 2 Provisional Regiment at the two battles of Sorauren to be one man killed and one officer and twenty-four men wounded.

211

went through the tongue, forcing with it some bones of the palate. I have not heard of him lately poor fellow; he will be sadly disfigured and must suffer a good deal.

Fehrszen whom you recollect with me in Dorsetshire had an opportunity of distinguishing himself which I am in great hopes will ensure his promotion. In these mountains we completely cheat the summer. There reigns a perpetual verdure, but we pay for it in a climate resembling that of Ireland, constant fog and wet. From the high ground a mile in front of us we look down on the smiling plains of France, and the Bay of Biscay over which I should not care if I was now rolling, but since we have been here it has not been clear enough to discover Bayonne, not more than six or seven leagues from us, and where the terrible English twice as it were at their gates have occasioned some alarm.

Badly off as we are, for the roads are so much out of order, that our supplies arrive in a very scanty manner, the French army must be worse off than we are. They have lost the whole or greatest part of their baggage twice in six weeks, and the officers we converse with do not scruple to abuse the Emperor and his ambition, in very plain terms.

For a person content to suffer much personal inconvenience for the sake of picturesque beauty these would be the mountains to come to; they far exceed either North Wales or Wicklow, in beauty, richness and diversity. The valley of Bastan is one of the finest things I ever saw, but it should be seen when the tints of autumn are on the trees. At present it is one green except the white spiral tents of the English perched on every height on which a tent can stand.

It is yet a doubt whether the great Marshal Soult will not make another push to relieve Pamplona, which may hold out till the first week in September. It is supposed he lost 20,000 men in the last attempt. A similar loss without attaining his object would drive the little Corsican mad; I do not envy his feelings when this last news reaches him.

[The remainder of the letter was removed by Bingham as private].

G.R.B.

Two letters (to his brother Major General Richard Bingham dated Camp near Lesaka 15 August; and to his mother from the same location, dated 17 August) were omitted by Bingham as being mere repetitions of letter 108 to Lieutenant Colonel Mansel.

Letter 110   Camp near Lesaka, 24 August 1813

To Mr Gundry

My dear Sir,

As I know you hear from time to time of my proceedings from my mother, I am the less anxious to trouble you with further communications except when I have something more suitable to your taste than a detail of marches and battles, and I am now about to undertake a task to which I feel myself quite unequal, to attempt to describe what we have seen of the Pyrenees.

These mountains are divided into the higher and lower Pyrenees; the former commencing near Jaca, at the source of the River Aragon, or a little to the eastward of it, and extend to the Mediterranean in a continual ridge much broken and rising into peaks and abrupt points and were, when we caught a glimpse of them in May last, covered with snow. The lower Pyrenees extend west from the River Aragon nearly to the ocean.

On the Spanish side they may be said to begin at the Ebro, for the ascent from thence although not perceived is considerable, nor do you immediately perceive at any distance these mountains that form the barrier between such mighty kingdoms, but a succession of hills present themselves, each of which is higher than the preceding one; beautifully wooded, the valleys well inhabited, and in a high state of cultivation.

The valley of Roncesvalles, so famous in romance, is far from beyond those I have seen in picturesque beauty. The three villages Espinal, Burguete and Roncesvalles, are in sight within a short distance, standing in a country wooded like a park, and of the richest verdure, the high pointed roofs so constructed to throw off the snow, the gilt balls on the tops of the churches all give it a very different appearance to anything else you see in Spain. Four or five months in each year, the inhabitants of this happy valley are deprived of all communication with the rest of the world, by the snow which covers the country to a considerable depth. Although on the Spanish side, you are by no means sensible that you are at such an elevation, yet when you look down on France you are at

213

once perceptible of it; your view on that side is unbounded; the prospect is unconfined, and you cannot behold these fertile plains without regretting that they are delivered into the hands of one man to enable him to domineer over the rest of the world.

The valley of Bastan is much more extensive than that of Roncesvalles, and is not at so considerable an elevation. It is very thickly inhabited, and exhibits every mark of wealth and comfort. Good roads, a luxury nowhere else to be met with in these mountains, cross the valley in every direction and many well placed chateau and bridges covered with ivy and masses of beech wood varies the prospect every mile you pass.

The inhabitants of these mountains are a very different race from those dwelling in the lower parts of Spain. They have a language of their own, Basque, not at all resembling the Castilian, and it is very difficult to learn. It is a written language, and in tour through the Pyrenees a vocabulary is given but I have not been able to obtain a sight of it; it is common to both sides of the mountains, and is spoken on the French side as well as the Spanish.

The productions of these mountains are more approaching our northern climate. Vineyards are replaced by orchards, from which they make good cider and there are neither olives, oranges or any other of the southern fruits. You might fancy yourself in Wales, or the north of England, but for large fields of Indian corn, or maize, which are frequent in the narrow plains. At Roncesvalles however it is too cold for that even and you find in its stead, hay and oats.

Amongst the mountains we have completely cheated the Spanish summer, and the agues and fevers accompanying it. There is always a breeze, fresh and delicious, and the mornings and evenings are particularly pleasant. The general state of health shows the superiority of the climate; the four divisions consisting of nearly five thousand men, two days since had only fifty-nine on the sick list, four of whom only required carriage, a smaller number than I ever remember with a strong regiment in England or Ireland.

From hence to Passages, the nearest harbour is not more than eighteen miles, yet the steepness of the mountain you have to pass, and the badness of the roads, and the dread of the army moving during your absence, has hitherto deterred me from attempting to go there. We profit however from our vicinity to the sea to get fish, which we have not had an opportunity of procuring for three years before, and this deprivation makes the treat greater.

214

The month of October we understand will render these mountains impassable from the depth of snow, and we expect will close our campaign for this year, and I mean to ask for leave of absence, if peace, at the idea of which they are much elevated in France, does not dismiss us before that time, and I look forward with great pleasure to once more shaking hands with all my friends after so long an absence, and shall not fail paying my respects to you at Ramsgate. Till that wished for moment, adieu &c.

G.R.B.

Letter 111   Camp near St Antonio,[1] 9 September 1813

My dear Mansel,

I should have written to you a week ago, but I have been confined by an inflammation in the eyes, and it was not until yesterday I ventured to write a line. I went to see the storm of San Sebastian and in doing so missed a sharp skirmish in which my battalion was engaged.[2] One man of the 53rd was killed, and Sergeant Robertshaw [3] and sixteen wounded, and eighteen of the Queen's. This and the loss of three volunteers killed at the storm of the town, has reduced us below five hundred bayonets, and if (notwithstanding the dreadful wet weather we have experienced in these cursed mountains) we were not remarkably healthy we should have been a skeleton long before this.

We are now encamped about four miles from Lesaka, very near the clouds and often above them; constructing a redoubt, a chain of which it is intended to make the line of the Pyrenees as strong as the lines near Lisbon.[4] We however expect another turn out as Soult

1. I cannot identify a village of this name.
2. The town of San Sebastian was stormed on 31 August 1813 whilst at the same time there were serious attacks by Soult at San Marcial, Vera, Zagaramurdi and at the heights of Salain where the 2nd Provisional Battalion fought.
3. Sergeant John Robertshaw, 53 Regiment.
4. This is interesting, as it is the only statement that I have come across regarding a chain of redoubts being built on the Pyrenees by British forces, which is certainly in keeping with Wellington's usual modus operandi. In the *Duke of Wellington's dispatches, Volume X* page 568, Wellington writes 'I do not think we could successfully apply to this frontier of Spain the system on which we fortified the country between the Tagus and the sea'. Despite this statement, Bingham was certain that a chain of defences was planned and he refers to the scheme again in later letters.

is said to declare he will make one more push for Pamplona. I hope with no better success than the last. The surrender of this place will we hope put us into winter quarters. It cannot hold out ten days longer, if so long. We believe that the castle of San Sebastian fell yesterday.[1] We hear no firing in that direction today, and reports are abroad to that effect. If we move after the fall of these places, it will be in the direction of Suchet, for if there were even any serious plans for a campaign in the south of France, it must be for the present abandoned. It would not do to have these mountains impassable from deep snow, in our rear. Soult has laboured hard at Bayonne, and it is said now to be very strong. Certainly it is past being carried by a coup de main; large stores of provisions have been collected in the citadel, and another bridge is thrown across the Adour above the town. The volunteers who went to San Sebastian, fourteen in number of whom seven have returned, came back loaded with plunder; Edwards,[2] formerly Hovenden's[3] servant got upwards of three hundred pounds in doubloons. I am sorry to say the town is no more. Scarce a house is left standing. We blame the French, but I am afraid whoever set the town on fire; we (who had possession of it) made no efforts to extinguish the flames.

The usual difficulty about forage; the parties out from five in the morning till two, and our animals will all die if we remain with them at picket much longer, in this bleak exposed situation.

Lord Wellington has just gone past. The castle surrendered yesterday even[ing].[4] Adieu.

G.R.B.

1. Following the defeat of the first storm of San Sebastian on 25 July, Wellington required volunteers from the three neighbouring divisions to show the 5th Division how to do it. Two hundred men were supplied from the 4th Division. The second storm was successful on 31 August and the garrison retired into the castle on Monte Urgull.
2. Private Griffin Edwards.
3. Lieutenant Pierce Hovenden 53 Regiment. The note seems to indicate that something untoward had happened to him, but he remained with the regiment for a long period and was not injured; he had obviously ceased using Edwards as his servant possibly for a misdemeanour, although nothing is indicated in the Returns.
4. The castle surrendered following an extremely heavy bombardment on 8 September.

Letter 112   Camp near Etxalar, 13 September 1813

To Major General Bingham, at Brighton.

My dear Richard,

Ample details will have reached you long before this of the surrender of the castle of San Sebastian by capitulation, of the storm of the town, and of Soult's reverse in attempting to relieve it. I went to see the last two days bombardment and storm, and by this means was absent from my battalion at rather a critical moment, it being the only British battalion of the 4th Division engaged, but could anyone have supposed the Duke of Dalmatia would have delayed till the last day, his attempt on our covering army; for had he succeeded the town would have been ours, and I am not sure he would have dared take it from us.

The remainder of the 4th Division was on that day, 31st August, in the rear of the Spanish army, and witnessed their gallant conduct. General Freire was everywhere,[1] at the head of every charge, and can they be brought to a continuance of such conduct the contest will be no longer doubtful. Seventeen officers killed and nearly eighty wounded prove that whatever may have been the case formerly, on this occasion, they nobly did their duty, and they cannot have been said to be backward.

Either the French or ourselves set fire to the town [San Sebastian] but whatever party were originally the cause of it, the discredit of its total destruction may certainly be laid to our door, no exertion having been made to put the fire out, for the several days it continued burning. At first it might have been easily stopped by pulling down the houses on each side of those on fire. Certainly afterwards it would have been more difficult, but no effort was made, and the individuals of the 5th Division were too intent on helping themselves to wine and other articles of plunder, than in affording assistance to the unfortunate sufferers, and now the attempt to excuse it is worse than the deed itself, viz, that the inhabitants were all in the French interests. No doubt before the war there must have been great intercourse between Bayonne and San Sebastian, but what business have we to punish a whole town because they don't think as we do. There certainly is no proof, although since they have been clamorous at the

---

1. General Manuel Freire commanded the Spanish troops at San Marcial.

burning of the town, it has been asserted they took an active part in the defence during the siege.

Redoubts are now constructing which are (it is said) to be furnished with heavy guns, on the same plan as the lines near Lisbon. The line runs from Roncesvalles to Fuenterrabia, but it will require some time to finish, and when the cold weather sets in we shall be hardly able to stay here. Forage has been for some time so scarce that we have to send daily ten or twelve miles distance and as many home, for it. Corn for anyone under the rank of a General officer is out of the question except sometimes on the eve of a march, when you get what the general, his staff, or commissariat can neither carry or consume themselves.

As soon as Pamplona surrenders, which cannot be far distant, I think of applying for leave, which I see however will be very difficult to obtain. Sir Lowry Cole is anxious I should succeed to the command of a brigade, but the command of a brigade under the rank of major-general is so precarious and involves a person in a certain expense that I own I cannot see that it is likely to be of any advantage. However a person embarked in a cause must strive to get through it, but as Cole has very much the ear of Lord Wellington at present, I must be guided a good deal by his advice and discretion.

Suchet you may have heard advanced on Lord William Bentinck, raised the siege of Tarragona, blew up the works and drew off the garrison, fell back, and has taken up a position on the River Foix, near Vilafranca [del Penedes] and Vilanova [i la Geltru]. He must take care not to stay too long, for when Pamplona falls and these mountains are secured part by the snow and the remainder by these redoubts he may be hampered by the superior force brought against him. Adieu.

G.R.B.

[A letter to Mansel dated 24 September has been omitted by Bingham as containing merely repetitions of former letters.]

Letter 113   Camp near Etxalar, 1 October 1813

My dear Mary,

Agreeable to my promise I shall be more frequent in my communications and you shall have a portion of the family letters addressed to you. The favourable account of my mother, communicated in your last letter put me quite in spirits to go to Sir Lowry Cole's dinner, where I spent a very pleasant day. I met a French commissary, who had been taken prisoner a few days before, a very pleasant gentlemanlike person, who he stated had lost a considerable property at St Domingo, some years before. He expects to be exchanged immediately for Mr Larpent the Judge Advocate[1] who was captured by the French at Lesaka, during their last advance; and I gave him a letter for John at Verdun, which he promised to put into the post office at Bayonne for me. I am doubtful if he will ever receive it, but if he does it will give him great satisfaction. I was much entertained at one occurrence that took place at dinner. The French gentleman was quite unacquainted with the customs of English society; some one at table asked him to take a glass of wine, which he declined. The person next to him explained the manner in which we drink wine with each other at dinner, adding the compliment of healths, and he quickly appeared to understand it. Shortly after he asked some one to take a bit of mutton with him, and gravely said when he had got a mouthful on his fork: 'Your good health, Sir'. Nor do I see anything so ridiculous in it, for it is quite as natural to wish a man a continuance of his health when swallowing a bit of meat as when drinking wine.

I returned the next day, not having been invited to the installation of the Knights of the Bath, which took place on the 27th, the anniversary of the Battle of Busaco. Sixteen general officers were present at a very good dinner in a very crowded room; in performing the ceremony Lord Wellington could hardly keep his countenance, especially when he knighted Pakenham.

The weather has been very wet this last week and we are heartily tired of flies, fleas and mountain roads.

We are told nine ounces of bread and five of horse flesh is the daily ration at Pamplona, which I heartily wish would surrender; it would determine our future operations. The French it would appear mean to act on the defensive as they are hard at work constructing redoubts, batteries, and they have broken up all the roads within the frontier.

A brigade of Spanish troops have just arrived and have hutted

1. Francis Seymour Larpent, the Judge Advocate left a lively journal, giving much detail of life at headquarters; it was published in 1853.

opposite my quarter. They are very noisy neighbours as they are drumming and trumpeting all day and all night. Adieu.

G.R.B.

Letter 114　　　　　　　Camp near Etxalar, 2 October 1813

To Major General Bingham, Brighton

[Extract made by Bingham]
Since I last wrote we have had no movement although we have had various reports of movements which have never taken place.

It is said Pamplona can hold out to the 16th of this month. A rumour is afloat that in a sortie made a few days since they obtained three days provisions, but I can hardly credit this.

I wish it would fall as I mean to apply for leave of absence if we do not enter France, which many people think we shall. After all, a winter's campaign in an enemy's country will be no luxury.

Yesterday the enemy sent into our out posts a bulletin in four languages relating to the advantages said to be obtained by their army in Catalonia. Of course they have magnified it greatly. Of course before this reaches you, you will be in possession of all the details which we are not. We hear Adam's corps[1] (which is said to have been almost surprised) was twelve miles in front of the remainder of the army; they will never in my opinion distinguish themselves in that quarter as long as Donkin remains Quarter Master General.[2] We had a specimen of his military ability when we first landed in Portugal.

Letter 115　Camp near Vera [de Bidasoa], 14 October 1813

To Lieutenant Colonel Mansel

[Extract made by Bingham]
On the 7th we left Etxalar, to support the Light Division in an

1. Colonel Frederick Adam commanded the Advance guard of Lord William Bentinck's army on the East Coast.
2. Major General Sir Rufane Shaw Donkin had previously (1808–9) served in Portugal as Deputy Quartermaster-General. He was now Quartermaster-General in the Mediterranean.

attack on the mountain above the town of Vera, being a part of a combined movement from the sea, to the pass of Maya, to possess ourselves of the whole range of mountains on the right bank of the Bidassoa, giving us a better road and a considerably shorter line of communication and the advantage of overlooking the plains of France, and consequently of guarding against any assembly of the enemy's troops. Of this movement which occupied a space of perhaps fourteen miles we only saw that part to which we were attached; the Light Division carrying entrenchment after entrenchment, on an exceeding steep mountain, leaving us nothing to do as supports but to follow. They finally pressed the enemy so hard that about two hundred and fifty prisoners and four mountain guns fell into their hands, and we were within three miles of St Jean de Luz, apparently a neat pretty town on the coast and we were in full view of the gardens and country houses that surround Bayonne, the town itself being covered by a hill on this side of it. The Spaniards on our right as far as we saw behaved very well. Not so Longa's corps which was with us. It was very difficult to get them on at all and they conducted themselves with great barbarity towards the wounded that fell into their power; they stripped even to his shirt an officer who was only wounded through the leg, not able to move, and left him to perish with cold. They were equally handy in stripping our own people some of whom (I myself saw a cacadore) were naked before the breath was out of their bodies. The pretence is retaliation, but I recollect to have heard that the same thing took place on the part of the Spaniards in the year 1793 at Toulon.

The same afternoon we moved to this neighbourhood to support Giron's corps,[1] who had that morning carried Santa Barbe whilst the 7th Division carried three redoubts on a tongue of land that runs down to the French village of Serres. Yesterday morning at 1 o'clock the farthest of these redoubts, the one next the village having been given up to the Spaniards was surprised, and two hundred of their men taken prisoners. They have however stood their ground very well since, and have lost they say, eight officers and four hundred men killed and wounded. There was a smart skirmish the whole day, we were in support looking on, and feeling so confident that our tents were not even struck. We returned at

1. General Pedro Augustin Giron commanded the Andalusian Army of Reserve.

4 o'clock to dinner and Fehrszen and myself cracked a bottle of claret to the Lord's good health and prosperity. The redoubt in question having been voted too far from our line, was left in the enemy's hands, which has spoilt our foraging; the part of the village in our possession having been full of excellent hay and Indian corn; as the French have not touched their own country, receiving regular issues from their commissariat, who however pay for nothing.

If anything happens before Sunday I will give you a postscript, adieu.

G.R.B.

Letter 116   Camp near Vera, 29 October 1813

My dear Mansel,

Nothing has taken place since I last wrote to you. Everybody seems to talk of a winter's campaign in France, and we are making all sorts of preparations. Very fortunately we have today got up a stock of trowsers [sic] (cloth) and equipment of every description, but we must have I should think different weather to enable us to commence our operations. The season has been, either from being in the mountains or some other cause, excessively wet but these last two days the rain has fallen in such torrents accompanied with thunder, hail, and snow, that the road even between the camp and the village is nearly impassable, and our artillery which has arrived as far, can neither move one way or the other. The soil is a deep clay like that about the lines of Lisbon and you may guess what sort of a figure we shall cut in a winter campaign; the mud is now over shoe, the first step out of the tent, and one step forward is generally accompanied with one slide backward. As yet however we have very few sick, but we cannot expect to remain so if we keep the field; the men are very well fed and tolerably paid. The poor animals are dreadfully off, with nothing to eat but the grass they can pick up. Twenty miles distance to send for corn. If you had not been in this country you would not believe that while the officers are obliged to send so far for their corn on their own beasts, at a risk of losing their baggage, in case of a sudden movement, the commissary of the division employs twenty-two mules in bringing up the meat from the place where it is killed to the camp; you will ask why he does not kill near the camp? I answer he would lose his dirty perquisites; marrow, bones, cow heel, tripe and tongues; you

222

will next enquire if the general officers do not interfere? They do not. The corn is brought up for them, and they are accommodated with public mules to carry their own baggage &c, &c.

Seven men of the 53rd have died in the last month in the hospital in the rear; chiefly those wounded on the 31st August and several sent home as invalids, amongst them Sergeant Robertshaw whom I mentioned as my having made a Colour Sergeant for his gallant conduct, and Sergeant Jones the Paymaster's clerk;[1] in an evil hour on the 31st August he got drunk, a common occurrence with him, and wandering about the country, he having lost Maclean's baggage,[2] he fell in with the 51st Regiment who as he could give no good account of himself put a musket into his hand, and took him into action, where his thigh was broken by a musket shot, and he will never be able to serve again; he was a very worthless fellow.

If you knew the shifts I have been put to, to get through this letter, constantly changing from one side to the other, to prevent the rain falling either on my head or the paper. Adieu.

G.R.B.

[A letter to his mother dated Camp near Vera, 4 November is omitted by Bingham as being merely a repetition of the last two letters.]

Letter 117   Camp near Vera, 6 November 1813

[Extract made by Bingham]

My dear Mansel,

We have now had two dry days with tolerably sharp frost and tomorrow we expect to enter France. The French have not neglected the opportunity of strengthening their positions, which in front of this looks very formidable and there is no want of information on their part from German deserters. They have within these two days increased their numbers. We have a summons today to meet our lieutenant general on a neighbouring hill at 10 o'clock,

---

1. Sergeant John Jones had only been appointed to Captain Gilles' company of the 53 Regiment on 3 April 1813 from the Vale of Glamorgan Militia.
2. Assistant Surgeon Charles Maclean.

that is to say commanding officers of brigades and regiments and then we expect to receive our orders.

Just returned from the conference; not as I expected arrangements for our move, but a lecture on the necessity of preventing plunder and marauding on entering France. All I could get from the general was that if the weather continued favourable we should move on Monday. Everybody seems to think our superiority in number is likely to make it an easy matter, but I should be surprised if it turns out as easy as they suppose. Time will show. I am not very sanguine on the event of our French expedition. However in the mountains we cannot stay; all the higher are already covered with snow, and the rest will probably be so before the month is over. I need not tell you it's tolerably cold in a tent without a lining. Adieu.

G.R.B.

Letter 118   Ascain, Department Lower Pyrenees, 20 November 1813

My dear Sir,

We have been so much occupied the last few days, that I have not had time to write to any one, but now being comfortably established I hope for the winter in the Cure's house in this village, I will try to give you an account of all that happened to us after we broke up from our mountain bivouac on the 10th which we were not sorry to do, the lateness of the season together with the cold and the wet, making it anything but agreeable. Before daybreak then, on that day, we started, it having been determined to force Soult's strong line of entrenchments on the Nivelle, and to establish ourselves on the plain; this movement was of an extended nature from the sea on our left nearly to St Jean Pied de Port on our right, which was to be the point of attack, our left being only a feint, but as this movement was of so extended a nature, I shall not attempt to give you any account beyond what actually happened to us on the right of the centre, leaving you to make out from the great lord's despatch the position of the whole. Two or three dry days enabled us to get up three brigades of artillery (18 pieces) to the rear of the wood where we were encamped by roads supposed to be perfectly impassable to carriages of any description. Operations were to commence at dawn by opening a fire on the redoubt of Sare, the same at which the French had been at work strengthening since the 13th October, when they retook it from the Spaniards and which was to all appearance very strong. As soon as the fire of the artillery had made an adequate impression, the battalion which I commanded was to carry it by storm. Accordingly leaving our packs behind and carrying bags filled with leaves to facilitate our descent into the ditch, we moved off, and suffering but little from the fire of the work, established ourselves under cover of the hill within thirty paces of it. There was another redoubt to our right within four pounder range which part of the 7th Division were to carry, and before their attack began we had the fire on us; to save our people from this teasing fire before the artillery had made any impression on the redoubt, we jumped up and dashed at the gorge of it, but found the French had been too quick for us. We were only in time to secure a few prisoners who were making their escape.

Thus this work which had appeared so formidable was taken with a very trifling loss within half an hour after the commencement of the action. The next point to be attacked was the village beyond which was a height, defended by two large redoubts, with an abatis at the foot of the hill. Sare was soon in our possession, and being exposed to a cannonade from the heights I got my battalion in column behind the largest house in the place waiting further operations; in this house had assembled all the better description of women of the village, and whilst the cannonade was destroying the back part of the building and offices in the rear, we were chattering with the ladies in front, whose tongues ran faster than the roll of musketry on every side of us. We were not delayed long but soon moved out from our cover to assist in the attack of the abatis which the 27th carried in great style. I had forgot to mention that I left an officer in the great house at Sare, to protect its inmates, who justly dreaded the followers, more than the army itself. I heard afterwards they were very thankful for my protection. As for ourselves we continued to push on, not meeting with that firm resistance we had reason to expect from the nature of the ground and the strength of the defences. The redoubt immediately behind Sare having been evacuated, we pushed on beyond it, cutting off from their own army a battalion of the 88th who had stoutly defended a redoubt on the left from several attacks of the Light Division.[1] Following the enemy

1. The 52 Regiment forced this battalion to surrender.

close, our light company took from them a light six pounder and about this time Fehrszen, whose conduct through the day had been most conspicuous, was struck down by a spent musket ball. For a short time we lamented him as dead, until looking to the front I discovered him as active and as gay as ever, leading his company on in gallant style. About midday we brought up on a height from which we had a splendid though distant view of the position of both armies; almost in rear of the French right and apparently as near if not nearer St Jean de Luz than they were. The battle raged furiously on our right and several of these redoubts defied the efforts of our old friends the 6th Division to take them. In our front and just below us was a bridge over the Nivelle,[1] which the French had not destroyed, and we remained wondering why we were not ordered to force this pass which would have brought us in rear of the right wing of the French. Probably the protracted resistance on our right prevented our making this movement, which would indeed have been decisive. We had three divisions besides Spaniards at the point, mustering strong, notwithstanding the casualties of the morning. The loss in our battalion amounted to one sergeant, four rank and file killed, three officers, forty one rank and file wounded. Towards evening the 6th and 2nd Divisions obtained possession of the left of the enemy's position and the firing ceased all along the line. Some time after dark, when I had laid myself down comfortably amongst the heather for the night, I was roused by an aide-de-camp to tell me to take possession of the village of St Pé[e–sur-Nivelle] at the foot of our hill and rather to the right; so grumbling at the disturbance and the darkness of the night off we set to find the place. It was eleven o'clock before we got there and having as well as we could, found out the avenues to the place and posted our picquets. Fehrszen and myself took up our quarters at a large farm house and threw ourselves down on the sweetest cock of hay I ever remember to have met with; it perfumed our cloaks for weeks after. The inhabitants had absconded and there was nothing to be had in an empty house. About two in the morning we heard some cocks crowing under a tub. We soon had them in the pot; and excellent chicken broth we had for breakfast. Before the day dawned we got under arms and began to look over our quarters, which were very good. We found also a surgeon

1. The Bridge of Amotz.

who had been at St Domingo and who spoke English very well. Soult had ordered the inhabitants to retire but this order had been but partially obeyed, and of the absentees, after daylight many began to return. From these we heard the French had retired to their entrenched camp near Bayonne. Here we stayed lounging about till about noon, when off we set to join the remainder of the division on the route towards Bayonne. About sunset we fell in with the enemy and were ordered to drive back their picquets, which we did without loss, and we took up our ground in the Bois de St Pé, where as the night was cold our people suffered severely. The tents had not come up and our men had taken off their packs the more easily to carry the redoubt the day before, and we were without blankets. The fuel fortunately was abundant. The 12th we halted; a fine day, quite warm. We got up our packs and blankets with a firm resolve on my part, never to part with them again under any of the exigencies of the service. Our tents too came and we were happy fellows.

The left of the army pushed on towards Bayonne, from which we were not far distant. The night was dreadful, such a storm of wind, rain, thunder, and lightning we had not experienced for some time. I had placed my tent on a very tempting spot of the green sward, on a flat surface which made me overlook the circumstance of its being in the run of the valley; in a moment the flood rushed down, and tent and bed and self were washed away. The remainder of the night was passed in collecting my floating goods and chattels. The next day (14th) afforded no opportunity of drying our soaked articles. It was wet and we sat shivering and shaking and hoping and wishing for cantonments and speculating on what our next movement would be; looking like fowls on a rail, in a wet day, cold and miserable. The 15th was only showery, and in a fair interval I got as far as the General's who had a sort of house. The Portuguese brigade having gone into cantonments gave us great hopes we should soon follow. Do not wonder we wished for the shelter of a house, the Bois de St Pé in the middle of a wet November held out no great inducement for the most sanguine to long to keep the field. The night was again dreadful with torrents of rain and a heavy gale of wind. I had got clear of my smooth valley and although on rough ground stood the night out well. Fortunately we were well off in eatables and drinkables which was a great consolation and I contrived to entertain three officers at dinner under circumstances far from comfortable.

On the 17th the joyful news of cantonments arrived, and starting at eight, through a road up to the knees in mud, we arrived at this place at three in the afternoon, but our baggage did not get here till after dark; and now snugly settled at the Curé's comfortable house, we hope all our fatigue and toil is at an end till better weather will enable us to enjoy taking the field again, and we speculate the beating Soult got in the last affair, and the advance of the allies in the north may keep him on the defensive till the weather will enable us to open the campaign under more auspicious circumstances; that is to say as far as individual comfort is concerned, for I think in England you will say we have done our duty in this instance and be satisfied for some short time to come. Adieu.

G.R.B.

Letter 119   **Ascain, 27 November 1813**

To Mr Gundry

My dear Sir,

Many thanks for your kind letter of the 10th and for the interest you take in my health and affairs. I had before I received your letter talked to Sir Lowry Cole about leave of absence and had deferred at his request, making a regular application as several general officers and people of distinction had been refused; however on the receipt of yours I took the liberty of reading [to General Cole] that part of it relative to my mother and he immediately said he would use his best endeavours, adding that no time was to be lost. I therefore sat down in his house and wrote a letter which he approved, stating in the strongest terms the necessity of my being allowed to return to England. This Sir Lowry took with him to headquarters where he was going to dine; he took a favourable opportunity of submitting it to Lord Wellington who said he was sorry to be obliged to refuse a person he was pleased to say had such claims, and whose presence [at home] he was certain must be so necessary; but that the army was so situated that he had determined to give no more leave except to those who could demand it on the score of parliamentary duty; as soon however as my services could be dispensed with I should have the leave I wanted.

What are to be the movements of the army it is hard to say. It is whispered abroad that the Spanish Government have behaved ill,

228

and have threatened Lord Wellington because he would neither sanction or allow the excesses of their troops, the whole Spanish army should be withdrawn; for they were not content with plundering but in some instances have actually burnt the houses that were to afford us shelter. Honesty and upright conduct should be enforced at any rate, and Lord Wellington may hereafter profit by his policy.

On our entering France many of the inhabitants fled, having been ordered to do so by the Duke of Dalmatia. They have now nearly all returned and being for the moment relieved both from conscription and contribution seem pleased with the change.

The venality and severity of Napoleon's government can hardly be conceived; no man could go from one village to another without a passport, and for this passport he was always obliged to pay. They were quite astonished when our generals granted passes to go beyond our lines, without taking any remuneration; the great French generals so celebrated throughout Europe, having in their own as well as in other countries been guilty of such dirty acts to raise their fortunes that a well principled English country gentleman would have been ashamed of. Adieu.

G.R.B.

Letter 120   Ascain, 1 December 1813

My dear Richard,

I ought to have answered your letter of the 11th by the last packet, but I have been so unsettled of late and in fact daily expecting to obtain leave of absence, which however has been at last refused, so I must make up my mind to stay, and the first thing I have to do is to lose no time in thanking you for your long letter.

Of the details of the passage of the Nivelle, and of the forcing the French lines on that river, you will long since have been acquainted. The more brilliant successes that have more to say to the grand question of war or peace, than our operations, will have so occupied the public mind that you will have hardly time or inclination to attend to our affairs of minor importance and yet altogether it has been one of the neatest things done by us, this war, and to look over the French position, which we now do in our morning walks, we wonder how we got it so easily.

Lord Wellington certainly did deceive Soult who remained the whole day on his right where he obstinately persisted in believing the real attack would take place, nor did he entirely evacuate the right of that position till three o'clock in the morning of the 11th. Had we (with 4th, 7th and Light Division) pushed forward on the afternoon of the 10th across the Nivelle from the heights above St Pé, where we were formed, to Bidart, a great part of the enemy's corps must have fallen into our hands but whether the backward conduct of General Giron and the Army of Andalusia which was conspicuous through the whole of the day, or the progress made by the enemy on our extreme right where a corps opposed to Mina penetrated nearly as far as the valley of Bastan, prevented our General from executing this plan, no one here can say; we had possession of the bridges so there could on that account have been no obstacle.

On Soult's line were not less than forty closed redoubts, some of them furnished with artillery, but perhaps works on this extended scale may be rather a detriment to an army as they prevent drawing bodies of troops from one part of the position to the other. Now Lord Wellington was pretty certain no part of the French army would quit their works to attack him, so he played a sure game in bringing a mass of troops to force the centre of their line which, once performed, the rest had nothing for it but to retreat.

The roads in this fine country are quite as bad as the worst mountain roads in Portugal, and we are as badly off for forage as ever. Hay is now brought from England and sells for twenty guineas a ton. I fortunately found a house full, which with economy will last a month, but I was obliged to bring it home by night for fear of detection.

Major General Howard[1] being about to be appointed to the command of the 1st Division, Anson goes to the 1st Brigade of Guards and I shall succeed to the command of the brigade, but now in our tide of success so many are wishing to come out from England that I will not hold it long, besides there are so many colonels senior to me in the country I have no chance of being put in orders as on the staff, and a brigade without the emoluments trifling as they are is ruin. Adieu.

G.R.B.

1. Major General Keneth Alexander Howard was appointed to command of the 1st Division in the absence of Sir John Hope, Lord Hopetoun, who was shortly after wounded and made prisoner at Bayonne.

Letter 121   France, 18 December 1813

To Lieutenant Colonel Mansel

[Extract]

In the last battles of the 9th, 10th and 11th and 13th[1] we have borne no part, having been constantly in reserve. On the last day the 2nd Division greatly distinguished themselves and it was as gallant an affair as ever was witnessed with the exception of the old Buffs, who gave up a village entrusted to them to defend, without firing a shot.[2] Bunbury[3] whose character was before more than suspected is to be brought to court martial, at least Sir Rowland Hill said so at the time. Whether he will alter his opinion is another thing; at any rate he will be obliged to quit. In the 6th Division also they say a very distinguished character might have had his division up to support much sooner if he had liked, and that neither on the 10th November or on the 13th December did he show himself a glutton as to fire.[4]

You will be sorry to hear poor Cotton[5] only survived his wound three days; he is a great loss to the service I think.

General Barnes and Byng were conspicuous the other day, as was Sir John Hope on our left the day his division was engaged.

To our great surprise Picton has come out again;[6] it is said to

1. Collectively known as the Battle of the Nive.
2. On the 13th, at the action of St Pierre, the Buffs (1/3rd) had been ordered to dispute the passage of a defile with the French as they advanced, but Lieutenant Colonel Bunbury, commanding the regiment, hastily abandoned the village of Vieux Mouguerre to the French.
3. Lieutenant Colonel William Henry Bunbury. He resigned his commission rather than be tried.
4. This is a thinly veiled attack on Clinton who was back in charge of the 6th Division. The division was very tardy in coming up to support Hill's weakened line.
5. Captain Thomas D'Avenant Cotton, 7 Foot, Brigade Major to Byng's 2nd Division received a mortal wound on 10 December when leading an attack on a redoubt. He died on 13 December.
6. Sir Thomas Picton had gone home after the fall of San Sebastian for political reasons and was duly elected MP for Pembroke. He returned, having been offered command of the Spanish Army of Catalonia, but following a private discussion with Wellington who did not think it a good move; he took command of the 3rd Division again.

command the Catalonian Army, but as Suchet has retired into France they are on their way to join and it is not likely he will remain here in command of a division, but probably will return. The weather has been excessively wet and the roads are so dreadfully cut up that the baggage is never up; we were two nights last week without tents, and exposed to the heavy rain, this is not likely to increase our effective strength. In short I am tired of this winter campaign, and ardently look forward to peace as the only remedy for our evils. We get no corn, no forage, or indeed anything else. Adieu.

G.R.B.

Letter 122   Arrauntz, 29 December 1813

My dear Richard,

You are long ere this in possession of the details of the seven actions from the 9th to the 13th of this month, which is more than we are. The 4th Division was never engaged nor were we ever in any situation that gave us one opportunity of clearly understanding either the attack on the enemy of the 11th on the left, when several regiments of the 5th Division behaved exceedingly ill, the 4th and 47th are mentioned in particular on the attack of the 13th on our right,[1] when the 2nd Division distinguished themselves as much the other way. It was indeed a severe contest, Soult having brought a preponderating force to that quarter, and hoping to have overwhelmed every opposition. Since this, he has retired from Bayonne leaving two divisions in the entrenched camp, which will be a sad thorn in our side. If we advance we must mask it, and having three points from which they can debouch viz, towards St Jean de Luz, between the Nive and Adour, and across the bridge having the old citadel as a tête de pont. I doubt whether you can effectually bombard it and if you set down regularly to besiege it you must have a large covering army, and where is all this force to come from; the Spaniards, who officers and all, are little better than a banditti,

---

1. Hope's corps, consisting of the left wing of the army was caught unprepared, foraging and cooking, when suddenly attacked by the French. The regiments, including the 1/4th and 2/47th had no time to form and were scattered as the French drove on. They fought in uncoordinated pockets, barely holding on until support arrived.

are so much annoyed at our having put a stop to their plundering that they cannot be depended on, hating you if possible worse than they did the French; you will never venture to move them far from their own frontier. All the disposable force you have at home is gone to Holland.[1] Soult is daily receiving reinforcements, so unless Napoleon is pressed on the other side so as to prevent his augmenting Soult's force we shall be obliged to fall back and shall return to the mountains in the spring if we are not driven there before. These however are gloomy prospects I hope may never be realised.

These last few days the weather has been clear, but the roads are dreadful; on the other side of the Adour, are represented as worse, but this can hardly be possible.

It is said General Anson is to go to the Guards, which would give me the temporary command of the brigade, but I should not be put in orders as there are so many colonels with the army senior to me. The expected brevet may do something for me, and the rage for serving in Holland will take away several who were looking for appointments here.

I passed my Christmas day with General Cole; Lord March[2] the son of your chief was of the party. Do you wonder at my being tired of this campaigning when this is the fifth Christmas I have spent with the army, leaving me in nearly the same situation I was at first placed in, without prospect of promotion or advancement.

'All work and no play, makes Jack a dull boy', yet it is fortunate I did not get leave, as I had proposed at the same time with Wade,[3] Cole's Aide-de-Camp, as he was captured on the passage. Colonel Grant[4] was also on board and the portrait painter with all the likenesses for the great national work of Vitoria. Excuse a letter written

1. In 1814 the Dutch requested British help to drive the French garrisons from their country. Sir Thomas Graham, who had sailed home on health grounds following the capture of San Sebastian, was coerced into leading the forces. The British troops landed in Holland and attempted to take Bergen op Zoom and Antwerp, but were unsuccessful.
2. Charles, Earl of March, son of the Duke of Richmond, was a captain in the 52 Regiment at this time.
3. Major Thomas Francis Wade, aide-de-camp to Cole. His entry in the Military Calendar does not mention his being made a prisoner.
4. I cannot identify this officer with any certainty as there is no record of a Colonel Grant being captured at this time nor of a ship captured in these circumstances.

in the spirit of the blue devils, but my mother's illness and the prospect of everlasting war deprives me of my evenness of temper. Adieu.

G.R.B.

A few days after George Bingham obtained leave of absence and hastened home to take a last leave of his mother. He unfortunately was too late for on his arrival at Falmouth, he learnt that she had expired on 31 December, some days before he had left the army. In early 1814 Lieutenant Colonel Mansel returned to France with the six fully restored companies, and commanded the 2/53rd when they fought as a complete regiment again at Toulouse.

Whilst George was preparing to rejoin the regiment in France in April 1814, the announcement of Napoleon's abdication and the termination of hostilities was declared.

In September 1814 George married Emma Septima Pleydell, the youngest daughter of Edmund Morton Pleydell, of Whatcombe House, Dorset. George also became a Knight Commander of the Bath and of the Tower and Sword of Portugal in 1814 and was therefore henceforth a 'Sir'.

Chapter Five

The HMS *Northumberland* Journal

Following Napoleon's return to France from exile on Elba, his reclaiming of the throne of France and subsequent defeat at the Battle of Waterloo on 18 June 1815, he was forced to abdicate a second and final time. Forced to remove himself from Paris, Napoleon and his entourage travelled to Rochefort with the intention of seeking passage to the United States of America. Numerous plans were proposed for Napoleon's escape past the ever watchful patrols of the Royal Navy, but the high chance of an embarrassing capture caused Napoleon to decide to surrender formally to the British.

Following protracted negotiations, Napoleon eventually presented himself to Captain Maitland onboard HMS *Bellerophon* and put himself under the protection of the British government. The *Bellerophon* proceeded to England and anchored at Torbay on 24 July 1815. Following serious deliberations as to the fate of their prisoner, the British government decided that it was much too risky to allow Napoleon to reside in England and that he was to be kept on the tiny South Atlantic island of St Helena.

The island was owned by the Honourable East India Company as a depot on route to India but was temporarily to become Crown Land and garrisoned by the British Army. The 2nd Battalion 53 Regiment had been recuperating in England and was ordered to St Helena as part of the increased garrison and embarked at Plymouth on a number of transport ships. Sir George Bingham was put onboard Admiral Cockburn's flagship HMS *Northumberland*, to which Napoleon and his entourage were transferred on 7 August 1815, eventually landing on St. Helena on 13 October 1815.

George sailed without his new wife as he was aware that Sir Hudson Lowe was to be made Governor and as he was hoping to become a major general shortly, he fully expected to be ordered home to avoid having another officer on the island of the same rank as the governor. However, this problem was negated by Lowe being given the local rank of lieutenant general and he was to remain on St Helena commanding all the troops on the island until 1820. Lady Bingham therefore sailed from Portsmouth with Colonel and Mrs Wynyard[1] in the *Adamant* transport on 1 February 1816. On arrival at Funchal they met up with the *Regulus* transport which had sailed earlier on 26 January. Here Lieutenant Colonel Mansel of the 53rd transhipped from the *Regulus* to the *Adamant* to continue the voyage but the ship having missed St Helena, the *Adamant* did not arrive until 6 May 1816.

Sunday, 6 August 1815

Having embarked at Portsmouth, and working down channel in the *Northumberland* with the wind at west, we perceived at eight o'clock in the morning, three large ships apparently coming out of Plymouth; signals being exchanged they proved to be the *Tonnant* (having Lord Keith's flag onboard[2]) the *Bellerophon*, and the *Eurotas* Frigate. On their coming up with us Admiral Sir George Cockburn[3] went onboard the *Tonnant* 84[4]; we made all sail towards the land, and anchored west of Berry Head, on the outside of Torbay, and on the admiral's return, heard that Napoleon Bonaparte was to be removed the next day at 10 o'clock.

1. Colonel Edward Buckley Wynyard was appointed Military Secretary.
2. Admiral George Keith Elphinstone was Commander of Plymouth dockyard and acted as the British Government's intermediary with Napoleon regarding his exile. Keith had been the admiral in command when the British army landed in Egypt to defeat the French forces at Alexandria.
3. Rear Admiral Sir George Cockburn was responsible for the safe passage of Napoleon to St Helena and continued as acting Governor until the arrival of Sir Hudson Lowe in April 1816.
4. The *Tonnant* 80 was Admiral Keith's flagship; Bingham was mistaken in thinking it was an 84-gun ship. The *Bellerophon* 74 had received the surrender of Napoleon and his entourage and held them whilst the British Government decided their fate. The *Eurotas* frigate 38 was to take back to France those in his entourage who were not proceeding to St Helena.

Monday, 7 August 1815

Early in the morning the luggage of Napoleon came onboard, and several servants and persons of his suite to prepare the cabin that was to receive him; about two o'clock he left the *Bellerophon*, and came alongside the *Northumberland*, accompanied by Lord Keith.

The Guard was turned out, and presented arms, and all the officers stood on the quarter deck to receive Lord Keith. Napoleon chose to take the compliment to himself. He was dressed in a plain green uniform, with plain epaulets, white kerseymere waistcoat and breeches, with stockings, and small gold shoe buckles; his hair out of powder, and rather greasy, his person corpulent, his neck short, and his tout ensemble not at all giving an idea that he had been so great, or in fact was so extraordinary a man.

He bowed at first coming on deck and having spoken to the admiral, asked for the captain of the ship[1] – in passing towards the cabin he enquired who I was, the captain introduced me, he then enquired the number of the regiment, where I had served? And if the 53rd was to go to St. Helena with him? He then repeated to an officer of artillery the same questions – from him he passed to Lord Lowther, to whom he addressed several questions after which he retired to the cabin.

The admiral who was anxious that he should as early as possible be brought to understand that the cabin was not allotted to him solely, but was a sort of public apartment, asked Lord Lowther, Mr. Lyttleton[2] and myself to walk in. Napoleon received us standing; the lieutenants of the ship were brought in and introduced, but not one of them spoke French; they bowed and retired; we remained. Mr Lyttleton who spoke French fluently answered his questions; after we were tired of standing we retired. Half an hour afterwards he came on deck and entered into conversation with Mr Lyttleton. He spoke with apparent freedom and great vivacity, but without passion; he rather complained of his destination, saying it had been his <u>intention</u> to have lived in a retired manner in England, had he

1. Captain Ross.
2. Lord Lowther was MP for Westmoreland and the Honourable William Henry Lyttleton was MP for Worcestershire. These gentlemen seem to have come onboard solely to experience the historic event and disembarked before it sailed to St Helena. Lyttleton published a short account of his conversations with Napoleon in 1836.

been permitted to have done so. He replied freely to several questions put to him by Mr Lyttleton relative to what had happened in Spain and other parts – this interesting conversation lasted at least an hour, at the end of which he retired.

At six o'clock dinner was announced, he ate heartily, taking up both fish and meat frequently with his fingers; he drank claret out of a tumbler mixed with a very little water. Those of his attendants who were received at the admiral's table were Bertrand (Grand Marshal),[1] the Countess his wife, Montholon (General of Brigade and A.D.C.)[2] and Las Cases,[3] wearing the uniform of a captain in the navy, but called a counsellor of state. The discourse was on general and trifling subjects, after which he talked to the admiral, of Russia and its climate and of Moscow, without seeming at all to feel the subject; he spoke as if he had been an actor only, instead of the author of all those scenes which cost so much bloodshed.

We rose immediately after dinner, and the admiral begged me to attend Napoleon. He walked forward to the forecastle; the men of the 53rd regiment and the artillery were on the booms, they rose and took off their caps as he passed. He appeared to like the compliment, and said he was formerly in the artillery; I answered 'Yes, you belonged to the regiment De la Fére' on which he pinched my ear with a smile, as if pleased to find I know so much of his history. He walked for some time, and then asked us in to play cards; we sat down to vingt un – he showed me his snuff box, on which were

---

1. Comte General Henri-Gatien Bertrand was an engineer officer by trade, building the bridges across the Danube for the great battles of Aspern-Essling and Wagram. He then became Grand Marshal of the Palace and accompanied Napoleon to Elba and St Helena. He was a loyal, faithful servant, but he and his wife did not enjoy their time on St Helena.

2. Comte General Charles Tristan Montholon had been an ADC to a number of the Marshals before becoming an Imperial Chamberlain in 1809. He was ADC to Napoleon at Waterloo and chose to remain with Napoleon at St Helena. His history is shrouded in vague claims of promotion and wounds which cannot be substantiated and he seems to have fallen out with virtually everyone in Napoleon's entourage during his exile. Some have suggested he was implicated in the murder of Napoleon; guilty or not he was certainly a shady character.

3. Comte Emmanuel Augustin Las Cases was originally an officer in the royalist navy and became an exile, returning during the amnesty pronounced by the Consulate. A strange character, he was expelled from St Helena in 1816 but took his revenge on Hudson Lowe and the British government with the publication of *Memorial de Sainte Helene*.

inlaid four silver antiques (coins) Scylla, Regulus, Pompey and Julius Caesar, with a gold one on the side, of Timoleon.

Madame Bertrand told me he had found these coins himself at Rome. He did not play high at cards, and left about fifty francs to be distributed amongst the servants – the latter part of the evening he appeared thoughtful, and at a little past ten, he retired for the night.

Tuesday, 8 August 1815

The weather was squally, and there was a heavy sea; most of the party were affected by the motion of the vessel – Napoleon did not make his appearance.

Wednesday, 9 August 1815

Napoleon at dinner asked many questions, but appeared in low spirits; he brightened up afterwards and came on the deck; he asked if amongst the midshipmen, there were any who could speak French; one of them had been at Verdun[1] and understood it a little. The Captain of Marines (Beattie) appeared on deck. He enquired who he was, and where he had served? When he told him he had been at Acre,[2] he appeared particularly pleascd, and took him by the ear, which I find he has always been in the habit of doing when pleased; he talked a good deal with this officer, walking the deck with his hands behind him. At eight o'clock he retired to the cabin; he lost at cards,* and observed that good fortune had of late forsaken him. About ten o'clock he retired for the night.

* Note by Margaret Pleydell
[G.B. won from him four Napoleons which are now in the possession of Mr Pleydell.]
1. Midshipman Smith had been held in the fortress of Verdun with George's brother John, one of the prisons not only for captured British military personnel but also for the numerous British civilians taken on the continent when war recommenced.
2. Acre stands on a peninsula abutting the Mediterranean. The Turkish Governor Djezzar Pasha, backed by a Royal Navy flotilla under Sir Sidney Smith held out against Napoleon's besieging forces in 1799. With plague ravaging his troops, Napoleon was eventually forced to abandon his march into Syria and return to Egypt.

Thursday, 10 August 1815

Napoleon did not appear till dinner time; he was affected by the motion of the ship, and said very little; he made an attempt to play at cards but was obliged to give it up, and retire early.

Friday, 11 August 1815

Blowing weather, and Bonaparte invisible the whole day.

Saturday, 12 August 1815

Napoleon made his appearance early, and looked better than usual; he walked the deck supporting himself on my arm. How little did I ever think when I used to consider him one of the first generals in the world, that he would ever have taken my arm as a support. He spoke but little at dinner, but conversed for half an hour afterwards with the admiral, in the course of which conversation he denied having had any knowledge of the death of Captain Wright,[1] and said, he had never heard his name till mentioned to him by an English gentleman at Elba[2] – that it was not probable that having the cares of a great nation, he should interest himself in the fate of an obscure individual. This reasoning I own appears more specious than solid. Of Sir Sidney Smith he also spoke, and said that he had once (when commanding the army in Egypt) inserted in his orders that he was mad, as a means of checking the intrigues he had attempted to carry on with his generals.[3] At cards this evening he was affected with the motion of the vessel, and retired early.

1. Captain Wright was engaged in clandestine operations, ferrying agents in the pay of Britain to and from France. Captured, he was placed in the Temple prison and supposedly killed himself. His suicide was doubtful and it was claimed that Napoleon had ordered his death.
2. Having abdicated in 1814, Napoleon had been banished to the Isle of Elba with a force of 1,000 men. Sensing that the French public were unhappy with Bourbon rule, he slipped away to France where he rapidly reassumed power, until his defeat at Waterloo and second abdication shortly afterwards. This period is known to history as the 'Hundred Days'.
3. Admiral Sir Sidney Smith had been captured during a cutting out expedition off Le Havre and imprisoned in the Temple prison. Threatened with being convicted as a pirate (which carried the death penalty), he made a daring escape. Given command of a small squadron in the Mediterranean, he helped in the defence of

Sunday, 13 August 1815

The Chaplain dined with the admiral – Napoleon asked a number of questions relative to the reformed religion; he did not display much knowledge of the tenets of our church, or of the English history of the period of the reformation. He played with his attendants at cards as usual – the English did not join him.

Monday, 14 August 1815

Napoleon asked at dinner a number of questions relative to the Cape, and whether any communication was carried on by land, with any other part of Africa by means of caravans – his information on these as well as on other topics connected with geography, appeared very limited; and he asked questions that any well educated Englishman would have been ashamed to have done – the evening passed off with cards as usual.

Tuesday, 15 August 1815

Napoleon's birthday.[1] The admiral complimented him on the occasion, and his attendants appeared in dress uniforms. After dinner a long conversation took place which turned on the intended invasion of England; he asserted that it was always his intention to have attempted it – for this purpose, he sent Villeneuve[2] with his

Acre and was very active in clandestine efforts with a number of French generals in an attempt to cause a coup. He was a braggart and given to theatrical gestures, but was one of only a handful of naval officers present at the Battle of Waterloo.
1. His forty-sixth birthday.
2. Vice Admiral Pierre Charles Jean Baptiste Sylvestre de Villeneuve had commanded the right wing of the Admiral Bruey's fleet in Egypt, being the only part of the French fleet to escape from Nelson's grasp at the Battle of the Nile. He commanded the naval forces at Toulon, with which he sailed to the West Indies in an effort to draw the Royal Navy away from the Channel. Returning to Europe he was to pick up the Brest fleet and gain local superiority in the Channel to allow the French invasion fleet to cross in relative safety. Following a drawn battle with the blockading squadron at Brest, Villeneuve retired to Cadiz, effectively abandoning all hope of gaining control of the Channel. Hearing that orders for his arrest were en route, he sailed with a combined Franco Spanish fleet which was promptly annihilated by Nelson at Trafalgar. Villeneuve had been captured but freed on parole in 1806. He committed suicide before his arrest and trial could take place.

fleet to the West Indies with orders to refresh at one of the French isles, to return without loss of time, and immediately to push up the Channel, taking with him the Brest fleet as he passed (it was supposed that this trip, would have withdrawn the attention of our fleets). Twenty thousand men were ready at Boulogne (of which six thousand were cavalry) to embark at a moments notice; under cover of this fleet he calculated he would have debarked this army in 24 hours; the landing was to have taken place as near London as possible; he was to have put himself at the head of it, and have made a push for the capital – he added 'I put all to the hazard, I entered into no calculation as to the manner in which I was to return; I trusted all to the impression the occupation of the capital would have occasioned, conceive then my disappointment, when I found that Villeneuve after a drawn battle with Calder,[1] had stood for Cadiz – he might as well have gone back to the West Indies. I made one further attempt to get my fleet into the Channel, Nelson destroyed it at the Battle of Trafalgar, and I then as you know fell with my whole force on Austria, who was unprepared for this sudden attack, and you remember how well I succeeded.'[2]

At cards this evening he was successful, winning nearly 80 napoleons; he evidently tried to lose it again – he was in good spirits at the idea of success on his birthday, having been always of an opinion that some days are more fortunate than others. It was nearly eleven o'clock before he left the card table.

Wednesday, 16 August 1815

Bonaparte did not appear till dinner time. He was in good spirits, and asked as usual a variety of questions. After dinner in his walk

1. Admiral Sir Robert Calder commanding the blockade of the Brest squadron intercepted Villeneuve's fleet on route for the Channel. In a confused engagement on 22 July 1805 little was achieved. Calder was reprimanded for his conduct by the Admiralty and never held another active command. The action did however set the scene for the eventual defeat of Villeneuve at Trafalgar.
2. Facts are at slight variance with Napoleon's statement here. Napoleon actually gave up on the planned invasion of Britain following the action with Calder and Villeneuve's retreat to Cadiz. The French Army of invasion left the Boulogne area and crossed the Rhine as early as the 22 July 1805 at the commencement of that campaign which humiliated Austria. Trafalgar did not occur until 21 October, when the invasion threat was clearly over.

with the admiral, he was quite loquacious, having besides his usual allowance of wine (two tumblers of claret), drank one of champagne, and some bottled beer. He said, he apprehended that the measure of sending him to St Helena, might have fatal consequences; he hinted, that the people of France and Italy were so much attached to him, and his person, that they might revenge it by the massacre of the English; he acknowledged however, that he thought his life safe with the English, which it might not have been had it been entrusted to the Austrians or Prussians. Of this life he appears tenacious, one of his valets de chamber sleeps constantly in his apartment, nor does it appear either from his own accounts, or those of his attendants, that he was very prodigal of it, at the Battle of Waterloo, certainly the most interesting one of his life, and on which his future destiny turned; not one of his personal staff was wounded, and had he been in the thickest of the fight as Wellington was, they could not all have escaped – but to return to his conversation – he said that after the Austrian war, Beauharnais,[1] and the people about him, told him, it was absolutely necessary that he should marry again, to have heirs for the sake and succession of France. The Emperor of Russia offered him the Archduchess Anne – a council was held on the subject, and in taking into consideration this marriage, a clause providing for the free exercise of the Greek religion, and also that a chapel should be allowed in the Tuilleries, for the worship of that faith, was strongly objected to, by some of the members, as likely to render the marriage unpopular in France. At this moment Schwarzenburg[2] offered a princess of the house of Austria; Napoleon replied, it was quite indifferent to him so as they gave him no trouble on the subject, this business was speedily settled; this was at ten o'clock at night; before midnight the copy of a treaty was drawn out (copied nearly word for word from the marriage contract between Louis 16th and Maria Antoinette) signed by him, transmitted to Vienna, and Marie Louise became the new Empress.

1. Eugéne de Beauharnais stepson of Napoleon was made Prince of the Empire and Viceroy of Italy.
2. Field Marshal Karl Philip, Prince Schwarzenburg, was the Austrian Ambassador to France from 1809. He returned to commanding troops in 1812 and became commander of all the allied troops pitted against Napoleon in 1813–14.

Thursday, 17 August 1815

Napoleon did not make his appearance till dinner; he conversed a little, and retired early to the after cabin; he remained but a short time at the card table. In conversation last night with Sir George Cockburn it turned on Waterloo, he said that he should not have attacked Wellington on the 18th had he supposed he would have fought him;[1] he acknowledged that he had not exactly reconnoitred the position; he praised the British troops, and gave the same account of the final result as in the official dispatch; he denied that the movement of the Prussians on his flank had any effect;[2] the malevolent he said, raised the cry of 'sauve qui peut' and as it was already dark, he could not remedy it. Had there been any daylight (he added) 'I should have thrown aside my cloak, and every Frenchman would have rallied round me; but darkness and treachery were too much for me.'

Friday, 18 August 1815

Napoleon in good spirits, and looking well; he conversed after dinner for a considerable time with the admiral; he mentioned Marie Louise and said she was much attached to him. She was asked by the Queen of Naples,[3] why she did not join her husband in Elba? She replied her inclination led her to do so, but that she was prevented by her parents; the Queen replied that if she loved a man, nothing should prevent her following him, if there were windows in the house, and sheets to enable her to let herself down from them. He spoke with interest of his boy,[4] and

1. Here Napoleon means that he had expected Wellington and his polyglot army to continue retiring towards Brussels that day.
2. To state that the Prussian flank attack had no impact on the battle is disingenuous. The Corps of Lobau and latterly part of the Guard were siphoned off from the main battle to prevent a Prussian breakthrough. At the least, these additional troops could have swung victory in his favour.
3. Napoleon's sister Caroline had married General Joachim Murat in January 1800. Murat had eventually risen to the rank of Marshal and then King of Naples in 1808.
4. Desperation for a male heir had caused Napoleon to divorce Josephine. Marie Louise, his new Austrian Queen, succeeded in giving birth to a boy on 20 March 1811who was proclaimed King of Rome. At the first abdication the Prince travelled with his mother to Austria where he was brought up as the Prince of Parma

appeared pleased to relate that when the Queen of Naples said to the child 'Well my boy, your game is now over, you will be obliged to turn Capuchin' he replied 'I never will be a priest, I will be a soldier'.

In Germany he said, he had intercepted a letter written by the young Prince of Orange in which he said the Prince was not very lavish in his praises of our Royal family, but that a lady at Dresden, who had either been mentioned in it, or had some reason for wishing that it might not be made public, entreated him so earnestly not to send it to the Moniteur[1] that he withheld it.

Saturday, 19 August 1815

At dinner, Napoleon talked of Toulon with animation; he said the only wound he had ever received, was from an English sailor (by a pike) in the hand, at the storm of Fort Mulgrave,[2] the possession of which, led to the evacuation of that town . This led to talking of the Navy; he said the only good officer he had was one whose name he pronounced Cas-mo,[3] who when Admiral Dumanoir[4] was acquitted by a court martial (having been tried for leaving the Battle of Trafalgar, and for having afterwards surrendered to Sir Richard Strachan[5]) took the sword that was delivered to him by the president and broke it. The admiral asked him for some other naval character, whose name I have forgotten; he answered 'he behaved well in one action, I made him an admiral on the spot; the consequence was, the very next year he lost me two ships in the Bay

and later made Duke of Reichstadt. On Napoleon's second abdication he was proclaimed Napoleon II but was forced to remain in Austria. The 'eaglet' as the French called him, was always weakly and he died of tuberculosis on 22 July 1832.
1. The *Moniteur* newspaper was the official mouth-piece of Napoleon.
2. Toulon had opened its gates to allied forces in 1793 and was besieged by the revolutionary armies. Realizing the importance of Fort Mulgrave and Point l'Eguilette which commanded the outer harbour, Napoleon launched a major attack, in which he was successful but wounded (it is normally stated that he was wounded in the thigh, rather than the hand). His success forced the allied fleet to leave Toulon, abandoning the city to suffer severe French reprisals.
3. Actually Admiral Cosmao-Kerjulien.
4. Rear Admiral Dumanoir le Pelley escaped from the defeat of Trafalgar with four ships that had hardly been engaged. This squadron blundered into Admiral Strachan's squadron on 3 November 1805 and all four ships were captured.
5. Admiral Sir Richard John Strachan

of Rosas.'[1] In conversation with the admiral before dinner, he made the following remarkable observation, 'I was at the head of an army at twenty four; at thirty, from nothing I had risen to be the head of my country, for as First Consul I had as much power, as I afterwards had as Emperor. I should have died' (he added) 'the day after I entered Moscow; my glory then would have been established forever.' The admiral replied that to be a truly great character, it was necessary to suffer adversity, as well as prosperity; he assented, but said 'my lot has been a little too severe'.

Sunday, 20 August 1815

Napoleon at dinner again began to question the chaplain respecting the reformed religion, whether we used the crucifix? How many sacraments we used? Grace was said, and he asked whether it was a benediction.

He walked for a considerable time by moonlight; and seeing the admiral did not play at cards, refrained himself. He talked of Egypt; he said 'The mamelukes ought to be the first cavalry in the world; no Frenchman is equal to them, five Frenchmen would never stand against the same number of mamelukes, or even a hundred; but three hundred Frenchmen would by manoeuvring, and having reserves, beat an equal number, or even a greater.' He continued to say that 'Kleber[2] was a good General, but not a politician sufficient to prosper in that country. Having landed in Egypt with a small army, and cut off from any reinforcements, he was obliged to practise every artifice to gain the good will of the people; for this, he and his followers professed the Mohametan religion;' which he made no scruple in acknowledging he had done himself. He had great difficulty in bringing the sheiks to waive what is considered both by the Jews and Mohammedans an important part of the religion. The real difficulty to be obviated was that of drinking wine; he said the Franks were natives of a colder climate, and for

1. This must refer to Rear Admiral Perrée who was captured with his entire squadron of five small ships as they returned to Toulon from Java. To be fair to Perrée, he was confronted by the entire advanced division of Admiral Keith's fleet and was hopelessly outnumbered and outgunned.
2. General Jean-Baptiste Kléber became commander of the French army in Egypt when Napoleon departed secretly. He was stabbed to death by a fanatic on 14 June 1800.

so long a time had been accustomed to it, that they would not relinquish it, and proposed, they should be allowed a dispensation. A consultation was held, the result of which was, that the Franks might certainly drink wine, but that they would be damned for it. Bonaparte replied that they by no means wished to enter the pale of their church on such terms, and begged they would reconsider it; the next answer proved more favourable; it was decreed, that they should be allowed to drink wine, provided every day before they did so, they should resolve to do a good action. On being pressed to know what was considered a good action, it was answered, either alms giving, building (or contributing towards building) a mosque, or digging a well in the desert. Having promised faithfully to comply with the terms he concluded by saying 'We were received into the mosque and I derived from it, the most important results.'

Wednesday, 23 August 1815

We made the Madeiras, and Napoleon seemed pleased in viewing the land of Porto Santo which we passed at the time he was usually on deck.

Thursday, 24 August 1815

We were standing on and off in Funchal roads; the British consul dined onboard the *Northumberland*. He was asked a number of questions relative to the island by Napoleon; the heights, the number of inhabitants and such. The flippant, pert manner of this gentleman, greatly annoyed Bonaparte, and he remained silent for the rest of the dinner, after which he walked, leaning on the admiral's arm; but on the consul joining them, he immediately retired to his own cabin which he did not leave for the night.

HM Ship *Northumberland* 1815

My Dear Sir Lowry, [1]

The orders under which I embarked for St Helena were so sudden that I had no time to wish you an adieu previous to my leaving

1. Sir Lowry Cole.

England. I take the opportunity of doing so now, as letters are to be forwarded from Madeira. I suppose this will find you in France and I think you will like to know how your friend Napoleon is going on.

At first he was in rather low spirits. He has now recovered and having got over the sea-sickness is very entertaining. He passes his days, in which you know on board there is no variety, in the following manner. He breakfasts in his own cabin and seldom makes his appearance before two or three o'clock. He then plays chess with some of the French who have accompanied him, who are too good courtiers ever to win a game from him. We sit down twelve at table he eats voraciously and asks a number of questions. He rises almost immediately after dinner and walks the decks, talking with anyone who understands French, till eight o'clock. We then assemble in the Admiral's cabin and play vingt-un. At ten o'clock and sometimes before he rises and goes to bed.

He has one servant who sleeps in the cabin with him and one at the door. He answers with apparent frankness any question that is asked him relative to his former transactions. He talks of Lord Wellington as being equal in the field to himself, but more fortunate in politics. He tells the same story of the battle of Waterloo that he did in his official account, namely, that the day was lost by the malevolent raising of the cry of 'sauve qui peut'. But he adds that 'if there had been daylight I should have remedied that, for I should have thrown aside my cloak and every Frenchman would have rallied around me'. Why he did not try that expedient the next day he did not condescend to explain. I cannot find that he used much personal exertion or even exposed himself much during the course of the day. None of his personal staff were wounded, which they could not all have escaped had he been like our commander in the thickest part of the fight.

The staff, like true Frenchmen, will not allow themselves to have been fairly beaten even here. They as usual tell nothing but lies, disguising numbers, &c.. They cannot, however, refrain from allowing that our infantry and artillery are beyond praise. One of them said they were exactly what the French were before the battle of Austerlitz, since which time, according to the Comte de Montholon's account, they have never had an army, the introduction of titles having ruined it. Upon which, Madame his wife, who is on board, puts in that her husband has always been a republican.

On board Napoleon is always treated with great respect but without royal honours, except by his attendants. He continues to wear a plain green uniform with two plain epaulettes, the star of the Legion of Honour and three small crosses in his buttonhole, white waistcoat and breeches, silk stockings and small gold buckles.

I need not describe his person to you. He has grown fat and gives me more the idea of a greasy Portuguese priest than of a person who has made so great a noise in the world. On his snuffbox he has antique coins of Sylla, Regulus, Pompey and Julius Caesar, which box Madame Bertrand says he has carried with him on most of his campaigns.

I suppose the expected ship will bring me home, for if Sir Hudson Lowe comes out it is not probable Government will allow two Major-Generals to remain in the island.[1] Under this supposition I have left Lady Bingham at home. I wished to have escaped the voyage altogether, but was unable to do so. I should have been much fortunate had I been with you.

The thing I feel as most uncomfortable is that I was not able to procure in London any instructions for my conduct, except from Lord Bathurst,[2] to put myself on shore as well as on board under the orders of Sir George Cockburn, who is to be supreme and is to have the whole arrangement of the island with liberty to retain or send away the accompanying troops as he chooses, to call for troops from the Cape, &c.. He intends to be general as well as admiral and has horses and furniture embarked for the purpose.

I beg to be remembered to all my old friends, and only consider myself as truly unfortunate in not having been with you and them, instead of being Napoleon's gaoler, which is a post I cannot say I ever coveted!

I remain, my dear General
Ever sincerely yours,
G.R. Bingham

1. George became a brigadier general on 21 October 1815.
2. Henry Bathurst 3rd Earl, Secretary for War and the Colonies. He had done much to support Wellington's army in Spain and had much to do with the setting of the rules governing Napoleon's strict captivity on St Helena.

Friday, 25 August 1815

We left Madeira, and on the 27th passed through the Canary Islands; Napoleon spent his time as usual, and nothing scarcely occurred worth remarking. In one of his conversations, he talked of the new Prussian constitution, and complained of the admission of the people into the states. Freedom he said would answer in England but no where else. The admiral reminded him of what he had himself done in France; which he said he was obliged to do, to secure a momentary popularity; he seemed to think that no one would manage the French but himself, but by no means hinted that he had ever intended they should have more than the semblance of a free constitution.

Sunday, 27 August 1815

After dinner an argument arose on the subject of religion; the ladies were the principle speakers, but it was one with which they were evidently not acquainted. At length high words took place between Montholon and Gourgaud,[1] the latter wanting (as the former said) respect for his wife. The admiral put a stop to the argument, by rising from the table; but it is not difficult to perceive, that envy, hatred and all uncharitableness, are firmly rooted in Bonaparte's family, and that their residence at St Helena will be rendered very uncomfortable by it. The subject of religion was started, by the admiral's telling Napoleon that a Portuguese priest had offered to attend him to St Helena. Napoleon returned an answer that proved his perfect indifference to the thing; but the ladies requested to know whether there <u>was</u> anything of the kind in the island, which occasioned the argument above mentioned.

5 September 1815

There has been of late but little conversation with Bonaparte, and nothing worthy of observation till yesterday, when in his after-

1. Baron General Gaspard Gourgaud was originally an artillery officer. He became a personal staff officer to Napoleon in 1811. At St Helena he acted as a secretary to whom Napoleon dictated part of his memoirs. He continued to feud with Montholon and left the island in 1818 in an attempt to gain better conditions for Napoleon.

noon's walk, Egypt was mentioned. The admiral asked him if there was any truth in the report of the massacre of the Turks at Jaffa. He frankly confessed there was; he said these people had been made prisoners before, and had promised not to serve again; instead of which, they threw themselves into the town. They were summoned; and threatened with no quarter if they resisted; they did resist, and consequently were put to death.

He then talked of poisoning his own people, and said 'that is a story Wilson[1] got hold of; the idea though agitated was never carried into execution, and the circumstance that did occur, took place as follows. When retreating from before Acre, there remained some men in the plague hospital at Jaffa, whose death was certain; and whom it was impossible to remove. I knew that if these men were left to Djezzar Pasha, he would have impaled them, or made them suffer great tortures; to avoid which, as their recovery was quite out of the question, I proposed that a certain quantity of laudanum should be given to each. The chief surgeon of my army refused, he said his business was to <u>cure</u>, not to <u>destroy</u>. The affair was then debated in council, when some were in favour of the measure, and others against it. At last the surgeon declaring, that if a force was left for forty-eight hours, the men in question would all be dead. I remained twenty-four hours myself, and left a rearguard twenty-four hours more, when the men being all dead, the force was withdrawn.' He said he had had the plague himself, and that he constantly visited the plague hospitals, while in the command of the army on that station.

He talked of the Queen of Prussia, said she was a very fine woman, and that she had been brought into his company to get what she could; after he had paid her many compliments, and presented her with a rose, she asked for Magdeburg; he added, 'had she made her application sooner, I might have presented it to her, but affairs were gone so far and were so settled, that I could not have complied without having altered the whole treaty; when she found she could not gain from me what she wanted, she altered her behaviour to me. She was much attached to the Emperor Alexander, and at the conference at [blank] detained the king, under pretence of business, the whole day which she passed with Alexander at a country house, not far from this town.'

1. General Sir Robert Thomas Wilson had written a history of the Egyptian campaign in 1802.

Monday, 11 September 1815

I take up my pen to continue my journal, which however becomes daily less and less interesting. On this day Bonaparte observed to the admiral that on his return from Elba, he received shortly after his arrival at Paris, a private communication from Ferdinand the 7th,[1] stating that whatever demonstration he might make in concert with the allies, it should be confined to that; and that his troops should not enter France; adding to this many upstart expressions of esteem. He also said that a similar communication had been made from the Portuguese Regency, which accounts for their refusal of troops,[2] and their conduct towards Beresford and such. Yesterday at table he spoke of the Turks, and their manner of eating, taking up their rice, fowls or other meat with their fingers. This brought on a story (after he had left the table) from Madame Bertrand, that when Bonaparte was First Consul the Turkish Ambassador was at table when green peas made their appearance at the commencement of the season, into which he darted his fingers; and that Josephine seeing what he had done, ordered the dish to be instantly removed. General Gourgaud said it was impossible that a person of such good manners as she possessed could be guilty of so much rudeness.

Having brought General Gourgaud forward, I must notice one or two anecdotes of him; he seems the only man of ability amongst them, and I make no doubt is a good officer. That he is a true Frenchman, may be perceived by the following occurrences; reading some notes to the admiral taken at, or immediately after the Battle of Waterloo, he came on a sudden to this paragraph, 'I put myself at the head of the cavalry; I charged and killed with my own hand xxx' then checking himself he said 'oh this belongs to myself, I will go on with another part of my narrative.'

He was particularly noticed after the return of the Bourbons by the Duke de Berri,[3] who obtained for him the order of St. Louis; he remained in Paris till the royal family left it, and he was repaid by Napoleon for his desertion by being appointed his aide de camp.

1. The King of Spain.
2. Wellington and the British government had requested a force of 10,000 troops to be added to his army in Belgium; they were refused.
3. The brother of King Louis XVIII.

In relating this he said 'you must not be surprised, if shortly I should be recalled by the French government, and I think it probable, I shall be appointed A.D.C. to the Duke de Berri.[1]

Tuesday, 12 September 1815

Yesterday the captain of marines (Beattie) dined at the admiral's table. He had been in Egypt and the conversation turned on this, Bonaparte's favourite subject. He asked a variety of questions whether Captain B[eattie] had observed his tent on Mount Carmel, he said that a shell fell very near him one day at the siege of Acre, and that two men clasped him in their arms, choosing rather to destroy themselves, than that any injury should happen to their chief. One of these men was a private in the chasseurs, and is now a general. He lost his arm at the Battle of Borodino, and was made governor of the castle of Vincennes.[2] When the allies penetrated into France in 1814 he was summoned to surrender; answered when they restored him the arm he had lost in Russia, he would comply with their request. After dinner Napoleon was again questioned on the subject of his projected invasion of England; Sir George Cockburn said, that many people in the country were persuaded it was never intended otherwise than merely as a feint; and to put us to expenses; his answer was 'Mr Pitt never thought so; I had well weighed the consequences, and I calculated that if I did not succeed, the demonstrations would do me [a] great disservice; as it would make the English a military nation, and at the same time would give the ministers a command of money, since no other measure could authorise them to call for so large a sum as in this case was requisite. I was very well pleased to see the preparations the English made on the coast opposite Boulogne, at which place it was never my intention to have attempted a landing.

I kept up this farce by frequent embarkations and by the exercise of my flotilla. My real point of attack would have been somewhere

1. So much for his loyalty to Napoleon!
2. This has to refer to General Daumesnil but many of the facts are incorrect here. He was actually in the Corps of Guides in Egypt where he did help to save Napoleon's life. He lost a leg at Wagram, not an arm at Borodino and he did carry out a stout defence of the fortress of Vincennes. His story has recently been published as *Napoleon's shield and guardian: the unconquerable General Daumesnil* by E. Ryan and H. de Clairvail, 2003.

between Margate and Deal; I calculated that I could have possessed myself of the lines of Chatham, as a point of retreat.[1] I should have pushed for London; had I arrived there I should have offered very moderate terms of peace, taking care however so far to cripple you, that you could have done no further mischief, nor have disturbed my future plans. Whether I should have succeeded or not, I cannot say, but such were my projects.'

He then talked of Ireland, where he said he had as many friends amongst the Protestants, as amongst the Catholics. 'An expedition for that country was at one time nearly ready to sail; it was to have left Antwerp and have gone north about, and was to have landed thirty thousand men in the north of Ireland. Roger O'Connor was to have accompanied them[2] but I knew better than to trust him with the command; I granted everything they asked, relative to the settlement of the government of the country, if it should have been conquered. It mattered to me little whether they adopted a republican or any other form of government; my sole object was to divide it from England, and to have occupied the attention of the English in re-conquering or tranquillising it. Could the division once be effected, peace and the ultimate ruin, and subjugation of both countries would have been the consequence. I carried on my communications with Ireland by means of the smugglers; they were the most staunch friends I had. At one time they offered to carry off Louis 18th from Hartwell,[3] and to deliver him to me; I declined this, as I should not have known what to have done with him; but I found the smugglers exceedingly useful and intelligent.'

At breakfast this morning the conversation happened to turn on the rapacity of Marshal Massena; and General Gourgaud related,

1. The lines of Chatham were a ring of defences constructed during the Napoleonic wars to protect the land approaches to Chatham dockyard. The main forts being Forts Pitt, Clarence and, of course, Amhurst which is now open to the public.
2. This comment, following immediately after discussion of his planned invasion of southern England would seem to be linked. However the facts seem to be jumbled, as the Irish invasion mentioned here would appear to be the failed attempt led by Hoche much earlier in 1796. Wolfe Tone and Arthur O'Connor, the son of a wealthy protestant land owner of County Cork, were involved in the planning but were not allowed to go with the invasion fleet. O'Connor was captured in Margate in 1798.
3. The deposed King Louis XVIII was allowed to reside at the estate of Hartwell during his enforced banishment.

that after the Peace of Vienna, he carried away from the house in which he had been quartered, fifty pounds of wax candles the only thing he could lay his hands on. Marshal Ney, in the campaign of Austerlitz, levied enormous contributions, the whole of which he remitted to his banker at Paris, for his own use. Napoleon heard of it; when the campaign was ended, he drew on him for the amount, the draft was immediately answered, and no further explanation took place.

I forgot to mention that when Bonaparte was talking of having London in his possession, the Admiral asked him if he did not think it a politic measure to fortify all capitals, and why he had never fortified Paris? His answer was, that every capital ought to be put out of the power of any enemy to insult; many instances had occurred where the occupation of a capital had occasioned the conclusion of a war; for myself he added, 'I never was so firmly established as to be able to attempt it at Paris; I owed my empire to the popular prejudice, and I dared not so far insult it as to attempt fortification; which would not have suited the people of that city.'

Saturday, 16 September 1815

Napoleon yesterday talked of his Russian campaign, he said that he ought to have halted at Smolensk, that had he done so he should have entered on the next campaign with such resources, as would have ensured him success; he had a two- fold object in this campaign, one was to erect in the re-establishment of the Kingdom of Poland a barrier against Russia; the other was to compel that power to embrace the continental system.[1] He said he had encouragement given him before he entered Russia, to advance, and free the peasantry. He added, he entered Moscow almost without opposition, and that he remained there for two days with the most flattering prospects. On a sudden the town was observed to be on

---

1. The Berlin decrees of 1806 ordered the closure of all the borders of the French Empire and satellite nations to British goods in an attempt to destroy British commerce and strengthen French industry. Russia had joined the system following the Treaty of Tilsit in July 1807. However Russia's strict adherence to the policy soon waned as her own commerce suffered and it became a major cause of the war in 1812.

fire in several places; he thought it had been done by his own people, and in riding towards it, in order to stop it, soon discovered it to have been set on fire by the orders of Rostopchin.[1] Three hundred Russians were shot by his orders, having been found with matches in their hands; he himself remained in the Kremlin, as long as he was able, and had at last great difficulty in getting his horses through the burning town. The country house, to which he went, was three miles from the city; but the atmosphere was so heated, that they were obliged even at that distance from the conflagration to close the windows, and exclude the air entirely.

Thursday, 21 September 1815

We have seen but little of Bonaparte lately; he now seldom or ever plays at cards, never appears till dinner time, and stays but a short time on deck; he writes a good deal, or rather is dictating, for he writes so illegibly himself, that he generally employs Las Cases as an amanuensis.

The Admiral asked him yesterday, if when he meditated his invasion of England, he had any idea of the strength of the lines of Chatham? He said he had no exact plan of them, but that he had understood there <u>were</u> lines there; he said he had at that time his information from Goldsmith[2] (he heard we had been reading his secret history of the cabinet of St. Cloud) who transmitted every intelligence by the smugglers to him; he was aware he said that the same men furnished our government with information in return, but he had no other means of returning it himself. The English government endeavoured as much as possible to prevent a correspondence with France, and he (Bonaparte) appointed Gravelines, as the only place where he allowed any communication to take place; at the same time he watched them very narrowly.

A few days since, he said that he had been once only in a state of intoxication, that before he was even a general, he accompanied a

1. General Count Fedor Rostopchin, Governor of Moscow. He is generally regarded as the instigator of the burning of Moscow, to deprive the French of its resources.
2. Lewis Goldsmith had published *Histoire secrete du cabinet de Napoleon Buonaparte et de la cour de St. Cloud* in 1810. It was published in English the same year by J. M. Richardson of London.

lady to Nice where they drank three bottles of burgundy each and fell under the table. But he is by no means now a temperate man; he drinks regularly his bottle of wine at dinner; a bottle of claret is always carried into his cabin at breakfast, which never comes out again, but as his servants have no dislike to it, they possibly assist him.

Yesterday Gourgaud showed me a map on a very large scale, of the environs of Brussels, which the Emperor used the day of the Battle of Waterloo; the English position was marked in pencil, and a scale added near in red lead, to show the neighbouring distances. I also saw the swords of this party, which he (Gourgaud) brought up to be cleaned. One is most superb, belonging to Bonaparte; it is a small dress sword, exceedingly well finished, with a gold hilt; two eagles supporting a column composes the grip, surmounted with an imperial crown; bees, and eagles ornament it. Round the necks of the eagles are the crosses of the legion of honour; on one side is inscribed 'patria' on the other 'veni, vidi, vici' the latter not very applicable to Waterloo. The scabbard is of tortoise shell ornamented with bees and eagles, also inlaid with bees; it was made in 1811, and is said to [have] cost £450 in France. Napoleon has likewise a Mameluke sabre with this inscription on it 'This is the sabre the Emperor carried at the Battle of Aboukir'. It is very handsomely mounted in gold, and I should greatly prefer it to the other. Gourgaud talked to me of the number of people he had killed (in the course of his services) with his own hands, and he showed me <u>his</u> sword, on which he had displayed in the water work, a Cossack attacking and just on the point of killing the Emperor, with the following explanation; 'Gourgaud first orderly to the Emperor, shooting with a pistol the Cossack that attacked him near Brienne'.

Monday, 2 October 1815

As the voyage lengthens, Napoleon grows more tired of the confinement, and has less and less intercourse with any of us; his attendants are divided into parties, and do nothing but abuse each other behind their backs. In a conversation with Bonaparte, and the admiral, the former confessed that he could have raised more than 800 million of livres a year in France, even when he had extorted to the utmost in the last year of his reign. In answer to a question put to him relative to the greatest number of men he ever had in action under his command, he said he had 180,000 at the Battle of Eylau, and 1,000 pieces of cannon; the allies had nearly the same number. At Austerlitz he had 60,000, and the allies 90,000.

Thursday, 5 October 1815

The day before yesterday Napoleon got hold of the *Life of Nelson*,[1] which was read to him by Bertrand, and in which he appeared to be particularly interested; at dinner he talked a good deal about Corsica, and said we had committed one great fault when in possession of that island. 'Paoli'[2] he said, 'expected to have been made viceroy, when he introduced you into the island, and had you done so, and given him £20,000 per annum, you might have withdrawn your English troops. He would have defied the whole force of France and the island would have been yours at this time; he knew how to treat the Corsicans, who cannot be governed in the same manner that you would treat other nations.' Bonaparte said he had attained great supplies of wood from Corsica, although there existed a great prejudice against it in his navy, but he could furnish at the dockyard at Toulon ten masts from that island at the same price as one from Riga.

The conversation then turned on timber; he said he had as much in France alone as would have built a thousand sail of the line; he minutely described the manner in which the *Rivoli* 74 was lifted over the shoals near Venice where she was built; this was effected (with all her guns onboard) by means of a machine called a camel; he added 'forty-eight hours after this labour and expense she was captured'.[3] He frequently says with a sigh 'the French nation have

1. *The Life of Nelson* by Robert Southey was published in 1813.
2. General Pascal Paoli had been a hero of the young Napoleon having led the Corsicans in their revolt against their Genevan rulers. The French captured the island in 1768 but Paoli turned against them when the revolution broke out in 1793. He offered the island to the British in 1794 but he soon fell out with them as well. He went into exile in London and died there in obscurity in 1807.
3. The *Rivoli* 74 was brought out of Venice harbour on 20 February 1812 escorted by the *Jena* 18, *Mercure* 18 and *Mamelouck* 10. They were spotted and chased by the *Victorious* 74 and *Weazel* 18. On the 22 February they closed to action, the *Mercure* blew up and the *Rivoli* surrendered having lost half of its 800 crew killed or wounded.

not a turn for the sea! I never could have got a French ship into the order that this is.'

Tuesday, 10 October 1815

Saturday evening we were surprised on going into the cabin to find the ex-Emperor reading a fairy tale of course to a very attentive audience. It was a curious one for him to have chosen; it represented a poor man who by some means had served a genius, and was overheard by him exclaiming 'if I had only the necessaries of life, I should never require the superfluities'. The genius appearing to him at that moment, asked him what he considered [were] the necessaries of life? The answer was, 'if I could receive the wages I now earn, without the drudgery, I should never want more.' The genius counted him out four days wages, and told him, he should see him at the end of that time. Four days having elapsed, he again made his appearance; each time he appeared, fresh demands were made on him for necessaries, till at last he possessed slaves, women, rich dresses, town and country houses, gardens and parks, all of which became by degrees the necessaries, not the superfluities of life. He tired his patron, by asking for a poor man's patrimony, contiguous to his, which he said was a necessary, as it intercepted the view from his pavilion, and thus he lost everything and was reduced to his original condition. Bonaparte appeared to read well, but very fast, and several times laughed heartily.

Yesterday at dinner he produced a snuff box which had on it a beautiful portrait of the young Napoleon; he was represented in the uniform of the Lancers of the Guard; his hands clasped towards heaven, imploring its blessings for his father and his country; it was painted when he was about four years old, and during his father's misfortunes.[1] After dinner he walked four hours with the admiral, and conversed with great freedom; he gave him a sketch of his life, and said that until after the Battle of Lodi,[2] he entertained no idea beyond his profession. At that time he began to feel his consequence, and he formed a party at the close of the war. Being

1. Napoleon's father, Carlo Buonaparte was an impecunious lawyer but with great social aspirations, which caused him to constantly teeter on the brink of financial collapse. He died in 1785 when Napoleon was aged fifteen.
2. The Battle of Lodi was fought on 10 May 1796.

suspected by the government he constantly attended the sittings of the institute, and affected to appear absorbed in the mathematical pursuits; it was at this time Sir Sidney Smith applied to him to assist him in his exchange,[1] which he declined, saying, he had entirely withdrawn himself from public business. The government then wished to employ him as a diplomatist, which he refused, as he also did the command of an army destined to invade England. They then proposed an expedition to Egypt, which he instantly caught at, as a means of withdrawing himself from France, until his schemes were more matured. He foresaw that if he could escape the English fleet, his career would be a brilliant one.

The death of the Duke of Enghien he avowed;[2] he said the conspiracies formed against him by the royalists were numerous and it was a measure of necessity to secure his throne; indeed by his own account he appears to have lived a life of continual dread and anxiety, adding one more to the numerous examples of the thorns encircling a borrowed crown.

The rest of his conversation during the few remaining days of the voyage offered nothing worthy of remark. We reached St Helena on the 13th, and here ends my journal.[3]

1. Sir Sidney Smith was captured during a daring cutting out raid off Le Havre in 1796. His attempts to exchange thwarted, he was threatened with being tried for piracy but made a daring escape from the Temple prison.
2. Louis Antoine Henri de Vourbon-Conde, Duc d'Enghien, was an emigré who had fought in the Army of Condé but by 1801 had retired to Ettenheim in Baden. Royalist plots induced Napoleon to order the Prince's arrest while on neutral territory. He was snatched from his home on 15 March 1804, immediately tried by military tribunal at the Chateau de Vincennes and shot. His death caused the alienation of huge numbers of erstwhile supporters of Napoleon; indeed this event can be identified as the defining moment when many throughout Europe started to see him as a tyrant and launched the nationalist movements which eventually contributed much to his downfall.
3. Napoleon actually disembarked on 17 September 1815.

Chapter Six

Letters from St Helena

Letter 1   **30 November 1815**

My last letter[1] was from Plantation House, where I spent a very pleasant week with Governor Wilks[2] and his family; I left it Monday 20th to go to Jamestown to the admiral's ball, which was very well attended; dancing began about nine, and was kept up till seven the next morning with great spirit by the performers. As I had been staying with the Wilks's I danced with the ladies of that family, and at the admiral's request, with Madame Bertrand, who was there in great splendour, with a dress valued at £500, and Madame de Montholon with a necklace said to be worth twice that sum; 200 persons sat down to supper. After this I considered it my turn to give the next fête, and I determined by way of variety, and also with the idea of showing Mrs Wilks the camp (which she had not seen) to give a breakfast. This I carried into effect the day before yesterday, I had three large marquees placed thus

O
O x O

1. This indicates that there were previous letters from St Helena, but they have unfortunately been lost. The recipient of most, if not all, of the early letters is his wife.
2. Colonel Mark Wilks was Governor of the island of St Helena as appointed by the East India Company who owned it. With the arrival of the *Northumberland*, the island was taken from the control of the company and although remaining as governor, he was made subordinate to Admiral Cockburn, who was given overall authority for the safety and confinement of Napoleon. Wilks was soon replaced as governor by the government's own man, Sir Hudson Lowe.

with tables in each for thirty people; and I covered the space marked x with a sail; I lined it with the flags of different nations; three small trees growing within the space were heavy with Seville oranges. I made my regimental carpenters lay down some boards within this space, which formed an excellent floor; it was a stage 50 feet long and 48 broad. At ten o'clock, the company began to assemble; first I walked them round the camp, having received the governor at the head of the regiment; then we repaired to the pavilion, and began to dance. At two we sat down to a breakfast, or rather a cold dinner, with hot soups, and afterwards stood up to dance again. Several persons staid [*sic*] till after dark, when the remains of the morning repast, afforded us an additional refreshment and by eleven everybody had retired from breakfast. It was as well managed as circumstances would admit, a profusion of the most beautiful flowers, were presented to me; we covered the poles of the tents with moss, which grows in great plenty, and wreathed them with roses; on the tables were hoops, covered with what in England are green house and hot house plants, also figures of soldiers drawn by the commissary, and the *tout ensemble* was beautiful; it appeared as if it were all enchantment to the natives of St Helena, who are so slow in their actions, that it would have taken them one year to have accomplished what we did in six days.

G. Bingham

Letter 2   6 December 1815

Longwood is now ready for the reception of Bonaparte; I called at the Briars[1] to accompany him thither; he received me with some apologies in his robe de chambre, and excused himself from going, on account of the smell of paint; he appeared to be in unusual good spirits having on the table, English papers to the 15th of September. The greater confusion there is in France, the greater chance he thinks there is, of his being allowed to return, as he thinks the English government will be obliged to recall him to compose the

1. As Longwood house was not ready for the reception of Napoleon, temporary accommodation had been arranged at Porteous house, an inn situated in the heart of Jamestown. Napoleon did not like the house and arranged to stay in a summer house in the grounds of The Briars, owned by William Balcombe of the East India Company. He remained here over a month before moving into Longwood house.

confusion that exists in that unhappy country. I have just seen Captain Macky,[1] the officer who has the charge of him; he appears to wish to remain another day, there is no knowing what he is about, he does not know his own mind two minutes together.

George Bingham

Letter 3   21 December 1815

Since I last wrote, Napoleon has been removed to Longwood, he appears in better health, and has been in good spirits. I called on him on Monday, and had a long audience, in which he was very particular in his questions relating to our mess; entering into the most minute particulars, even so far as to ask who cooked for us, male or female? White or black? On Friday I met him as I was marching with my regiment,[2] he rides now every day within his bounds, (but never exceeds them) with a British officer, which he cannot yet reconcile himself to. His attendants as usual are split into parties, and they have procured the removal of Bertrand (who has at least the merit of being his oldest and most faithful servant) from the superintendence of his household.

G. Bingham

Letter 4   1 January 1816

Last Tuesday I introduced all the officers of the 53rd to Bonaparte; it was evidently an effort on his part, although the proposal in the first instance came from himself; he asked a number of questions, which were exceedingly absurd. He has been in great spirits since the last arrivals; he has heard that 'all the virtues' (with Sir Francis Burdett[3] at their head) were to advocate his cause, and his recall, and he sanguinely looks forward to the result.

G. Bingham

1. Captain James Mackay of the 53 Regiment. The surname is spelt this way in the Army List of 1815.
2. Note by Miss Pleydell. Sir George Bingham had not at this time received intimation of his promotion; nor was he informed of his appointment to brigadier general on the staff, till the arrival of Sir Hudson Lowe; his commission was dated 21 October 1815.
3. Sir Francis Burdett, the Liberal MP led a campaign for the return of Napoleon to Britain.

Letter 5 8 January 1816

Since I wrote last, I have dined with Napoleon; it was a most superb dinner, which lasted only forty minutes, when we retired into the drawing room to play cards. The dessert service was Sevre china, with gold knives, forks, and spoons;[1] the coffee cups were the most beautiful I ever saw; on each cup was an Egyptian view, and on the saucer a portrait of some Bey or other distinguished character. They cost twenty five guineas the cup and saucer in France; the dinner was stupid enough, the people who live with him scarcely spoke out of a whisper, and he was so much engaged in eating, that he hardly said a word to anyone. He had so filled the room with wax candles, that it was as hot as any oven; he said to me after I had entered the drawing room, 'you are not accustomed to such short dinners'. He has generally one, or two officers of the 53rd to dinner, or rather supper, for it is half past eight before he sits down.

   G. Bingham

Letter 6 12 January 1816

Yesterday I rode with Captain Brine of the *Mosquito* sloop,[2] and Sir Charles Tyler (arrived from the Cape) to see Bonaparte, but we were disappointed, for he would not show, complaining of indisposition. I have sent your father four Napoleons, that I won from the ex-Emperor, onboard the *Northumberland*, to serve as markers at whist.[3]

   G. Bingham

Letter 7 14 February 1816

I send you a little pen sketch of the house at Longwood,[4] as it appears from my tent; it does not appear here much like an Imperial establishment; it has however great depth and more room than there appears. The trees about the camp are gum wood, of a bluish green

1. This statement is of great interest regarding the 'enforced' sale of Napoleon's silver cutlery to make ends meet which occurred at a later date. This shows the sale to be a sham; Napoleon was not selling his best.
2. The *Mosquito* formed part of the squadron patrolling the approaches to St Helena.
3. See his *Northumberland* diary entry for 9 August 1815.
4. Unfortunately the sketch is not to be found.

colour, and at a distance give you the idea of an old umbrella. You see Fehrszen's marquee and servant's tent amongst the trees in the foreground, three trees are full of a species of canary bird that sing as sweetly but are not so handsome as ours; there are also amadavats,[1] and Java sparrows with red beaks, and there are the whole of the small birds in the island. When it was first discovered, it had not a living creature on it, partridges are now plenty, and there are a good many pheasants, more like the golden pheasant of China than our English birds, and some peacocks which are rather smaller than our tame ones. I saw two the other day; they rose very majestically to fly away when disturbed; they are not allowed to be shot, and the pheasants are reserved for the governor only. Yesterday I went to call on Bonaparte; he was going out in his carriage, and insisted on my going with him, and we had a drive together of three miles; he always asks after you, and today when he heard a packet was arrived from England, he said 'Now the colonel will hear from Lady Bingham'.

G[eorge] B[ingham]

Letter 8   19 April 1816

I have taken a cottage four miles from Jamestown;[2] I am already got into it, and am trying to put it in order for Emma's reception.[3] There are beautiful geranium hedges which continue in bloom nearly the whole year round, oranges, myrtles and all the beautiful cape bulbs; the climate is delightful, and I think we may promise ourselves a comfortable establishment in our new place of abode. I called on Napoleon last Sunday before the *Phaeton* had anchored to announce to him the arrival of the new governor, he received me in his bedroom en robe de chambre, and a dirtier figure I never beheld. He was pleased with the compliment, he received Sir H. Lowe[4] last

1. The amadavat is a small Indian song bird akin to the finch.
2. Knollcombe cottage.
3. This is the first letter that is obviously sent to another rather than his wife. The identification of the recipient has not been established with any certainty.
4. Lieutenant General Sir Hudson Lowe had seen much service in the Mediterranean including Corsica. He had then been attached to the Staff of Blucher and although in Belgium in early 1815, Wellington declined to use his services in the Waterloo campaign. He was appointed Governor of St Helena, superseding the uneasy pairing of Governor Wilks and Admiral Cockburn. He was recalled on the death of Napoleon and subsequently served as the Governor of Antigua and then on the Staff in Ceylon.

Wednesday with marked attention, behaving at the same time in a manner pointedly rude to Sir George Cockburn; you have no idea of the dirty little intrigues of himself and set; if Sir Hudson Lowe has firmness enough not to give way to them he will in a short time treat him in the same manner;[1] for myself it is said I am a favourite, though I do not understand the claim I have to be such. Cockburn has certainly used great exertions to make him as comfortable as circumstances would permit, and for this, and for the care he took of him onboard the *Northumberland,* he did not deserve to be treated as he was on that day, which was nothing more or less, than when he was going to introduce Sir Hudson, and to say 'My charge ends, I beg to introduce my successor' they shut the door in his face saying 'It is the Emperor's orders that the governor goes in alone.' There have been the usual fracas continued in the family; about a week since it was intimated to Madame Bertrand that she was so fond of the English and partial to their society, that she might save herself the trouble of attending at dinner. The Emperor had dined in his own room the day before, fearing he could not have kept his temper, and have displayed a scene before the servants. Madame then made known, that Napoleon was frequently in the habit of using language neither kingly or even gentlemanly towards his attendants, and that the ladies even were not respected in these fits of rage. The interdiction lasted a week, at the end of which time it was signified that the Emperor <u>permitted</u> her to come to dinner. Napoleon received the intelligence of the death of Murat, and Ney, with the greatest indifference; of the former, he observed that he was a fool, and deserved his fate; he said he had behaved very ill to him, and had refused to lend him money when at Elba. Of the latter; he said he had done him more harm than good, and did not appear to care the least about either.

G. Bingham

1. George's comments are very interesting; the new Governor was welcomed warmly, but once it became clear that he was not going to ease the restrictions on Napoleon and his entourage, they quickly set to vilifying him. This primary evidence, written way before the problems between the governor and his ward became apparent, shows that the path towards conflict was already set. Only a man so weak as to agree to every demand of Napoleon, could have escaped the furore that was to come, but would instead have been unacceptable to the British government and rapidly recalled.

On Tuesday last, I went with Sir George Bingham, and Colonel Mansel[1] to pay a visit to Bonaparte; when we first arrived, he was out airing with his attendants, and after waiting for some little time in Captain Poppleton's[2] room, we were informed of his return, and were shown into a small ante room, where at an inside door stood his footman dressed in green and gold, to open and shut it when necessary for his Imperial master. When he was quite ready to receive us, we were ushered into his presence. I think him much better looking than I had expected, though his complexion is exceedingly sallow; he was extremely factious, and in excellent humour, and after asking me a few frivolous questions, he desired me to walk in the garden; handed me out, and did me the honour (as I afterwards found it was intended) to walk with his head uncovered. He told me I had an excellent husband, that I ought to be very happy, as he loved me dearly; that he was also a gallant soldier, and that soldiers always made the best husbands. He asked me several questions about Louisa,[3] and made some remark relating to her husband and herself; but this I lost, as owing to his speaking so remarkably fast, it is sometimes with the utmost difficulty he can be understood.

Not withstanding the constant rain, I take a great deal of exercise on horseback, and as I have a most quiet animal, I ride without the least fear up Ladder Hill, and other tremendous places, to the astonishment of the St Heleneans. I assure you I pass here for a very superior horsewoman, which gave rise to a question from Napoleon, whether in England I often went a fox hunting? Having a vast idea that the English ladies are exceedingly fond of that amusement; I told him it was one I was by no means partial to, or ever took part in. Napoleon has been much out of spirits of late, I fancy from the little probability he sees of ever being able to make his escape from this island; he has within the last few days taken to play at shuttles. Of all his followers Madame Bertrand is the one

1. Lieutenant Colonel John Mansel 53 Regiment had travelled to St Helena with Emma.
2. Captain Thomas Poppleton 53 Regiment was orderly officer at Longwood between June 1816 and July 1818. He had been slightly wounded at Salamanca.
3. Louisa Mansel, wife of the Colonel.

for whom I feel the most interest; she is poor woman! so thoroughly unhappy, that it is quite melancholy to see her; she is extremely pleasing and elegant in her manner. Just before I arrived the French attendants had an offer made them of returning home, but they preferred signing a paper which now precludes all future idea of leaving the island. Bertrand it is said agreed to this from an honourable motive, having promised Napoleon to remain with him during his captivity; poor Madame I fancy would gladly have laid aside all the honour, had it been left to her arrangement.

Emma Bingham

Letter 10   Dead wood Camp 14 June 1816

We neither hear or see much of Bonaparte now, I fancy he confines himself much more than usual to the house, which will tend to increase his corpulence; he appears to be dropsical, and his complexion very sallow; in short he looks exceedingly out of health. I understand the Governor is rather desirous to move him, nearer to Plantation house (his own residence) being suspicious of his attempting his escape, which makes Sir Hudson uneasy, and feel somewhat alarmed; for this he has not the slightest cause, as he is perfectly secure both by sea and land. I should regret his removal from Longwood as there is not on the island so beautiful a piece of ground as this. I have an excellent suite of barrack rooms, from the windows of which is seen a very grand, and noble view, comprising sea, wood, a fine extensive plain, immense heights, rugged rocks, fortifications, barracks, tents, and people of all colours, even the whole making a pretty panorama.[1] I went to fish one day last week and met with good success; the fish we caught weighed from one to two pounds, some of which I sent to Bonaparte, he was much pleased with them, and said they were the best he had eaten, since he was on Mount Cennis.[2]

J. Mansel

1. This description differs markedly from that of Napoleonists, who usually describe the location of Longwood as on an unhealthy, barren plain.
2. Mount Cennis is in the Italian Alps at the end of the St Bernard pass.

Letter 11   **Deadwood Camp, 16th June 1816**

Since I wrote last I have fulfilled my engagement with Emma, by spending a pleasant day with the Bingham's at their cottage. Yesterday Sir George took me a beautiful ride; I don't know that I ever beheld scenery so magnificently grand, as came to my view suddenly and unawares; but how to describe it to you I am at a loss, for my pen cannot do it justice, I shall however attempt a short account.

After having ascended by narrow paths, which wind round immense precipices, for which this island is noted, we got upon a ridge of hills three thousand feet from the base, when the grandest natural panorama I ever saw opened up to the view. The objects appeared an immense distance beneath us, interposed with beautiful villas, and neatly laid out gardens, situated upon minor precipices, well wooded, and commanding pretty prospects, innumerable vallies [sic] well cultivated with potatoes and various kinds of vegetables, bananas and other produce of the island. We stood a little below Diana's peak (the greatest height in the island) which is covered with wood and fine vegetation on both sides, which are also well stocked with cattle; on our right and left the hills were wooded, but further on, and in our front, forming a kind of half circle, tremendous barren and rugged mountains appeared to view bounded by the sea. After having admired this prospect we descended by a narrow path that winded round the hills, crossing ravines frequently till we get within 1,500 feet from the bottom, and then changed our direction towards another part of the island, inclining to the camp, by such narrow paths, and break-neck precipices, as affected Bingham's head; but I being a Welshman,[1] and accustomed I suppose to mountains such as Wales present, did not experience the unpleasant sensations he complained of. After this wonderful tour of part of St Helena, we parted about a mile from camp, Sir George taking the left road, and I the contrary one. It was near five o'clock before I arrived, and was highly pleased with the excursion.

John Mansel

1. The Mansels were from Glamorganshire.

Letter 12   Deadwood Camp, 21 June 1816

Sir George Cockburn embarked and sailed the day before yesterday; I assure you he quitted this island universally regretted. The 53rd, 66th, St Helena Regiment and artillery[1] were drawn up in line from the gate of the wharf to the landing place, and presented arms, while the music played; he did not wish for this compliment, though at the same time he felt himself flattered by this mark of respect and attention. He walked with his hat off along the line attended by the governor, Sir Pulteney Malcolm,[2] the Austrian,[3] Russian,[4] and French[5] Commissioners, members of council, heads of departments, Marshal Bertrand, and an immense concourse of people, all really very much affected at his departure, both by expression, and gesture. When Sir George came to my position, he begged I would convey to the regiment his sentiments of regret at parting with his old friends the 53rd, and wished us health and prosperity; he is much attached to us.

Emma was prevented being present at this grand military spectacle, by the weather, which was very unfavourable in the morning; and we had a soaking in our march to the town; but it cleared up before we arrived, except light passing showers now and then. The weather is today very cold, blowing hard, heavy rain, thermometer 58.

M . . . . . . [6] wishes to know whether Bonaparte ever practises any religious observances, or whether there is any catholic chapel provided for the French establishments; I fancy he does not think now of the first, even as he formerly did when his designs were often perpetrated under the plea of a religion, that but suited his purpose at the time, and for the latter, there is nothing of the kind on the island.

John Mansel

1. This constitutes the entire garrison on the island which was commanded by Sir George Bingham.
2. Rear Admiral Sir Pulteney Malcolm superseded Sir George Cockburn to the command of the naval station at St Helena.
3. Baron Barthelemy von Stürmer was resident on the island as the Austrian Commissioner from June 1816 to July 1818.
4. Count Alexander Antonovitch Balmain was resident as the Russian Commissioner from June 1816 until May 1820. Whilst on the island he married Lady Lowe's eldest daughter by a previous marriage.
5. The Marquis Claude Marin Henri de Montchenu was the Commissioner from the government of Louis XVIII.
6. Although left blank in the manuscript, it almost certainly refers to George's sister Mary who was married to Tryon Still.

Letter 13   **Knollcombe Cottage, 23 February 1817**

Seven weeks have now passed since Colonel Mansel left this for England, and I can fancy him increasing the happiness of your domestic circle assembled round the breakfast parlour fire; I was delighted at his having secured so comfortable a passage home.[1]

On the 17th we were at a ball and supper given by the admiral and Lady Malcolm, in honour of their son's birthday, who is just three years old.

On the 20th we are engaged to a ball and supper at the Briar's (Mr Balcombe's); we live quietly with the exception of these sort of things which occur occasionally. Our dinner visits at Plantation house take place about once a month generally speaking. The theatre comes on exceedingly well and we have now a very tolerable set of performers.

On the 28th we are to have races and Major Harrison is to ride a horse of Sir G.B., the chestnut, which Colonel Mansel will remember.

I believe I told you in my last that Sir George had been to visit Bonaparte; he was not in good spirits, but very civil; he now begins to take more exercise.

He asked Lady Malcolm one day whether we burned incense in our churches, on being answered in the negative, he said it was the only thing worth going to church for. I dined a short time since at the Briars, and curious enough, the dessert set was exactly similar to that at Whatcombe;[2] the glass net work; and I could when looking on the table almost fancy myself seated at that, in the dining room at home.[3]

E[mma] B[ingham]

1. Notes by Margaret Pleydell. He sailed home onboard the *Orontes* frigate, Captain Cochrane.
2. Whatcombe house, Dorset was the family home of the Pleydell family.
3. Notes by Margaret Pleydell. This extract is here entered from the singularity of the circumstance. The method of forming this net work in glass, is now unknown, it being lost, with the person who invented, and never revealed it. Three sets only were supposed to have been manufactured in England; one of which was in the possession of Queen Charlotte, another is in the possession of the Earl of Shaftesbury, besides that in our family. Frequent and unsuccessful attempts have been made to match it.

Letter 14 Knollcombe Cottage, 13 May 1817

We have had nothing but deaths and sickness, subscriptions for widows, and fatherless children; Mr Rainsford who was sent out by Government as a bumbaillif died shortly after his arrival, leaving six children totally unprovided for; they have been sent home in a whaler with a subscription of £700. Captain Meynell[1] of the *Newcastle* has been a fortnight at Plantation house, and for more than the last week has not been expected to live an hour, but the fever has now fixed on his liver, and all immediate danger has subsided; he is in a day or two to be carried in a cot to the *Newcastle* in order to take a cruise, as a voyage is particularly recommended for a liver case. I cannot be too thankful for the continuation of good health I enjoy, when we have been surrounded with so much sickness, that Mr Bryce[2] thought it necessary to read the prayer (during the church service) for plague and sickness, which I never heard before. Although there has been great sickness and very many deaths, yet the disorders are occasioned only by the change of seasons and none of any contagious kind. It certainly frightened many, who would scarcely believe but that there must be the plague or something very bad, in some parts of the island. Major Fehrszen[3] has been very ill for some time and almost all the officers both of the 53rd and 66th. Captain Fuller[4] indeed, of the former regiment suffered severely from inadvertently taking a medicine intended for his horse, and this mistake nearly cost him his life; but he is now getting about again. We have had nothing gay here except the races last month, with a ball and supper in the evening well attended, Sir George's horse one of the successful racers. I have lately seen Napoleon, and George saw him the day before yesterday. He is looking better, than he ever remembers to have seen him; he takes little exercise, although more than he did some time ago. Mrs Wynyard has not yet seen him, and we are going together soon to

---

1. Captain Henry Meynell survived to live to a ripe old age.
2. The transcript of the letters states the name as Bryce, but there is no record of such a person. It seems more likely that it should read as the Reverend Richard Boys, who was senior chaplain of the East India Company in St Helena.
3. Major Fehrszen commanded the 2/53rd in the absence of Lieutenant Colonel Mansel.
4. Captain Frederick Fuller of the 2/53rd.

pay him a visit. All the French people are struck with her resemblance to Marie Louise. I shall write another letter when the *Newcastle* is relieved by the *Conqueror,* which must be very shortly.

E. B.

Letter 14   **Knollcombe Cottage, 24 July 1817**

We have been very gay here recently, a ball on Friday last was given to above two hundred persons by the officers of the garrison; the next evening we were at the play, and on Monday at a ball given by Mr Balcombe to the officers of the 53rd on the occasion of their departure from St Helena.[1] The officers called one morning (accompanied by Sir George) on Bonaparte, to take leave of him; when he wished them all prosperity and happiness; and at the same time thanked them for the polite manner in which they had performed the duties allotted to them. I have sent you a copy of General Orders, on the regiment quitting the island; thinking you may like to see them.

The governor gave a large farewell dinner to the officers of the 53rd; Lady Lowe and myself were the only ladies present, and the day following another dinner to the new officers of the 66th.[2] Lady Lowe was that day too ill to appear, and I sat down to dinner, the only lady with thirty eight of the officers; when I got up from the table I set off to the play alone leaving the gentleman to follow me.

I have desired to have sent to me some common brown earthen large pans to hold the water we drink; as it is fetched from a very good spring nearly half a mile from us, and from standing in tubs made from old wine casks, which is all we can get here, it is sometimes not drinkable.

E. B.

1. The 2/53rd sailed from St Helena in 1817, returning to England, where it shared the fate of most second battalions under the 'peace dividend' and was promptly disbanded.
2. The 1/66th arrived at St Helena in 1817 from India, joining the 2/66th which already formed part of the garrison of the island. The second battalion was disbanded on the island and the fit and able men transferred into the first battalion.

Letter 15   **Knollcombe Cottage, 2nd September 1817**

Sir George and myself spent a couple of hours with Bonaparte, about a week since; he was in excellent spirits, and entered on a variety of subjects as usual. He showed me his wife's picture, with her infant son in her arms. He asked me why I did not come more frequently to see him; he told me he understood that my house was uncommonly well managed, also that I dressed extremely well, and made me tell him what I wore at the ball I attended a day or two previous to my visit at Longwood. When talking of our house, Sir George told him, that he should be happy to show him our little cottage, if he would pay us a visit; Bonaparte answered, that he should visit us frequently, if our house stood within his district.[1] When talking of the ball, he was much amused to hear that I had danced with the governor, with whom he is not on the best of terms.
       E. B.

Letter 16   **Rock Cottage,[2] 20 September 1817**

We are going on much as usual, improving our place, and making the most of the very few amusements the island affords us; we have for the last three weeks, been staying with the Wynyards at Rock cottage; and with Major Harrison have formed a very merry quintet. The races went off very well, and Sir George's horse carried off [the] 100 dollar plate; the ball we did not attend; this amusement is to improve every time; it takes place twice a year, and affords conversation for at least a month before and a month after.
       E. B.

Letter 17   **Knollcombe cottage, 22 September 1817**

You will doubtless hear much in England of an earthquake which has been felt at St Helena, and I now write you a confirmation of it. On Sunday night 21 September at a quarter before ten, Sir George, Major Harrison, Mr Trevennion and myself, were sitting around the fire, conversing on various topics, when suddenly, as

1. The limits within which he was allowed to ride freely.
2. Rock Cottage or Rock Rose Cottage was near Sandy Bay. The Wynyards owned this property but normally resided at Alarm house.

we at first imagined, a violent gust of wind arose, shaking the whole house with a very rumbling noise like a wagon; the room and chairs where we were sitting, were violently agitated; we went as fast as possible to the front door, and found we were out in a fine moon light night, with very little wind; we all exclaimed 'it must be an earthquake', and such it proved to have been; it lasted about 20 seconds and we have much to be thankful for, in this little spot under circumstances of so much danger. In the town it was felt very forcibly, and occasioned the church bell to ring for some time.

 E. B.

Letter 18   Knollcombe Cottage, 28 October 1817

[Extract]

Bonaparte has not been very well lately, his legs, and gums, have been much swollen, but he is at present considerably better. I believe that is all the information I have to give respecting him, by this opportunity.

 E. B.

Letter 19   Knollcombe cottage, 30 December 1817

My dear Sir Hudson,

 In answer to your note of yesterdays date referring to a passage in a letter of Count Bertrand respecting the limits allowed for exercise to Napoleon Bonaparte unaccompanied by a British officer and the opinion he states to have been offered on the subject, I must again assure you that I have never made any remarks or held any conversation with either of the individuals at Longwood relative to it. I have myself always considered the space allowed as ample and quite sufficient for the preservation of health and such officers as have landed here and whom I have occasionally accompanied to Longwood have been invariably struck with the injustice of any complaint on that point, nor can I call to my recollection ever having heard of any person who has experienced sentiments similar to those alluded to by the Count since I have been on the island.

 I remain my dear Sir Hudson
 Ever faithfully yours
 G. R. Bingham

Letter 20   Knollcombe Cottage, 16 August 1818

Yesterday we made a cruise round the island, in the *Racoon* (Captain Brine); we spent a very pleasant day, having a very pleasant party on board. We shall be sorry to lose Captain Brine who is about returning to England. I hope you will also see <u>us</u> there soon; I could not help wishing yesterday that I was on my voyage home, instead of cruising round this miserable spot. Our farm answers beyond our expectation, and our green forage more than pays our meat bill which is pretty well for St Helena. You have no idea what beautiful butter I make, with my new butter print, which you were so good as to send me; it is the only one on the island. We have of late been much interested on the subject of the abolition of slavery; and it was resolved at a meeting which was held on Saturday, that every child born after next Xmas day is to claim its freedom; the boys when they have attained their 18th year, the girls on their 16th, thus enabling them by that time to maintain themselves; but their morals and education are so terribly neglected, that it is quite dreadful, and one half of the slaves are not christened at this moment. There is a piece of ground unconsecrated, allotted for the burial place of these unhappy victims of neglect. Sir George has been a magistrate for three months, and wishes if possible to reform in some measure their sad practises. We give our patronage to the school, which gets on pretty well. We are trying to persuade the people to educate the children of their slaves, but I don't know whether we shall succeed.[1]

    E.B.

The following letters were sent to the Bingham's consequent to their departure from St Helena. It is usually stated that Sir George

---

1. The trade in slaves had been abolished on British ships by Parliament in 1807; however the West Indian merchant lobby had ensured that existing slaves were not covered by the Act. It was thought that the end of this trade would improve the lot of the existing slaves as they became a more valuable commodity. This unfortunately overlooked the fact that slaves could be acquired via ships of other nations and there was little real improvement in the situation. The British Government followed an admirable policy of attempting to persuade countries to ban slavery in return for territorial gains at the Congress of Vienna at the culmination of the Napoleonic Wars. It unfortunately took until 1833 to pass an act abolishing all slavery throughout the British Empire.

and Lady Bingham left the island in 1820 when Sir Pine Coffin arrived, but it is clear that they left in May 1819. He was granted leave to return home to attend to private affairs and because he was hurt that the Court of Directors had not confirmed his appointment as a member of Council at St Helena, to which the Governor had provisionally nominated him. Sir Hudson Lowe stated his feelings on the loss of Sir George Bingham in his dispatch of 28 May 1819 to Lord Bathurst.

It would be difficult to express in too strong terms the high sense I entertain of Brigadier General Sir George Bingham's very important and useful services during the period he has been under my command; of his attention towards the comfort as well as the discipline of the troops placed under his immediate orders; of the cordial, zealous, and effectual assistance and support I have derived from him on every occasion in the execution of my own duties; and of his vigilance in every point where the public service could be benefited by it; but I cannot afford a stronger proof of the perfect sincerity with which I take the liberty of thus expressing my sense of his conduct than by making known my most earnest desire that he may be enabled soon to return here, and to resume the performance of those duties which he has hitherto executed with so much credit to himself, and so much real advantage to the public service.

George, on his arrival home learnt that he had become a Major General on 12 August 1819.

It would appear that the following letters were sent to him following his departure by his friends Colonel Edward Wynyard and Major Charles Harrison.

Letter 21   17 July 1819

Since you have left the island, Bonaparte has manifested some inclination to discontinue the practise of showing himself daily; the Governor and Sir Thomas Reade[1] in consequence were at

---

1. Sir Thomas Reade was Deputy Adjutant General in St Helena and effectively Deputy Governor.

Longwood for some time on Sunday last, and several messages passed between the Governor and Count Montholon through the orderly officer, the result of which was, that after the governor went away, his Imperial Majesty walked in the garden for some time.

Letter 22   24 July 1819

I saw Bonaparte the other day when giving directions about a sod wall he desired to have, to shelter his little garden before the library from the wind; he appeared very much the same as when I had last a glimpse of him; he went all over the new house the other day, and I believe expressed his approbation of it.

    E[dward].W[ynyard].

Letter 23   14 August 1819

I told you in my last that Napoleon had shown a strong disposition towards seclusion again; a short time ago he did not appear for some days; he however came to his senses again; but about ten days since he had a relapse, and did not show till yesterday, when the governor was about to proceed in a way that I believe I should have had to superintend. I need not attempt to impress on your mind what a set of rascals they are at Longwood, but I will relate to you how it was brought about. When Bonaparte shut himself up, the governor wrote him a letter inclosing him a copy of his instructions from Lord Bathurst,[1] relative to his being seen every day; this letter both Bertrand and Montholon refused either twice, or three times to receive. On the 11th instant, the governor sent Colonel Wynyard up with the letter, and directed him to take me with him. His instructions were to give the letter to Captain Nicholls,[2] (orderly officer) who was first to offer it to Montholon, but he was ill, and

---

1. Lord Henry Bathurst was Secretary at War and Colonies from 1812–27. He wrote a ream of 'Instructions' to Sir Hudson Lowe, which formed a set of guidelines strictly controlling all aspects of Napoleon's exile on St Helena. It has been shown by William Forsyth in his 3 Volume *History of the Captivity of Napoleon at St Helena* published in 1853, that much of the bile heaped on Sir Hudson Lowe should really have been directed at Lord Bathurst and the government.
2. Captain George Nicholls 53 Regiment acted as Orderly officer at Longwood from September 1818 to 9 February 1820.

could not be seen; he was then directed in my presence to offer it to Bertrand. We proceeded to Longwood, Captain Nicholls said 'Here is a letter for General Bonaparte from the Governor, will you take it?'

The reply was 'I have seen that letter before' and he refused to take it. Captain Nicholls was then instructed to say 'There is an officer of the Governor's personal staff waiting with a letter from the Governor, will you inform him of it?'

Bertrand's reply was 'If the governor will communicate with the Emperor in the usual manner through me, I will do it.'

We then left him, the neat part of the instructions to be carried into execution was, that Colonel Wynyard was to go to the front door of the house, knock, and ask to be admitted to the presence of Bonaparte; in the event of no one answering, he was to try the door, and if open to continue to proceed, till he came to the room in which he was, but not to use any force.

The door was locked; Colonel Wynyard having executed these orders, he ordered me to accompany Captain Nicholls by another door which leads from the kitchen to the dining room; this we did, but to no purpose. Colonel W. then went away, and reported the whole to the governor, who was perfectly satisfied. Yesterday morning I again received an order from Gorrequer[1] to go immediately to Longwood; when I arrived there I found Captain Nicholls had received instructions to see Bonaparte.

By the bye, I must tell you that the rejected letter was sent up again on the 12th, and Bertrand took it, but said the Emperor would throw it into the fire. Nicholls sent for Marchand and said 'I am directed by the governor to see Bonaparte.'

Marchand's reply was (Verling[2] was the interpreter) 'The Emperor had a bad night last night and is now in his bath'.

---

1. Major Gideon Gorrequer had already served as aide de camp to Sir Hudson Lowe before the latter was ordered to St Helena. Gorrequer accompanied Lowe to St Helena as aide de camp and Acting Military Secretary. Wynyard was appointed as the official Military Secretary but did little of the work of that office at St Helena, whether through Wynyard's lethargy or Lowe's preference for utilizing the services of his long standing ADC. Gorrequer's diaries were published as *St Helena during Napoleon's exile* by James Kemble in 1968.
2. Dr James Roche Verling replaced O'Meara as the doctor resident at Longwood to attend the French staff. However, Napoleon suspected Verling, being an appointee of the Governor's and he was never allowed to attend him personally.

Nicholls said, 'Will you deliver a message to Bonaparte to say I must see him?'

Marchand flatly refused, and said it must be done by the Grand Marshal. Nicholls had then nothing to do but as before to try the doors which were locked. He then retired to make his report, and I left him of course expecting to be called on again in the afternoon, or as soon as the answer could come from the governor. Just after I had left Nicholls and he had made out his report, Bertrand came to him and asked him what he wanted? Did he wish to see the Emperor?

He replied, yes it was all he wanted; Bertrand said 'If you will go past the window of the room in which the bath is you will see him'. He went back to his room, took off his red jacket, put on his blue greatcoat, returned, found the window open and his Imperial Majesty up to his neck in water. The object was thus attained and he retired, but what do you think of our friends at Longwood now? I have related what passed in my presence at Bertrand's; he wrote to the governor the following day, and said, that he had observed to Captain Nicholls that his prince being confined to his bed and very unwell, had occasion for medical assistance, and not matters likely to irritate, which he considered a personal insult. What an egregious liar! It appears almost incredible, but so it was; nothing passed but what I have told you.

C[harles] H[arrison]

Letter 24   23 August 1819

Since I last wrote to you, and since the bath scene, Napoleon has been very sulky again, and did not show for many days. On the 13th after many letters, and messages had passed, the governor went to Longwood with his staff; he took me with him, and we remained there till seven o'clock in the evening, the governor sending messages by Verling, and Nicholls, without receiving any satisfactory answer. At last he set off, and I was ordered to be in readiness the following morning; when however he finds the governor is determined, he always contrives (though he was said to be dreadfully ill in bed) to show himself; for the next morning he was not only seen, but was heard vociferating most loudly. This last business has rendered him more despicable than ever, for after the governor had left Longwood, that evening Napoleon wrote to him, to say, he might tell the Prince Regent of England, that if he attempted to force open his doors, he should walk over his corpse at the threshold, meaning that he would defend himself to the last; this is a great secret of course. Notwithstanding all this, he showed himself the next morning, as I have told you; all this business gave him the vertigo, and Arnott[1] was sent up, but he would neither see him, or Verling; this was on the 19th.

C[harles] H[arrison]

Letter 25   9 September 1819

The *Hyaena* sails I believe on Sunday and I must tell you the result of Mr Stokoe's trial[2] which took place on the 30th, and lasted until the 2nd instant when the sentence was pronounced, which was that John Stokoe having been found guilty of the whole of the charges (10 in number) be dismissed His Majesty's service, but in consideration of his long services the court recommended him for half pay; rather an extraordinary recommendation after having found him guilty of such serious charges. The charges were principally founded on disobedience of the admiral's orders; but the evidence of the admiral[3] branched out into such collateral matter, that Mr Stokoe's connection with the people at Longwood was as clearly proved as possible. I <u>did </u>intend to have sent you a copy of the charges; Reade promised them to me, but I cannot get them. I dare say however you may have seen them in London. Mr Stokoe could not get any one to assist him in his defence; none of his friends would come forward. His defence was bad, irritating, and I think disrespectful, but I believe he was pretty confident he was taking leave of the Admiralty, and he did not care what he said. He talked

1. Dr Archibald Arnott was surgeon to the 20 Regiment which had arrived at St Helena in March 1819.
2. Dr John Stokoe, surgeon on HMS *Conqueror*, was called to attend Napoleon during a bout of illness in January 1819 which he initially declined, but eventually agreed to do. He became Napoleon's personal physician, but did file reports on Napoleon's health to Lowe. The reports were a source of embarrassment to Lowe, hinting at liver disease caused by the climate of St Helena; he was examined by Admiral Plampin and sent home as an invalid. Evidence coming to light of his role as a surreptitious messenger for Napoleon caused him to be sent back to St Helena to be court- martialled when he was dismissed from the service.
3. The admiral at this time was Rear Admiral Sir Robert Plampin who had succeeded Sir Pulteney Malcolm.

of the overwhelming authority of his prosecutors, aided and assisted by local prejudices and the subtleties of the law. I was there the whole trial, and I shall not forget the firmness, perspicuity, and force, (added to which a little bitterness) with which the old admiral went through the whole of the evidence, and he not only astonished the doctor by producing documents, he could have had very little idea were in the admiral's possession, but he made a certain knight (Sir J. Reade) stare with all eyes, when he produced every note, every letter, and also minutes of every syllable of conversation, that had taken place, from the very commencement, between himself and Mr Stokoe relative to his visits at Longwood.

I never recollect having met with so clear headed an old gentleman. You recollect about the time the business was going on, he was accused of apathy, and lukewarmness; as it has turned out I defy any one to have acted a more firm and decided part. You remember the surgeon of some ship coming from Ascension (I believe it was Brine's[1]) mentioning a conversation that had taken place between himself and Mr O'Meara,[2] when the latter hinted, that the governor had obliquely suggested to him poison; the admiral not only called on this surgeon for a written statement of the conversation, but wrote an official letter to Mr Cuppage (Governor of Ascension) on the subject; both of which letters were produced, with their answers, and both these gentleman declared, that Mr O'Meara had positively hinted to them, that the governor had proposed to him to administer poison to Bonaparte. I cannot now tell you of the consummate impudence of the court at Longwood, notwithstanding what has been going on, which I have stated to you in a former letter. On the arrival of the *Abundance* they wrote to the governor to say, that 'Having understood the Emperor's physician (Stokoe) had arrived in the *Abundance,* the Emperor directed he should immediately be sent up to Longwood.'

When however they found that the physician was sent out to be tried, and that he called on Counts Bertrand and Montholon, who

1. Captain Brine of the sloop *Mosquito.*
2. Dr Barry O'Meara, the head surgeon on HMS *Bellerophon* was persuaded to accompany Napoleon to St Helena as his personal physician. O'Meara had numerous altercations with Sir Hudson Lowe and was eventually dismissed and sent home in July 1818. His book *Napoleon in Exile or a Voice from St Helena* published in 1822 was the start of the vilification of Sir Hudson Lowe.

were summoned as his principal evidences, Montholon was so ill that he could not attend, and Bertrand did not understand the English laws, and did not go. Mr Stokoe relied strongly on the evidence of these people, and his friends have treated him with marked attention as a reward due to his services. Since I last wrote I have had another official visit to Longwood; about 8 o'clock on the evening of the 29th ultimo, I received a dispatch to proceed thither immediately with letters addressed, one to Napoleon Bonaparte, one to Bertrand, one to Montholon, and another of the same tenor in French to be read to the servants. Croad[1] was the interpreter on the occasion; the instructions signified that these letters were to be delivered by Nicholls as directed. Bonaparte was as usual inaccessible, Bertrand could not be seen, because he was with Napoleon, and Montholon was so ill he could neither see Nicholls or receive the letter. Not being able to execute the instructions relative to the delivery of the letters the instructions went on to say that the communication should be read to the servants either collectively, or individually, whichever could be most easily accomplished, in order to make the whole, or as many as possible acquainted with the purport. This communication stated, that in consequence of Napoleon Bonaparte not having shown himself for some days, so as to enable the orderly officer to make the report required by the governor of his actual presence at Longwood, in the event of the governor's being obliged to carry into execution the instructions received from home, he cautioned all the persons and servants at Longwood against interfering in any way whatever, and should any resistance be made, or any accident take place, he would immediately arrest them and they should abide the consequences.

I suggested to Nicholls that we should send for Marchand, and explain to him through Croad, that there was a communication to be made to the foreign servants of the establishment at Longwood, from the governor, and desiring him to assemble them in Nicholl's room. This, Marchand said he could not do, without an order from the Grand Marshal. We then proceeded to the servants' room where we got hold of Pierron,[2] St Denis,[3] and a new man of

1. Lieutenant Frederick Croad, 66 Regiment.
2. Pierron or Piéron was butler to Napoleon.
3. Louis Etienne Saint-Denis, or the Mameluke Ali, was valet de chambre to Napoleon. His *Souvenirs* were published in 1926.

Bertrand's. Croad commenced reading, and they listened respect-fully and attentively; after having done this, I left them, and saw the governor the next day, who was perfectly satisfied with what had been done, and I have heard nothing of them since; but I believe his Imperial Majesty has shown lately.

C[harles] H[arrison]

Letter 26   1 December 1819

Things are now going on very quietly. Napoleon is out every day, and has for some time past been employed in making some alter-ations in his little garden. I saw him about a fortnight ago walking round the new house;[1] I was not very close to him, but he appeared to walk as well as ever; he is constantly walking about now, and does not avoid any one who approaches him.

H[arrison]

Letter 27   18 January 1820

I think little or no alteration has taken place since I wrote last, excepting that the great man at Longwood is quite an altered person; he is now out of doors constantly, and is making curious and inter-esting improvements in the garden immediately round the old house. I have not seen them as he never quits the spot, and unless one takes the opportunity of going when he is at dinner, you must fall in with him. I understand he was so much delighted with the arrival from Jamestown, of some frame work which was to line a pond, for gold and silver fish, that he gave the carter a glass of wine, or brandy with his own hand. He keeps Montholon and all his people constantly at work at his improvements, and is frequently seen in a nankin jacket and straw hat in the midst of them. I do not hear that they have troubled the governor lately, who unsolicited has extended his limits very considerably; some people think he will come out again but as yet there is no demonstration of the kind, all the other people have taken advantage of the extension, and one day Montholon rode

---

1. The house at Longwood was not really adequate for the residence of Napoleon and his entourage. A replacement had been designed and manufactured in England then shipped out in pieces to be reassembled on site. It was virtually completed by spring 1821, but Napoleon did not move into it before his death.

round the new limits with Gorrequer, he has likewise visited De Fontaine.[1] The new doctor Antommarchi[2] I understand showed a great disposition to be troublesome by making frequent complaints to the governor through the proper channel, that he was stopped by the sentries, when endeavouring to pass at improper hours; he is however now silenced in a manner which will show you that the Court of Longwood is still kept up with all its Imperial consequences. Antommarchi took upon himself at last to write to the governor direct; and Montholon significantly remarked, 'He has written to the Governor, and has got his answer.' Nothing has been heard of the doctor since. The extension of the limits has been affected without any considerable increase of duty to the troops; the picquet house above Huts Gate is converted into a signal station and the picquet by day, done away with, so that there is only a picquet at Bates' branch in addition. There is a code of signals established, peculiar to Longwood, and the governor is acquainted when any of them go out. The carriage has been neatly fitted up, and three or four new horses sent for. I have seen his Imperial Majesty several times lately at a distance; he appears to be fully as active, and to walk, as well as when I first saw him. The new house does not get on quite so well as it might do; they are now at a stand still, for things expected from home almost before you left us. Preparations are making for the removal of the barracks where they will be quite out of sight of Longwood.

C[harles] H[arrison]

Letter 28   12 May 1820

The people at Longwood continue perfectly quiet; Napoleon constantly employed in his garden. I have heard that great objections are made to the iron railing,[1] and that he has observed he

1. Actually John de Fountain who had worked for the East India Company on St Helena.
2. The Corsican Dr Francesco Antommarchi had been chosen by the Bonaparte family in Italy for Napoleon's personal physician. He arrived in September 1819.
3. The iron railings for the new house became a contentious issue. Napoleon saw them as forming an iron cage around him, but he was assured that it was merely a decorative feature of the house. It would be set well out of view of the house and form an enclosure for his ornamental gardens and prevent the ingress of cattle. Some of the rail can be now seen outside Anne's Place, the only restaurant in Jamestown.

would never enter the new house whilst it had so much the appearance of an iron cage. The house since the arrival of the *Mary* from England makes great progress, and except the railing Napoleon does not in any way object to it. My little neighbour Ibbetson[1] is going on very well as Purveyor at Longwood, and there has not been a single complaint [in] I don't know how long.

    C[harles] H[arrison]

Letter 29   6 July 1820

As for the affairs at Longwood, everything is going on as smoothly as possible, and Napoleon has sent Montholon lately over to Plantation House, to express his satisfaction at something that had or was going to be done; and this more than once.[2]

Letter 30   18 August 1820

Napoleon is going on well, and has taken to riding again; he has asked for an extension of his limits, and preparations are making for removing the present cordon of sentries out of his sight, besides which another new road is in contemplation. I shall not be surprised to see him pass the Huts some of these days. Admiral Plampin asked to see him before he left, and they returned him the old answer, 'If any one wished to see him, the application must come through the Grand Marshal of <u>the Palace</u>'. I shall not fail to give you an account of all the alterations that may take place here, with regard to our prisoner, as you must always feel interested about him. He certainly is much relaxed in his feeling towards the people in power here, and he now frequently sends Montholon over to Plantation House on matters relating to himself.

    C[harles] H[arrison]

1. Denzil Ibbetson, an Army Commissary, had come out with Napoleon in the *Northumberland*. He succeeded Balcombe as Purveyor to Longwood in March 1818.
2. This is a very interesting comment, much at variance with the version of his captivity portrayed by the mythical 'Napoleonic tragedy'. The British officers clearly felt that Napoleon was generally content with his lot and grateful for their attempts to ameliorate his sufferings as a prisoner.

Now to our friend at Longwood, a wonderful change has taken place there likewise. I have said in former letters that there were strong indications of his coming round, and I told you that the governor had made such a disposition of the picquets and sentries, that you could scarce see the one or the other of them from the road. About three weeks ago between six and seven o'clock in the morning the signal man came down to say, that Bonaparte was riding full gallop attended by two servants only, in this direction; but before I got out, he had passed and rode round the cordon; as I did not myself see it I could scarcely believe it, but I afterwards clearly ascertained it was him. This ride so knocked him up, that he could scarcely move for a few days. On Wednesday last I was called up again between seven and eight, when I saw Napoleon attended by Bertrand, Montholon, and four servants approaching in Imperial state; I observed also that two of the servants carried hampers or panniers. The cavalcade passed my house slowly, and proceeded in the direction of Plantation House. I could not conceive where they were going, and waited impatiently their return, which did not take place till near twelve o'clock; previously to which time, a servant had been dispatched for the carriage; and on the hill just above me he dismounted, got into it, and drove quietly home. It turned out afterwards that without having previously said a word to any one, they all rode to Sir William Doveton's[1] (I must tell you his house is now within the limits) where he had his panniers emptied (which contained his breakfast) on a cloth in front of the house on the green. Sir William, and Mr and Mrs Greentree[2] were there, but they could not persuade him to take his breakfast in the house; after he had finished however, he went all over the house, and (curious enough) observed the furniture of the house was altered since he was there before, and remarked there were formerly two sofas. You recollect he went there with Sir George Cockburn, shortly after his arrival; when he was very much

1. Sir William Webber Doveton was a St Helenian; he was a Judge, member of the Council and Treasurer and Paymaster for the East India Company on the island. His house was at Mount Pleasant near Sandy Bay.
2. Mr Thomas Greentree was the storekeeper for the East India Company. Mrs Greentree was Sir William Doveton's daughter.

smitten with Mrs Greentree, and almost pulled old Sir William's ear off. Since this eventful day, the weather has been very wet; when otherwise, I understand he intends to continue his rides.

C[harles] H[arrison]

Letter 32   2 February 1821

I said in my letter to Lady B that I thought our friend at Longwood was breaking fast; I scarcely know however what to make of it as almost every day induces me to form a different opinion. He certainly has grown very large, and is become very inactive, and I understand he is supported in and out of his carriage; but about ten days ago he was on horseback again, but not out of the grounds, so that it is impossible to say whether he is really in the state he appears to be in, or that he only wishes it to be supposed such. I heard yesterday that he has made a proposition to the governor in terms which he (the governor) thinks reasonable. You are aware that Bertrand has long wished to get away, but as he could not leave this, unless under the protection of our government which I suppose was not thought politic, Napoleon now proposes, that both Bertrand and Montholon shall be sent to England at the disposal of our government, and that they shall be replaced by others (of course) of his own choosing. Besides which, he is dissatisfied with his present surgeon, who I fancy has not had sufficient experience in the world to enter into his extensive views. It is impossible to draw any inference from these projects, and whether he wishes to send these people home to further his own plans in the present unsettled state of Europe, or that he is now reconciled to his fate, and does not wish them to remain longer in a state of banishment is difficult to decide. Certainly every thing appears going on very quietly at Longwood. The new house is quite ready for the reception of Napoleon, but I do not know when he takes possession of it. I am going thither this afternoon I fancy for the last time to see the interior of the house, it is beautifully finished.

C[harles] H[arrison]

Letter 33   31 March 1821

The *Duke of York* China ship sails this day, and I must write to say that it is not at all unlikely that I may have the pleasure of seeing you ere long. The reason of the change likely to take place, I will not vouch for, as such profound secrecy is observed and enjoined on the occasion; but you will recollect in several of my late letters, I have expressed my opinion that Napoleon has been declining fast, for some time past, and the impression on my mind at this present moment is that he is now on his death bed; for the last fortnight he has been in so bad a state, that what little sustenance he takes will not remain on his stomach, and for this last week he has taken to his bed, and has (I have reason to believe) been in a perfect state of stupor. Arnott is in constant attendance, but I have not been able to make out whether he has seen him. There are dragoons going constantly backwards and forwards, and yesterday the governor must have been sent for express, for a dragoon galloped past this, and the governor returned with him in a very short time. He called here in his way home, and wrote a note, but he never said a syllable to me. I find it impossible to get at the real state of the case, and what I have said must not go beyond Lady B and yourself, as I merely say what I really believe to be the truth, that Napoleon is dying; the people about him have said so for some time; I cannot reconcile it to myself why the governor should keep the thing so close, for if my premises are just, some of these days or I may say hours, the death of Napoleon will be announced when literally not a soul on the island knows that he has been ill. If I am wrong in the opinion I have formed, (for what I have said is merely founded on opinion) there is no harm done, but if it should happen, I have prepared you for the worst.

C[harles] H[arrison]

Letter 34   3 April 1821

My letter of the 31st of last month, or three days ago, would naturally lead you to expect one from me very soon after, and I am glad now I can give you the real state of affairs, which information I gained this afternoon, and which may be relied on. The circumstances I am about to detail are curious, but as you know the character so well, you will not be astonished at any thing that might otherwise appear extraordinary. Whether this is a plot got up, or not, it is impossible to say, but a short time must discover. It appears as I said in my last, that Napoleon has been very unwell for some days past, and had taken to his bed, during the whole of

289

which time, Arnott has been in attendance, but it comes out had not seen him, but was frequently asked, what he would do, and how he would act under such and such circumstances; which he contrary I believe to the custom of medical men candidly gave his opinion upon. Whether this advice was acted on I know not; but on Sunday night (the night before last) he was sent for between 10 and 11 to see the Emperor, who was very ill; and when he arrived at the house, he was told he was personally to visit him. He consequently proceeded to his apartment, but what was his astonishment when the door was opened, to find the room was in a state of perfect darkness; for the candles were not only put out, but the window shutters closed, and the doctor was led to the bedside, when an arm was stretched out, which the doctor seized and after having examined the pulse said, 'Whosever arm this is, the pulse indicates that the person is in a state of extreme debility, but I am not apprehensive of any serious consequences, and I will prescribe'. This was accordingly done, and the next morning Arnott was introduced into the Imperial presence after which he pronounced that he was in a very debilitated state, but that he was better than when he felt him the night before, and that his disorder proceeded more from the state of his mind than his body. He has seen him again this morning, and the report he makes is, that he continues better. That he has been very ill, there can be no doubt, as Arnott is the first British medical officer, that he has seen, who has not signed his allegiance to him;[1] but whether he will get over it, or whether it is only one of their schemes, I shall not decide, till I hear he is out of bed and going about again.

C[harles] H[arrison]

Letter 35   22 April 1821

I don't know what to think of the invalid, but I now begin to firmly believe it is all humbug. He still continues confined to his bed, but from what I can collect is considerably better. His new doctor (Arnott) attends him twice a day regularly, and he tells me he is the most extraordinary man he ever had to deal with in his life, and the

---

1. O'Meara and Stokoe, his previous British doctors had both been taken into Napoleon's service before they were allowed to examine him. Arnott was still a surgeon in the 20 Regiment and owed no allegiance to Napoleon.

conviction on my mind is, that if he were to be told there was a 74 arrived to take him back to France he would find the use of both his mental and bodily faculties.

C[harles] H[arrison]

Letter 36   2 May 1821

This morning before I was dressed Sir Thomas Reade came from the direction of Longwood, and stopped at my gate, to tell me that Bonaparte was then dying, and it is supposed, he cannot live over tomorrow. He has within these three days, had most violent fits of vomiting, and for the two last, has refused all medicine, or the slightest sustenance; and he is now labouring under incessant hiccupping, which I fancy is the last symptom of complaint, and the probability is, that he will have terminated his earthly career, before I shall have closed this.

C[harles] H[arrison]

Letter 37   3 May 1821

Bonaparte is still alive; Sir Thomas Reade was with me during the whole of the night, in momentary expectation of receiving an account of his death; but it appears that his hiccup has ceased, and that he dozed for several hours, which renovated him for a short time; but about three o'clock this morning, he became speechless, and seemed not to know any one.

(½ past 2 p.m.)
The governor has just past, and told me that there is no great alteration. Montholon has consented that some medical people shall see him when he becomes insensible, and there is since a signal passed for the surgeon of the flagship, so I suppose the next report will be that he is no more.

(Six o'clock p.m.)
He is totally insensible, and his eyes are fixed, with every appearance of immediate dissolution.

C[harles] H[arrison]

Letter 38   4 May 1821

(10 o'clock a.m.)

Bonaparte is still alive, the symptoms are now more favourable; yesterday afternoon when in a state of insensibility, they put into his mouth a bit of soaked biscuit, with ten grains of calomel, which he swallowed, and which had the desired effect. This has made such a change, that the report this morning is, that he is much better, but very weak, and the hiccup still continues. The change has astonished us all, but there are not the slightest hopes of his recovery.

(One o'clock p.m.)

Doctor Shortt[1] who has just passed, tells me there is a wonderful change for the better; that he has taken some jelly and wine, and is more himself again; the hiccup has also ceased; what an extraordinary thing it would be, should he get over this attack.

C[harles] H[arrison]

Letter 39   7 May 1821

I was so employed all yesterday and the day before, that I could not continue my reports, having been at Longwood all the day, and part of the night. The once great Napoleon Bonaparte departed this life without the slightest struggle on the evening of the 5th of May at ten minutes before six o'clock. The governor and staff were there, and we were going in to see the body, when Montholon requested we would not go near him for six hours, as it was the custom with them to devote that time to prayer, after the departure of a friend; this was arranged, that the governor, admiral,[2] brigadier general,[3] and the French Commissioner should assemble at daylight, the following morning when we all went in and beheld poor Napoleon's corpse. A sight which I cannot do justice to in describing; for instead of a horrid ghastly appearance which I

1. Dr Thomas Shortt had succeeded Dr Alexander Baxter as head of the colony's medical department in December 1820.
2. Rear Admiral Robert Lambert had succeeded to the command of the St Helena naval station on 14 July 1820.
3. Brigadier General Pine Coffin, who had arrived 23 August 1820 to replace Sir George Bingham.

expected to have seen, there was an inexpressible something in his countenance that gave one an idea of every thing serene and placid; and the strong and marked expression was really beautiful. After we had had a sight of him, it was arranged that his body should be opened at two o'clock; and the persons fixed upon to witness this operation, were Sir Thomas Reade, the orderly officer[1] and myself, which was highly gratifying to me. And though it was a scene at which I had never before been present, I stood it as well, and was as anxious to see the seat of his disorder as any one of the seven surgeons[2] in attendance; particularly as they were themselves in doubt as to the nature of the disease. They commenced upon his lungs, which were declared to be as sound as any man's in the world; they then examined his heart, which was perfectly natural, and in an equally sound state. The part to be seen the most interesting, as it was supposed (recollect only supposed) might be the seat of his disorder, was his liver; but to my astonishment, it had the appearance of being, and was declared to be, as sound a liver as was ever seen; they cut into it, and all was perfectly correct. The next part to be examined was the stomach, and at a moments glance (even of my eye) it was evident the seat of his disorder was discovered; for there was a nasty black looking hole, into which you might have put your finger, and when the stomach was cut out and washed, the whole appeared in a sad disordered state, and the faculty simultaneously declared, that he had a cancer in his stomach of which disorder he had died, and which was not the effect of the climate, but an hereditary disease, for it appears his father died of the same thing. He had fixed on the spot here where he is to be buried, and the ceremony will take place the day after tomorrow; the workmen are now making the vault under the willow tree at the bottom of Mr Ibbetson's garden. After the body was sewn up again it was dressed in full uniform by his own people, boots, spurs,

1. Captain William Crokat was orderly officer at Longwood 26 April–6 May 1821. He took the dispatch home announcing the death of Napoleon.
2. There were actually eight surgeons present if you include Antommarchi; the other seven were all British surgeons. They were Dr Thomas Shortt; Dr Archibald Arnott; Dr Francis Burton (Surgeon of the 66 Regiment); Dr Charles Mitchell (Surgeon of HMS *Vigo*); Dr Matthew Livingstone (Surgeon to the East India Company); Dr George Henry Rutledge (Assistant Surgeon of the 20 Regiment) and Dr Walter Henry (Assistant Surgeon of the 66 Regiment, who left an account of the autopsy).

cocked hat and such, and laid out in state, for two hours to be seen by any one who chose to go in and look at him.

C[harles] H[arrison]

Letter 40   St Helena 6 May [1821]

Bonaparte expired yesterday evening at ten minutes before six; just at the very instant the sun sunk below the horizon, he breathed his last sigh. He had been confined to his bed since the 17th of March; he consented to receive Doctor Arnott's visits from the first of April, but as he threw up everything almost that went down his throat, would scarcely take any medicine, would not or could not take any nourishment and has been sinking ever since the first day he took to his bed. Indeed for many months he was constantly subject to fits of vomiting, and took very little sustenance. Antommarchi probably trifled with the disease, from his dread of mercury. On the 3rd however, on a consultation with two other medical men (Shortt and Mitchell) he was induced to adopt their recommendation, and ten grains of Calomel were given to the patient, which produced a great effect, and might _perhaps_ have saved him, had it been administered in time; but it showed his interior was a mass of corruption.

He has died in a manly proper manner; no complaint, no murmur, no invective, no lamentation or nonsense; extreme unction was given to him before his death, and from six in the morning yesterday, till six at night, the whole of his attendants from the highest to the lowest surrounded his bed in deep silence, (Madame Bertrand and the rest of the females) till the moment of his dissolution. His last day, was one of gradual extinction, but I should think of little pain, judging of his appearance as a corpse. Never did I behold one so divested of all that is painful or horrifying to behold in death; there was a serenity, a placidity, a peaceful slumbering aspect in his countenance (when all the authorities, staff, naval, and military, went to see the corpse this morning at six) that produced a strong effect on every one who saw him. He was, general and unanimous exclamation declared, the finest corpse ever seen; there was something so noble, so dignified in his countenance, that a heart of stone, his most bitter enemy, could not have beheld without interest and admiration. Some sketches were afterwards taken, but they are quite below the original. I never saw his face look so _handsome_, (and really you may use the term) as at that moment; all the exuberant fat, the jowl, in fact all the superfluous flesh and sallowness had disappeared, and left a well proportioned countenance, such as he might have had some twelve or fourteen years ago. A doyen of those who saw him concurred in saying, he did not look at the utmost more than forty, and he certainly did not; even less I think. His hair though thin, retained its natural dark brown; not a wrinkle, or the slightest contortion in the face. At the moment I am scribbling the body is opening, to find out if possible the disease he died of. It will I think turn out dispepsy, and hepatitis; but I shall add when I know. He is to be buried with military honours, probably tomorrow, (as you are aware his corpse was by a second instruction not to be sent home) as a general of the highest rank, by the side of the spring near Torbett's[1] country house, below Mr Ibbetson's at Hutt's gate, from whence he had two bottles of fine pure water, brought to him by a Chinese morning and evening (silver bottles) under the shade of a cluster of weeping willow trees, which we have been looking at, this forenoon; and I do not think a more appropriate spot could have been selected. He fixed upon it himself, in the event of being buried here.

Montholon has requested the spot may be consecrated by our clergyman, and afterwards by their own priest Vignali (the old Abbé Buonavita being on his passage home).[2] The night preceding his death, an old, favourite gum wood tree opposite Montholon's quarters, fell down broken from the roots. The *Waterloo* store ship arrived two days previous, and just before he expired, the little horse, formerly Miss C. Somerset's and his favourite, got the head stall off ran out of the stable, and was for a long time galloping about the house. These circumstances will by some be considered as presages of his fate. Montholon has applied for his heart; it is not however to be given up now, but most probably will be enclosed in a leaden case, and buried in the same, from whence it may be afterwards withdrawn, should government approve of its being delivered up to his friends. He has left a will, but the question on our side, whether to be or not to be opened is not yet resolved; his followers desire it.

1. Mr Richard Torbett.
2. The priests Vignali and Buonavita had arrived with Antommarchi; they had been sent by his family to give him spiritual succour. Napoleon did enjoy the services they provided and openly declared himself a Catholic.

At half past five o'clock yesterday morning he was speaking of his son, and knew everyone about him; in his usual way the day before, he 'tutoyed' [sic] his servants, spoke French to some, Italian to the others. He has been long sinking depend upon it; he has frequently said for some months past 'Il n'y a plus d'huile dans la lampe' meaning, he was wasting fast. The new house was just ready for him, and it was agreed to take down the railing in the part of the lawn of which he complained calling it a cage.

I have scarcely been in bed for the last two nights and mostly at Longwood, awaiting the catastrophe for several days till late from a very early hour. The report of the disease of which Bonaparte died is just come in, and it appears it was of the pylorus or schirrus in the stomach, where it had eaten a hole through some part of it, which of course destroyed all the powers of digestion, and caused the constant vomiting he had been so long subject to. The sore was approaching the nature of a cancer, or was gangrened. The faculty who opened him, say it must have been a long time in progress, and was incurable. There was no hepatitis, but a little adhesion of the liver, however dispepsy was part of the disease; his father died of the same disorder at Barege,[1] and Napoleon had in consequence, himself expressed a wish to be opened, in order to ascertain whether he died of the same complaint, that in case it should prove hereditary, his son might be benefited by the knowledge of the malady with which he might here after be attacked. His sister Princess Borghese (Pauline) it is supposed is affected in the same way, being in like manner subject to frequent fits of vomiting, and want of appetite.

This explanation of his illness will correct all former hypotheses at the beginning of this scrawl respecting the cause; his inside was full of a fluid, thick, and like coffee grounds.

Yours and such

Gorrequer

This final letter from St Helena was actually written to Colonel Wynyard from Colonel Gorrequer, but appears in the Bingham papers. I believe that the letter has never been published and is of great interest as it deals with the funeral of Napoleon in great depth.

1. Carlo Buonaparte actually died at Montpellier in 1785.

Letter 41   Undated

My dear Wynyard

I scarcely know where I left off in my last letter, but I think I told you how Bonaparte looked, when we took a view of him the morning after his death, extended upon his little camp bed; and of the statement that had been made by the medical man after his decease. After the dissection had taken place, his attendants dressed him out in a new plain uniform of a colonel of chasseurs, of the late Imperial Guards; cocked hat on, booted and spurred, sword buckled on and such. A handsome blue cloak or mantle with the collar and cape, richly embroidered in silver, spread underneath the corpse. This was the same he wore at the Battle of Marengo and took with him in all his subsequent campaigns, though apparently little worn. In this state all the officers, respectable inhabitants, and great part of the men of the 20th, were admitted to see him. Almost every body who chose had in fact access to the room, before, and after the body was placed on the coffin; his followers appearing pleased at the concourse of persons that came there. Some attempts at likeness were made before, and after he was dressed out, I have not seen any however really like. The best performers were those who attempted it after the dissection; but by that time there had been an immense change in his appearance; his features were then those of a corpse, though still of a handsome one. Had a good likeness been taken of him at the time we first saw the body, it would have been much admired at home. You will see the print shops crowded with him soon; a cast of plaster of paris was also taken of him and a bust made from it; which is now in the possession of Madame Bertrand, but this was unfortunately at the last moment, when the body was in the state that it was scarcely possible to remain in the same room. He had conceived (very justly) that the original instruction for the conveyance of his remains to Europe might be counter ordered; and therefore, solicited that pretty spot I mentioned in my last; close to a fountain near Torbett's cottage, below Ibbetson's, under two weeping willows, in the event his being interred at St Helena; at the same time, desiring his heart should be sent to his wife. His wishes on this point however, it has not been thought proper to accede to here, but the heart has never the less been enclosed in a small silver vase preserved in spirits of wine, and soldered up and the diseased part

297

of the stomach in like manner put into another, and both deposited in the coffin along with the body; so that the heart may still be got at, should the widow on deliberation at home be allowed to become the possessor of it. On the 7th the body was put into a wooden coffin, lined with tin (in full uniform as above described) which was then placed in a leaden one, and then into a third made of mahogany. Within the interior shell were deposited along with the corpse 12 coins of the French Empire and Kingdom of Italy, (eight gold and four silver); a silver plate; a silver handled knife and fork; silver ewer instead of a lamp, and a silver cup or small vase. The 9th having been fixed upon for his burial with the honours due to a full General, all the troops on the island, marines from the flag-ship, St Helena volunteers and such, assembled, and formed a line on the crest of the hill above the road leading to Hutt's Gate, to the guard house at Longwood; close to which, the right of the line extended.

A funeral car had been made from his old sociable, or barouche; and was drawn up with four carriage horses, harnessed to it, at the foot of the garden in front of what was formerly the billiard room in the old house. The coffin was then carried by a party of the 20th Grenadiers from the room he died in, (the receiving or drawing room) and placed upon the car when we (the high rank) followed.

The procession was then formed as follows-

Priest Vignali dressed out in rich golden embroidered canonicals on foot led the van, with a 'benitier' of holy water in his hand; next walked Henry Bertrand with an 'encensoir'; then followed the car with body; the Marengo mantle, and a sword placed on the coffin, flanked by 12 grenadiers of the 20th; six on each side. Immediately behind the car was his favourite little horse formerly Miss Charlotte Somerset's; and then called 'King George'; but afterwards named 'Sheik' by Bonaparte. Doctors Antommarchi and Arnott next appeared; then succeeded Madame Bertrand, with her daughter, and youngest boy, in a phaeton; and following them, were all the rest of the attendants, with the two counts, this group being the chief mourners. Then came on the midshipmen of the men of war in harbour on foot, succeeded by a cavalcade of civil, naval and military officers; juniors first, closed by the French Commissioner, the admiral and governor. This cortege proceeded slowly on, along the front of the line, the whole resting on their arms reversed; and the bands playing a solemn dirge; when it reached the left, the troops filed off; joining the rear of the procession, until they arrived opposite to Torbett's cottage; where the horsemen dismounted; and the coffin having been removed from the car, was borne by detachments of grenadiers of the different corps; the pall supported by Counts Bertrand, and Montholon; Napoleon Bertrand and Marchand followed in the same order as before. The body was then deposited in the grave; the troops having meantime, extended to the right and left of the artillery; which halted opposite to the burying place, which had been consecrated by the Protestant and Roman Catholic priest. Three rounds of 11 field pieces were fired over it, and the troops withdrawn. The grave was 12 feet deep, and 5 feet wide in the clear; the sides, and bottom, of masonry 2 feet thick; and a kind of sarcophagus (composed of four large slabs of free, or Portland stone taken from a platform of one of the batteries, with two smaller ones for the ends) supported by 8 square stones a foot high, placed at the bottom of the grave, finally received the body; the stones, forming this sort of sarcophagus, were united together with roman cement, and immediately over this, were placed two layers of island free stone, two feet thick; which besides being well cemented together, were connected with iron cramps. The upper part of the grave was then filled up with earth; and lastly another large slab of Portland stone covered the mouth of it with a border of masonry all round it. The sepulchre has been enclosed with a railing, and an officer's guard mounted over it ever since; there is therefore no chance as you may well suppose that any clandestine removal can take place. The weather was beautiful on the day of the funeral, and the sides of the hills which surround the ravine, being covered with the population of the island, the ladies in their best attire, produced together with the military ceremony, a very beautiful, imposing, and awful effect.

Extreme unction was administered to Napoleon before his death; when he expired a 'chapelle ardente' was fitted up, mass and prayers were said frequently, and everything from his death, to the funeral, was extremely well conducted, and the most perfect propriety marked the conduct of all.

Napoleon behaved with princely liberality to Doctor Arnott, who attended him from the 1st of April only; (having at last admitted an English medical officer to see him; more however I believe, to avoid being constrained to receive the visits of the orderly officer, than from any expectation of being cured of his disease, the nature of which he had long suspected, his father having died at the age of 36 of the same disorder at Barege where he was opened; and Princess Borghese (Pauline) labouring it is supposed now under the same. For besides a rich gold snuff box, the last he himself used, still half full of snuff, and upon the lid of which, he had with his own hand engraved with a pen knife the letter N, he caused him to be presented with six hundred Napoleons; and he has got some little remembrances too, from the Bertrands.

Bonaparte has left to Lady Holland, a beautiful gold snuff box, with a very valuable antique cameo set in the lid, which has been one of the most admired in the collection of the Vatican; and made a present of to him, by the pope, at the Peace of Tolentino, in 1797, as a token of gratitude, for some favourable articles introduced by him in the treaty. Inside the box, on a card, was written by Napoleon's own hand 'L'Empereur Napoleon, à Lady Holland, témoignage de satisfaction et d'estime'. On 16th of April he made a codicil to his will wholly in his own hand writing, by which he left all he possessed on this island, to be equally divided between Counts Bertrand, and Montholon; and Marchand excepting only, three small mahogany boxes, about as large as common sized dressing cases; principally containing snuff boxes, with antique cameos, and medals, set in the lids; some with portraits of sovereigns and members of his family; others presented to him, by crowned heads, cities, states &c. These boxes, he sealed up himself, and made four of his followers annex their seals to his own; desiring, they should be delivered to his son, when arrived at the age of sixteen.

Two days after the funeral, his rooms in the old house, were laid out exactly as they were during his lifetime; his dressing table, and apparatus, beds, furniture, apparel, in short to the most minute article, were each exhibited; all the effects he left behind him, plate, the beautiful set of porcelain presented to him on his marriage with Marie Louise, his wardrobe and coats and hats that he had worn at various battles; the old radical straw hat, he used to work in the garden &c.; all laid out very neatly in the billiard and drawing room, and the whole house thrown open for three days, to every body, who chose to go and look at the display; and I believe everybody went that could, except the lowest class.

We have many wild reports of the immense sums left by Napoleon to his followers; as one instance, to Montholon <u>100,000 sterling a year!!!</u> And so on. We however saw nothing but a codicil; whether the will itself, was at home or concealed we can't tell; for my part I am impressed with an idea that all the jewels he has been said to possess, the millions deposited in various banks in Europe, and America, as well as other immense resources at his disposal, will turn out to be in general a fallacy; though it is natural enough to suppose, he secured enough to reward those who came out, and staid [sic] with him here. He had very little plate indeed, and we certainly saw no articles of particular value; the Sevre china, presented to him by the city of Paris on his marriage, and the plate were probably the most valuable, the former only consists of a few plates, cups and saucers and such.

We were all surprised at the simplicity and plainness of his wardrobe and the few things of value left behind him; not a diamond, or jewel of any kind. What he brought here with him was mostly part of his camp equipment, extremely compact, and portable, for the purpose of carrying on mules or bât horses.

There has been great anxiety among some of the people here to obtain a little bit of his hair, and some have succeeded (as they hope) through the means of his attendants. I did not try to get any or might have had it; I was satisfied with some of his hand writing.

Yours and such

Gorrequer

Bibliography

Anon, *The Royal Military Calendar*, T. Egerton, London, 1820

Chandler, D.G., *Dictionary of the Napoleonic Wars*, Arms & Armour, London, 1979

Clinton, H.R., *The War in the Peninsula*, Warne, London, undated

Clowes, W.L., *The Royal Navy a History*, Chatham, London, 1899

Cockburn, Sir G., *Buonaparte's Voyage to St Helena*, Lilly, Boston, 1833

Esposito, Brigadier V.J. & Elting, Colonel R.E., *Military History & Atlas of the Napoleonic Wars*, Arms & Armour, London, 1980

Forsyth, W., *History of the Captivity of Napoleon at St Helena*, Murray, London, 1853

Gregory, D., *Napoleon's Jailer*, AUP, 1996

Gurwood, Lieutenant Colonel, *Duke of Wellington Dispatches*, Murray, London 1834

Hart, Lieutenant A. G., *Annual Army List 1840*, Murray, London 1840

Haythornthwaite, P.J., *The Napoleonic Source Book*, Guild Publishing, London, 1990

——*Wellington's Military Machine*, Guild Publishing, London, 1989

Jones, Sir J.T., *Journal of Sieges in Spain*, Weale, London, 1866

Kauffmann, J.P., *The Black Room at Longwood*, Four Walls Eight Windows, New York, 1999

Kemble, J., *Napoleon Immortal*, Murray, London, 1959

——*St Helena, Gorrequer's Diary*, Heinemann, London, undated

Latimer, E.W., *Talks of Napoleon at St Helena*, Mc Clurg, Chicago, 1903

Martineau, G., *Napoleon Surrenders*, Readers Union, Newton Abbot, 1973

——*Napoleon's St Helena*, Murray, London, 1968

Mullen, A.L.T., *The Military General Service Roll 1793–1814*, London Stamp Exchange, London, 1990

Myatt, F., *British Sieges of the Peninsular War*, Guild Publishing, London, 1987

Napier, W.F.P., *History of the War in the Peninsula*, Boone, London, 1835

Oman, Sir C., *A History of the Peninsular War*, Oxford, 1902

——*Wellington's Army 1809–14*, Arnold, London, 1913

O'Meara, B.E., *Napoleon in Exile*, Simpkin, London, 1822

Rosebery, Lord, *Napoleon the Last Phase*, Humphreys, London, 1906

Warden, W., *Letters from St Helena*, Ackermann, London, undated

Index